The CPM Gold Yearbook 2008

CPM Group

WILEY

John Wiley & Sons, Inc.

Published by John Wiley & Sons, Inc., Hoboken, New Jersey.
Published simultaneously in Canada.

No part of this publication may be reproduced, stored in a retrieval system, or transmitted in any form or by any means, electronic, mechanical, photocopying, recording, scanning, or otherwise, except as permitted under Section 107 or 108 of the 1976 United States Copyright Act, without either the prior written permission of the Publisher, or authorization through payment of the appropriate per-copy fee to the Copyright Clearance Center, Inc., 222 Rosewood Drive, Danvers, MA 01923, (978)750-8400, fax (978) 646-8600, or on the Web at www.copyright.com. Requests to the Publisher for permission should be addressed to the Permissions Department, John Wiley & Sons, Inc., 111 River Street, Hoboken, NJ 07030, (201) 748-6011, fax (201) 748-6008, or online at http://www.wiley.com/go/permissions.

Limit of Liability/Disclaimer of Warranty: While the publisher and author have used their best efforts in preparing this book, they make no representations or warranties with respect to the accuracy or completeness of the contents of this book and specifically disclaim any implied warranties of merchantability or fitness for a particular purpose. No warranty may be created or extended by sales representatives or written sales materials. The advice and strategies contained herein may not be suitable for your situation. You should consult with a professional where appropriate. Neither the publisher nor author shall be liable for any loss of profit or any other commercial damages, including but not limited to special, incidental, consequential, or other damages.

For general information on our other products and services or for technical support, please contact our Customer Care Department within the United States at (800) 762-2974, outside the United States at (317) 572-3993 or fax (317) 572-4002.

Wiley also publishes its books in a variety of electronic formats. Some content that appears in print may not be available in electronic formats. For more information about Wiley products, visit our Web site at www.wiley.com.

Library of Congress Cataloging-in-Publication Data:

ISBN-13 978-0-470-37706-2

Printed in the United States of America

10 9 8 7 6 5 4 3 2 1

Founded in 1807, John Wiley & Sons is the oldest independent publishing company in the United States. With offices in North America, Europe, Australia and Asia, Wiley is globally committed to developing and marketing print and electronic products and services for our customers' professional and personal knowledge and understanding.

The Wiley Trading series features books by traders who have survived the market's ever changing temperament and have prospered-some by reinventing systems, others by getting back to basics. Whether a novice trader, professional or somewhere in-between, these books will provide the advice and strategies needed to prosper today and well into the future.

For a list of available titles, please visit our Web site at www.WileyFinance.com.

CPM Group's Gold Yearbook 2008
March 2008
Volume 22, Number 1

CPM Group
30 Broad Street
37th Floor
New York, NY 10004
USA

Telephone:	212-785-8320
Telefax:	212-785-8325
E-mail:	info@cpmgroup.com
Website:	www.cpmgroup.com

Jeffrey M. Christian, Managing Director
Doug Sherrod, Director, Investment Banking
Alec Kushnir, Investment Banking
Mark Hansen, Director of Business Development
Adam J. Crown, Executive Vice President, Sales & Marketing
Nichola Eliovits, Sales & Marketing
Lennys Ramos, Administrator

Carlos Sanchez, Associate Director, Research
Catherine Virga, Senior Research Analyst
Rohit Savant, Senior Research Analyst
Max Pyziur, Senior Research Analyst
Griffin McGee, Research Analyst
Ify Isiekwe, Research Analyst
Chintan Parikh, Research Analyst
Madhusudan Daga, Consultant
Bhargava Vaidya, Consultant

CPM Group provides a range of research and consulting services related to precious metals and commodities. These range from research studies on individual markets and market segments to materials management services. In addition to publishing precious metals and commodities research, CPM Group produces special reports. In 2005 CPM Group produced special reports on topics which have piqued investor interests, such as Uranium and Fuel Cells.

The core of CPM Group's product is its consulting services. These include specific projects related to the special needs of individual producers, refiners, fabricators, institutional investors, financial institutions, governments, central banks, and others. CPM Group provides advisory services related to hedging production and raw materials requirements, and manages positions for producers, consumers, and institutional investors. CPM Group's financial engineering includes impartial advice, structuring, placements, and management of hedging and investment positions.

CPM Group provides investment banking advisory programs for commodities-oriented corporations, and metals, materials, and asset management services for producers, consumers and institutional investors.

Annual Research Reports
> **The CPM Gold Yearbook (published by John Wiley & Sons)**
> **The CPM Silver Yearbook (published by John Wiley & Sons)**
> **The CPM Platinum Yearbook (published by John Wiley & Sons)**
> **The CPM Gold Long-Term Outlook: Ten Year Projections**
> **The CPM Silver Long-Term Outlook: Ten Year Projections**
> **The CPM Platinum Group Metals Long-Term Outlook: Ten Year Projections**

Monthly Research Reports
> **Precious Metals Advisory**
> **Base Metals Advisory**
> **Softs Commodities Advisory**
> **Energy Advisory**

Weekly Research Report
> **CPM Commodities Views**

Specialized Reports
> **The Sustainability of Recent Molybdenum Prices**

Visit www.cpmgroup.com for additional information.

Preface

The gold market in 2007 helped re-define volatility. Gold prices rose to record levels, while supply and demand trends moved in exaggerated patterns. All of this has spilled over into 2008, which promises to be even more volatile in many ways.

The **CPM Gold Yearbook** is meant to provide readers with the basic supply and demand statistics and analysis needed to make sense of market and price trends. CPM Group must pay thanks and honor to the companies that sponsor and help underwrite this annual report. This year's sponsors include Anglogold Ashanti, Barrick Gold Corporation, CME Group, Dubai Gold & Commodities Exchange, Goldcorp Inc., Hecla Mining Company, Kitco Inc., Luismin, S.A. de C.V., Multi Commodity Exchange of India, Noah Financial Innovation, NYMEX, Commodities Now, The Institute of Scrap Recycling Industries, Inc., and The Prospector Exploration & Investment Newspaper.

I am taking a more personal tone to this preface this year. The first time I authored one of these annual gold reviews was in the first quarter of 1981, when they were the **J. Aron Gold Review and Outlook**. The report that year needed to explain all of the momentous events that had occurred in the gold market during 1980. It was quite a task, encompassing gold prices propelled to record highs by 14% inflation, 22% interest rates, the deepest post-war recession, U.S. hostages in Iran, Soviet troops in Afghanistan, Soviet and Iranian assets frozen around the world, anemic financial markets, bank failures, and one of the most controversial U.S. presidential elections of that century.

For 20 years afterward I did not believe that I would see those sorts of wild economic, political, and market conditions again. By 2000 things began to change. When we released the **CPM Gold Survey**, in November 2000, we said the political and economic landscape, which had been so sanguine for two decades, was likely in the years ahead to become more hostile than it had been even in 1978 - 1980. In that environment, we concluded, gold prices could rise to surpass the January 1980 peaks. Slightly more than seven years later, the gold price has posted new records.

This year's report has been a bit more difficult to organize than usual. The gold market is in disarray. Companies involved in trading and refining gold have been overwhelmed by volumes of business, and have been so overloaded that they are less certain than in years past as to how much metal is being bought and sold in various markets for specific applications or purposes.

This year is expected to be an even more extreme than 2007 both in terms of the economic and political conditions that affect gold prices, and gold market trends and developments themselves. This report was written in January, a month that already lived up to that expectation.

We hope you enjoy the information, analysis, statistics, and insights of this edition of the CPM Gold Yearbook. We look forward to producing next year's report for you even more, as we expect it will have some very interesting tales to tell.

Jeffrey M. Christian
Managing Director
3 February 2008

The Following Organizations Assisted in the Preparation of the Gold Yearbook

AngloGold Ashanti
NYSE: AU

AngloGold Ashanti, one of the world's leading gold producers, has a portfolio of long-life, relatively low-cost assets with a variety of orebody types in key gold-producing regions around the world.

AngloGold Ashanti produced 5.6 million ounces of gold in 2006 of which 2.6 million ounces (45%) came from deep-level hard-rock operations in South Africa and the balance of 2.5 million ounces (45%) from shallow and surface operations, and 0.5 million ounces (10%) from underground operations around the world. Today, AngloGold Ashanti has 21 operations located in 10 countries on four continents, together with a substantial project pipeline and a focused, global exploration programme. AngloGold Ashanti currently operates in South Africa, Argentina, Australia, Brazil, Ghana, the Republic of Guinea, Mali, Namibia, Tanzania and the United States.

Greenfields exploration is underway in Western Australia, Colombia and the Democratic Republic of Congo (DRC), and through exploration partnerships and joint ventures in Colombia, Russia, China, the Philippines and Laos. In 2006, 119,089 metres of greenfields exploration drilling was completed, a four-fold increase on that of 2005.

Headquartered in Johannesburg, South Africa, AngloGold Ashanti's primary listing is on the Johannesburg Stock Exchange (ANG). It is also listed on the following securities exchanges: New York (AU), London (AGD), Australia (AGG) and Ghana (AGA), as well as Euronext Paris (VA) and Euronext Brussels (ANG).

Contact Details: Investor Relations
                          investors@anglogoldashanti.com
                          www.anglogold.com

Barrick Gold Corporation
TSX: ABX, NYSE: ABX

Barrick is the world's largest gold producer, with a portfolio of 27 operating mines, many advanced exploration and development projects located across five continents, and large land positions on the most prolific and prospective mineral trends. The Company also has the largest reserves in the industry, with 123 million ounces of proven and probable gold reserves, 6 billion pounds of copper reserves and 964 million ounces of contained silver within gold reserves as at December 31, 2006.

In 2006, Barrick produced 8.64 million ounces of gold at a cash cost of $282 per ounce, in the bottom third of the global cost curve. In addition, the Company produced 367 million pounds of copper at a total cash cost of $0.79 per pound. For 2007, Barrick is targeting gold production of 8.1-8.4 million ounces and copper production of approximately 400 million pounds. Total cash costs are expected to be about $335-$350 per ounce of gold and about $0.90 per pound of copper.

The Company has a successful track record of mine development, having completed the construction of the Tulawaka, Lagunas Norte and Veladero mines in 2005, the Cowal mine in early 2006, and the re-opening of the Ruby Hill mine in early 2007. Barrick has many more projects at various stages of exploration and development. This robust and unrivalled pipeline of projects is due to the Company's ongoing commitment to exploration, even in times of lower gold prices. Barrick is actively exploring for gold in more than 15 countries around the world.

Barrick has the gold mining industry's strongest and only 'A' rated balance sheet, which positions the Company to take prompt advantage of attractive development, exploration and acquisition opportunities as they arise without needing to pause for financing.

Contact Details: Deni Nicoski
                          Vice President, Investor Relations
                          dnicoski@barrick.com
                          www.barrick.com

CME Group

In a world of increasing volatility, customers around the globe rely on CME Group as their premier source for managing risk. Formed by the 2007 merger of the Chicago Mercantile Exchange and the Chicago Board of Trade, CME Group is the largest and most diverse exchange in the world. We offer futures and options on the widest range of benchmark products available on any exchange - interest rates, equity indexes, foreign exchange, commodities and alternative investments - providing you with the tools you need to meet your business objectives and achieve your financial goals. CME Clearing matches and settles all trades and guarantees the creditworthiness of every transaction that takes place in our markets.

Furthermore, CME Group offers the widest range of commodity derivatives of any U.S. exchange, with trading available on a range of grains, livestock, metals, oilseed, dairy and other products. Representing the staples of everyday life, these products offer you liquidity, transparent pricing and extraordinary opportunities in a regulated centralized marketplace with equal access to all participants.

Contact Details: Rich Jelinek
                               Associate Director of Commodity Products
                               commodities@cmegroup.com
                               www.cmegroup.com

Dubai Gold & Commodities Exchange

The DGCX commenced trading in November 2005 as the regions first derivatives and commodities exchange. Being located in the Middle East it fits the critical time zone between the markets of Europe and the Far East. As a truly international commodities and derivatives exchange, DGCX offers a range of products, with electronic trading accessible from anywhere in the world.

DGCX is a Dubai Multi Commodities Centre (Government of Dubai) initiative in partnership with Financial Technologies (India) Limited and Multi Commodity Exchange of India Limited (MCX). Management of DGCX comprises senior personnel from commodities, securities and financial services industries. These professionals bring experience, expertise and a track record to ensure the success of DGCX.

Dubai is the ideal and obvious location for the region's electronic commodities derivatives exchange. Its geographical position is a strategic strength as are the sophisticated infrastructure and enlightened leadership of the Emirate of Dubai.

DGCX is a technology driven, de-mutual organization committed to provide a world-class trading platform for a wide array of commodities and to implement the best global practices, with the highest level of transparency.

DGCX offers huge advantages to existing participants in physical commodities markets in the region previously unable to hedge their price exposures as well as opportunities to the region's burgeoning investment community. These advantages include:

·A fully automated, state-of-the-art, electronic trading platform accessible from anywhere in the world
·Uninterrupted trading hours from 08:30 am - 11:30 pm (GMT +4)
·An effective regulatory structure
·Futures and Options trading on a range of commodities
·Robust risk management and surveillance systems
·Settlement guarantee provided by Dubai Commodities Clearing Corporation (DCCC), a subsidiary 100% owned by DGCX

Contact Details: info@dgcx.ae

Goldcorp Inc.
TSX: G, NYSE: GG

Goldcorp is a leading gold producer engaged in gold mining and related activities including exploration, extraction, processing, and reclamation. The Company's assets are comprised of 10 operations and 7 development projects throughout the Americas. Over 70% of Goldcorp's reserves are situated in NAFTA countries.

Goldcorp is one of the world's largest gold mining companies and in 2006 the Company doubled its reserves and resources from 5 million to 10 million ounces through the acquisition of assets from Barrick (Placer Dome) and Glamis Gold Ltd. Gold production is forecast to increase by over 50% in the next five years.

Goldcorp's strategy is to provide shareholders with quality returns from our world class assets. The board, management and employees of Goldcorp continually work together to deliver results to our shareholders and to create value within the communities in which we operate. Goldcorp has a solid pipeline of projects including the 100% owned Eleonore gold project in Quebec, Canada and the 100% owned Peñasquito project in Zacatecas, Mexico. These two valuable assets, along with several others, will allow for growth in production for years to come.

Goldcorp has one of the best management and operational teams in the industry and we are dedicated to growing shareholder wealth into the future.

Goldcorp is one of the world's lowest cost and fastest growing multi-million ounce gold producers. The Company has a strong and liquid balance sheet and does not hedge its gold production.

Contact Details: Jeff Wilhoit
                          Vice President, Investor Relations
                          info@goldcorp.com
                          www.goldcorp.com

Hecla Mining Company
NYSE: HL

Established in 1891 in northern Idaho's Silver Valley, Hecla Mining Company has distinguished itself as a respected precious metals producer with a rich history of mining. Hecla is the oldest U.S.-based precious metals mining company and the lowest-cost primary silver producer in North America, with exploration properties and operating mines in four world-class silver and gold mining districts in the U.S., Mexico, and Venezuela. Hecla's operations include the Lucky Friday unit, a silver mine in northern Idaho. Lucky Friday is the deepest operating mine in the United States and has produced 130 million ounces of silver in the mine's 65-year history. Hecla also has a 29.73% interest in the Greens Creek mine in Alaska; the world's fifth largest silver mine.

Although the largest portion of the company's value resides in its silver properties, Hecla also produces gold from the La Camorra unit in Venezuela. Hecla is in the midst of the most aggressive exploration program in its history, focusing on its large and prospective properties in central Mexico and surrounding its mines in Idaho and Alaska. The company's common stock has been traded on the New York Stock Exchange since 1964 under the symbol "HL."

Contact Details: Vicki Veltkamp
                        Vice President, Investor & Public Relations
                        vveltkamp@hecla-mining.com
                        www.hecla-mining.com

Kitco Inc.

Since 1977, Kitco Metals of Montreal has earned the reputation of being the world's premier online retailer of precious metals. Kitco offers a complete line of high-quality pure gold, silver, platinum, and palladium bullion coins, bars, and precious metals buying as well as a range of highly secure storage programs to individual investors and corporate partners worldwide.

Most individuals are familiar with Kitco by virtue of its extremely popular internet website. Kitco's precious metals website has the distinction of being the most frequently accessed precious metals news and price information website on the internet, as well as frequently being ranked in the top 2,000 most popular websites worldwide. About 5 million individual page views are recorded each week on Kitco's homepage, *www.kitco.com*. Out of one million Internet users online at any given moment, close to 1,000 are visiting Kitco's website.

Whether it is for purchasing gold coins or bars, checking live, 24/7 precious metals prices, researching detailed price charts, or reading up-to-the-minute news and gold market commentaries, investors from all over the world know they can rely on Kitco's unsurpassed information quality and competitive online and telephone gold buying services. In addition, the Kitco site covers the base metals and silver markets, and also offers discussion forums to its users.

Contact Details: Jon Nadler
                          Senior Analyst, Head of PR
                          JNadler@kitco.com
                          www.kitco.com

Luismin, S.A. de C.V.

Luismin is the Mexican subsidiary of Goldcorp Inc.

Luismin owns and operates two gold and silver mines and holds numerous exploration projects throughout Mexico. The San Dimas mine located in the border of the Durango and Sinaloa states, Nukay a small operation acquired with los Filos, which is located in the state of Guerrero. These mines hold exploration and exploitation concessions with a total area of approximately 40,000 hectares. This extensive land area covers the mines, as well as the most prospective surrounding areas and forms an important asset for Luismin's future exploration programs.

Luismin has a long history of mining in Mexico, with some current operations dating back to the 1890s. Luismin has an experienced management team and a proven record of increasing production while maintaining reserves over long periods of time.

All of the mines are underground, operations using mechanized cut and fill mining methods. After milling, cyanidation, precipitation and smelting, dore bars are poured and then transported to refineries in Mexico and United States. Production from the mines in 2006 was 208,400 ounces of gold and 8,931,700 ounces of silver.

Multi Commodity Exchange of India

MCX is an independent and de-mutulised multi commodity exchange. It was inaugurated on November 10, 2003 by Mr. Mukesh Ambani, Chairman and Managing Director, Reliance Industries Ltd.; and has permanent recognition from the Government of India for facilitating online trading, clearing and settlement operations for commodities futures market across the country. Today, MCX features amongst the world's top three bullion exchanges and top four energy exchanges.

MCX offers a wide spectrum of opportunities to a large cross section of participants including producers/ processors, traders, corporate, regional trading centre, importers, exporters, co-operatives and industry associations amongst others. Headquartered in the financial capital of India, Mumbai, MCX is led by an expert management team with deep domain knowledge of the commodities futures market. Presently, the average daily turnover of MCX is around USD1.55 bn (Rs.7,000 crore - April 2006), with a record peak turnover of USD3.98 bn (Rs.17,987 crore) on April 20, 2006. In the first calendar quarter of 2006, MCX holds more than 55% market share of the total trading volume of all the domestic commodity exchanges. The exchange has also affected large deliveries in domestic commodities, signifying the efficiency of price discovery.
Being a nation-wide commodity exchange having state-of-the-art infrastructure, offering multiple commodities for trading with wide reach and penetration, MCX is well placed to tap the vast potential poised by the commodities market.

Key shareholders: Financial Technologies (I) Ltd., State Bank of India and it's associates, National Bank for Agriculture and Rural Development (NABARD), National Stock Exchange of India Ltd. (NSE), Fid Fund (Mauritius) Ltd. - an affiliate of Fidelity International, Corporation Bank, Union Bank of India, Canara Bank, Bank of India, Bank of Baroda , HDFC Bank, SBI Life Insurance Co. Ltd., Merrill Lynch and Citigroup

Contact Details: info@mcxindia.com

Noah Financial Innovation

Noah Financial Innovation ("Noah") is a niche South African-based stock broking company with an enviable track record of providing innovative, tailored execution and independent research services to institutional investors. Noah's business model is specifically designed to cater for unbundled execution and research services in accordance with global market trends.

Contact Details: Prinolan Pillay
                        Research Sales
                        ppillay@noahfi.com
                        www.noahfi.com

NYMEX

The New York Mercantile Exchange, Inc. is the largest physical commodity futures exchange and the preeminent trading forum for energy and precious metals. It is also the largest exchange for the trading and clearing of precious metals based on product volume.

The Exchange is a trading forum providing market liquidity and price transparency. The financial guarantees offered through the NYMEX clearinghouse mitigate the risk of counterparty default.

Futures and options contracts that provide for the physical delivery of gold, silver, copper, and aluminum trade on the COMEX Division while platinum, palladium, crude oil, gasoline, heating oil, and natural gas trade on the NYMEX Division. Trading in these contracts is by open outcry, and electronic futures trading is also available on the CME Globex® platform under a technology services agreement with the Chicago Mercantile Exchange. The physically delivered futures contracts trade on CME Globex simultaneous with the trading floor and seamlessly continue trading when the floor closes in the afternoon and as it reopens the following morning. Trading can be conducted for 23 ¼ hours a day via CME Globex.

A series of electronically traded metals futures contracts were introduced for trading on CME Globex in late 2006, including fractional COMEX gold, silver, and copper futures; COMEX Asian gold and NYMEX Asian platinum and palladium; and COMEX London aluminum, copper, and zinc.

The Exchange also lists approximately 350 energy and related futures and options contracts on the NYMEX ClearPort® electronic platform which can be traded or transacted off-exchange and submitted for clearing.

NYMEX Holdings, Inc., the parent company of the Exchange, trades on the New York Stock Exchange under the symbol NMX.

Contact Details: marketing@nymex.com
                          www.nymex.com

Commodities Now

Commodities Now is the quarterly magazine and associated website for the globally traded commodities markets. The primary focus is on the base and precious metals, power and
energy, and agricultural and soft commodities markets. It is the trends and developments
within these sectors that are addressed, such as supply and demand, trading and risk management, and technology through to regulation. Read by professional commodity market
participants around the world, Commodities Now has regular updates on the bullion and
precious metals markets with contributions and special reports from leading metal market
and mining specialists such as CPM Group, TheBullionDesk, Dow Jones Newswires and
many more. *Commodities Now* also produces an annual LME Week Supplement looking
at base and precious metals and mining.

The associated website: *www.commodities-now.com* provides daily news and research of
interest to players throughout the commodity complex with prices and charts from leading precious metals exchanges included.

Contact Details: Guy Isherwood
                        gish@commodities-now.com
                        www.commodities-now.com

The Institute of Scrap Recycling Industries, Inc.

The Institute of Scrap Recycling Industries, Inc. (ISRI) is the "Voice of the Recycling
Industry." ISRI represents over 1,500 companies in 21 chapters nationwide that process,
broker, and consume scrap commodities, including metals, paper, plastics, glass, rubber,
electronics, and textiles. With headquarters in Washington, D.C., the Institute provides
education, advocacy, and compliance training, and promotes public awareness of the vital
role recycling plays in the U.S. economy, global trade and environment.

Contact Details: Bob Garino
                        Director of Commodities
                        bobgarino@isri.org
                        www.isri.org

The Prospector Exploration & Investment Newspaper

The Prospector newspaper is North America's leading source of in-depth information
about news making junior mining companies. Published in Vancouver, the bimonthly
journal includes company profiles, area play analysis, commodities studies, and investment advice from leading stock analysts. The Prospector also produces Internet Daily
Mining News, the only daily source of mining news coverage of its kind.

The CPM Gold Yearbook, 2008

Charts and Tables

Official Transactions

Fabrication Demand

Prices

Review and Outlook

Review and Outlook

Six years into an unprecedented bull market, gold prices soared to record levels in 2007. Last year saw gold prices surpass their record high settlement price of $834 on 21 January 1980. Gold prices, basis the nearby active Comex futures settlement price, approached this previous peak on 26 December, settling at $829.50. Prices continued to strengthen, settling at $831.80 on 27 December. It finally set a new record high settlement price, of $842.70, on 28 December, before subsiding slightly to settle at $838.00 on 31 December, the last trading day of the year.

Even before gold prices had broken the previous daily settlement high, they had reached record levels in terms of weekly, monthly, quarterly, and annual averages. Gold prices averaged $700.11 in 2007. This was 15.4% higher than the $606.67 average for 2006, and 14.4% higher than the $611.98 average in 1980. The low settlement price for 2007 was $606.90, higher than the average for all of 2006.

The move to record prices in gold reflected continued strong investment demand for physical gold, around the world. Investors have been buying gold to protect against a falling dollar and volatile currency markets. Other investors have been buying gold as a portfolio diversifier, as protection against falling and volatile stock markets and low yields on interest-bearing bonds and notes. Still other investors

The Price of Gold

Monthly Average London PM Fix, Through January 2008.

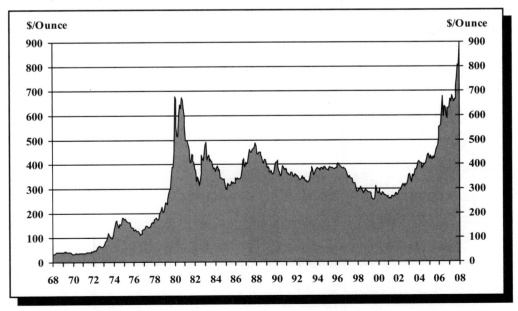

have been buying gold as a safe haven against political turmoil, worrying about everything from invasions and bombings of their countries to home-grown revolution and general political malaise. Still others have been buying gold as an inflation hedge, as a form of savings, as protection against financial market problems, and as a commodity that seems to have fundamentals suggesting still higher prices are yet to come. All of these factors have been stimulating historically high levels of investment demand on a sustained basis, pushing prices higher. Lower mine production and surprisingly strong fabrication demand for gold for use in jewelry in developing economies and electronics also have helped stimulate higher gold prices.

Prices continued to rise in January 2008, and accelerated their increase. Gold settled at $860.00 on 2 January 2008, and then rose to break above $900.00, on 11 January. Gold continued to rise through January, reflecting investor discomfort regarding economic, financial market, and political concerns. Extremely high open interest in the nearby active February Comex futures contract added to the upward momentum. The February Comex gold futures contract reached $927.10 on a settlement basis on 28 January and an intraday high of $936.30 on 30 January, as bullion traders who were short the February Comex contract were buying back their shorts and rolling them into April, June, and August contracts.

Supply/Demand Balance

Projected Through 2008.

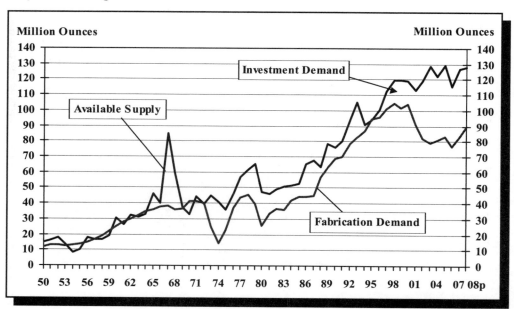

Throughout January 2008 gold prices stayed above $860 on a settlement basis. This was in stark contrast to the 1980 experience. In 1980 gold prices settled above $800 for only two days, Friday, 18 January and Monday, 21 January. Gold futures prices settled at $740.50 on Wednesday, 16 January 1980. This was locked the daily futures price limit of $50 higher than the day before.

They rose another $50 to $790.50 the next day, and then to $823.00 on 18 January and $834.00 on 21 January. The intraday high on 21 January was $873. The next day, Tuesday, 22 January, saw the nearby active February contract fall the daily limit of $50 on the exchange, settling at

$784.00. The spot contract, which had no daily maximum limit, plunged $143 to settle at $682.

The period of prices above $800 is more sustained this time around, perhaps because the factors that have been driving gold prices higher are more sustained and prolonged. Indeed, the entire cycle of gold and other commodities prices has been elongated compared to past periods.

Looking forward, insofar as the rise in gold prices has been propelled by investors worried about the plethora of economic, financial market, and political problems they see facing the world, the period of high gold prices should be expected to continue for as long as

Investment Demand's Effect on Gold Prices

Price Change Through December 2007.

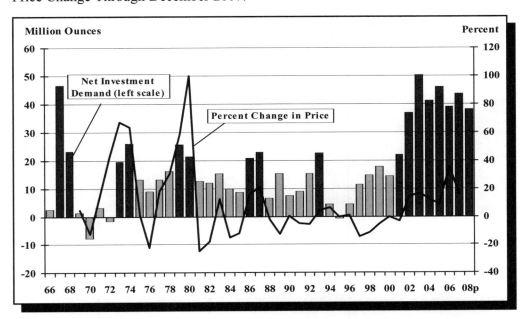

Gold Statistical Position
Million Troy Ounces

	1977	1978	1979	1980	1981	1982	1983	1984	1985	1986	1987	1988	1989	1990	1991	1992
Mine Production																
South Africa	22.5	22.6	22.6	21.6	21.1	21.4	21.8	21.9	21.6	20.5	19.4	19.9	19.5	19.4	19.2	19.6
Canada	1.7	1.7	1.6	1.6	1.7	2.1	2.2	2.5	2.8	3.3	3.7	4.3	5.1	5.3	5.6	5.2
United States	1.1	1.0	1.0	1.0	1.4	1.5	2.0	2.1	2.5	3.7	4.9	6.5	8.5	9.5	9.5	10.6
Australia	0.6	0.6	0.6	0.5	0.6	0.9	1.0	1.3	1.8	2.5	3.5	5.0	6.8	7.9	7.6	7.6
Peru	-	-	0.1	0.2	0.2	0.2	0.2	0.1	0.1	0.1	0.2	0.2	0.1	0.1	0.1	0.3
Indonesia	-	-	0.1	0.1	0.1	0.1	0.1	0.1	0.3	0.3	0.4	0.5	0.5	0.6	0.8	1.2
Other Market Economies	5.1	5.0	4.7	5.6	6.2	6.4	6.9	7.8	8.7	9.8	9.9	11.1	11.0	11.8	13.2	14.2
Total	31.0	31.1	30.7	30.5	31.2	32.4	34.2	35.7	37.9	40.3	42.1	47.5	51.6	54.5	56.0	58.6
% Change Year Ago	-	0.1%	-1.2%	-0.7%	2.3%	4.0%	5.5%	4.3%	6.2%	6.3%	4.5%	12.7%	8.6%	5.7%	2.8%	4.6%
Secondary Supply	5.7	5.7	10.9	21.2	10.5	11.1	11.7	10.4	9.0	13.0	12.8	11.1	9.7	10.7	11.3	12.0
% Change Year Ago	-	0.0%	91.2%	94.5%	-50.5%	5.7%	5.4%	-11.1%	-13.5%	44.4%	-1.5%	-13.3%	-12.6%	10.3%	5.6%	6.2%
Transitional Economy																
Sales	13.2	13.2	6.4	2.9	9.0	6.5	2.7	3.9	7.6	13.2	10.1	10.1	11.0	10.0	10.0	11.0
% Change Year Ago	-	0.0%	-51.5%	-54.7%	210.3%	-27.8%	-58.5%	44.4%	94.9%	73.7%	-23.5%	0.0%	8.9%	-9.1%	0.0%	10.0%
Total Supply	50.0	50.0	48.0	54.6	50.7	50.0	48.6	50.0	54.5	66.5	65.0	68.7	72.3	75.2	77.3	81.6
% Change Year Ago	-	0.0%	-4.0%	13.7%	-7.1%	-1.3%	-2.8%	2.8%	9.0%	22.0%	-2.2%	5.6%	5.2%	4.1%	2.9%	5.5%
Industrial Demand																
Electronics	2.6	3.0	3.5	3.1	3.1	3.0	3.4	4.0	3.6	3.7	3.7	3.9	4.1	4.2	4.1	3.8
Dental/Medical	2.7	2.9	2.8	2.0	2.2	2.0	1.8	1.8	1.9	1.9	1.7	1.9	1.9	2.0	2.1	2.3
Other	1.6	1.8	1.7	1.4	1.3	1.2	1.4	1.2	1.2	1.3	1.1	1.2	1.5	1.5	1.5	1.4
Total	6.9	7.8	8.1	6.5	6.6	6.1	6.5	6.9	6.6	6.8	6.5	7.0	7.5	7.8	7.7	7.5
% Change Year Ago	-	12.4%	3.9%	-19.1%	0.6%	-7.4%	7.0%	6.5%	-4.9%	3.5%	-5.2%	7.7%	7.2%	3.5%	-1.0%	-2.4%
Jewelry																
Developed Countries	20.9	22.8	21.2	12.4	15.4	17.0	16.5	18.5	20.2	20.2	19.9	22.5	26.5	28.5	28.5	29.9
Developing Countries	16.0	14.6	10.5	6.8	11.4	13.6	12.6	16.2	17.3	17.4	18.6	27.1	29.1	32.4	34.0	40.8
Total	37.0	37.4	31.6	19.2	26.8	30.6	29.1	34.7	37.5	37.7	38.5	49.6	55.6	60.9	62.5	70.8
% Change Year Ago	-	1.2%	-15.5%	-39.3%	39.7%	14.3%	-5.0%	19.3%	8.2%	0.4%	2.2%	28.8%	12.1%	9.5%	2.6%	13.3%
Total Fabrication Demand	43.9	45.2	39.7	25.7	33.4	36.7	35.6	41.6	44.1	44.5	45.0	56.6	63.1	68.6	70.2	78.3
% Change Year Ago	-	3.0%	-12.2%	-35.2%	29.7%	10.0%	-3.0%	17.0%	6.0%	0.8%	1.1%	25.8%	11.5%	8.8%	2.2%	11.5%
Official Transactions																
Int'l Monetary Fund	-6.0	-5.9	-5.5	-2.2	-	-	-	-	-	-	-	-	-	-	-	-
United States	-	-4.1	-11.8	-0.4	-0.2	-0.1	-0.6	-0.6	-0.1	-0.6	0.3	-0.5	0.1	-	-	-
Canada	-	-	-	-1.2	-0.5	-0.2	0.0	0.0	0.0	-0.4	-1.2	-1.4	-1.0	-1.0	-1.8	-3.0
Other	-2.7	-1.7	-0.2	11.2	5.2	1.3	-1.7	-0.9	1.6	2.0	-2.0	7.2	-5.3	-1.0	-1.0	-9.1
Total	-8.7	-11.7	-17.5	7.4	4.5	1.0	-2.4	-1.5	1.5	1.0	-2.9	5.3	-6.2	-2.0	-2.8	-12.1
% Change Year Ago	-	34.5%	49.6%	NM	-39.2%	-77.8%	NM	-37.5%	NM	-33.3%	NM	NM	NM	-67.7%	40.0%	332.1%
Net Private Investment																
Official Coins	4.6	9.2	9.3	7.7	7.3	5.3	5.7	4.1	4.8	10.8	7.0	4.7	5.0	3.9	5.1	2.8
Bullion	8.5	5.7	15.4	12.5	4.6	5.8	8.6	4.4	3.7	9.6	15.5	1.6	9.7	4.0	4.2	11.9
Medallions	1.7	1.6	1.1	1.2	0.9	1.2	1.1	1.4	0.4	0.6	0.5	0.5	0.7	0.7	0.7	0.7
Indian Demand	-	-	-	-	-	-	-	-	-	-	-	-	-	-	-	-
Total	14.8	16.5	25.8	21.4	12.8	12.3	15.4	9.9	8.9	21.0	23.0	6.8	15.4	8.6	10.0	15.4
% Change Year Ago	-	11.4%	56.6%	-16.8%	-40.3%	-3.7%	25.1%	-36.1%	-9.9%	136.7%	9.2%	-70.3%	125.4%	-44.3%	16.5%	54.6%
Total Stock Demand	6.1	4.8	8.3	28.8	17.3	13.3	13.0	8.4	10.4	22.0	20.1	12.1	9.2	6.6	7.2	3.3
% Change Year Ago	-	-21.6%	73.9%	248.8%	-40.0%	-23.0%	-2.3%	-35.9%	24.2%	112.1%	-8.9%	-39.5%	-24.2%	-28.5%	9.3%	-53.5%
Total Demand (Fabrication Plus Stock Change)	50.0	50.0	48.0	54.6	50.7	50.0	48.6	50.0	54.5	66.5	65.0	68.7	72.3	75.2	77.3	81.6
Price Per Ounce																
High	$168.20	$245.00	$517.80	$834.00	$597.00	$486.00	$510.10	$404.60	$348.80	$441.10	$497.10	$487.00	$418.90	$422.40	$403.20	$359.30
Low	127.30	166.90	217.60	463.00	388.50	298.00	372.60	307.30	282.00	327.00	392.10	394.00	358.10	346.80	348.10	329.70
Average	148.11	193.36	307.82	611.98	459.02	376.23	424.12	360.36	317.40	368.00	446.74	437.16	382.40	383.90	362.44	343.76
% Change Year Ago	-	30.6%	59.2%	98.8%	-25.0%	-18.0%	12.7%	-15.0%	-11.9%	15.9%	21.4%	-2.1%	-12.5%	0.4%	-5.6%	-5.2%

Source: CPM Group.
Notes: There maybe discrepancies in totals and percent changes due to rounding. Net official sales are indicated by negative numbers.
The price is the Comex nearby active settlement, 2007 through December. Longer term projections are available in CPM Group's
Gold Supply, Demand, and Price: 10-Year Projections report. e -- estimates. p -- projections. NM -- Not meaningful.
January 31, 2008

1993	1994	1995	1996	1997	1998	1999	2000	2001	2002	2003	2004	2005	2006	2007e	2008p	
																Mine Production
19.9	18.8	16.8	15.9	15.8	14.9	14.5	13.8	12.7	12.7	12.1	11.0	9.6	8.8	8.0	8.0	South Africa
4.9	4.7	4.9	5.3	5.5	5.3	5.1	4.9	5.1	4.9	4.5	4.2	3.8	3.4	3.3	3.4	Canada
10.6	10.5	10.2	10.5	11.6	11.8	11.0	11.3	10.8	9.6	8.9	8.3	8.4	8.0	7.8	7.9	United States
7.7	8.0	8.4	9.2	10.0	10.0	9.7	9.6	9.2	8.8	9.1	8.3	8.3	8.0	7.9	8.0	Australia
0.7	1.1	1.8	2.1	2.5	3.0	4.2	4.2	4.5	5.1	5.5	5.6	6.7	6.5	5.4	5.5	Peru
1.5	1.9	2.4	2.6	2.8	4.0	4.5	4.2	5.6	4.7	4.6	3.1	4.5	3.0	3.5	2.5	Indonesia
14.6	15.2	15.8	16.2	16.9	18.3	20.0	19.6	19.3	19.5	20.2	20.6	21.2	22.4	23.6	24.8	Other Market Economies
59.9	60.2	60.3	61.8	65.1	67.4	68.8	67.7	67.0	65.2	64.9	61.1	62.4	60.0	59.3	60.0	Total
2.3%	0.5%	0.1%	2.4%	5.5%	3.4%	2.2%	-1.6%	-1.0%	-2.8%	-0.3%	-5.9%	2.3%	-3.9%	-1.1%	1.1%	% Change Year Ago
12.6	13.8	14.5	17.0	15.5	22.6	20.0	21.2	22.0	26.0	29.4	27.4	28.0	26.3	32.4	33.9	Secondary Supply
5.0%	9.5%	5.1%	17.2%	-8.8%	45.8%	-11.5%	6.2%	3.5%	18.4%	13.0%	-7.0%	2.4%	-6.2%	23.3%	4.6%	% Change Year Ago
																Transitional Economy
11.0	10.0	11.0	11.5	12.0	15.0	17.0	16.0	15.0	17.0	17.0	18.0	18.0	18.0	19.0	20.0	Sales
0.0%	-9.1%	10.0%	4.5%	4.3%	25.0%	13.3%	-5.9%	-6.3%	13.3%	0.0%	5.9%	0.0%	0.0%	5.6%	5.3%	% Change Year Ago
83.5	84.0	85.8	90.3	92.6	105.0	105.8	104.9	104.0	108.2	111.3	106.4	108.5	104.3	110.7	113.9	Total Supply
2.4%	0.6%	2.1%	5.2%	2.6%	13.3%	0.8%	-0.8%	-0.9%	4.0%	2.9%	-4.4%	1.9%	-3.9%	6.2%	2.8%	% Change Year Ago
																Industrial Demand
3.8	3.9	4.0	4.3	4.9	4.8	4.9	5.0	4.7	4.6	4.7	4.9	5.5	7.5	8.9	9.4	Electronics
2.1	2.2	2.6	2.6	2.7	2.6	2.6	2.7	2.6	2.5	2.5	2.5	2.4	2.4	2.4	2.4	Dental/Medical
1.4	1.5	1.5	1.7	1.7	1.6	1.6	1.6	1.6	2.0	2.0	2.0	1.9	3.1	4.6	5.5	Other
7.3	7.6	8.1	8.6	9.2	9.0	9.1	9.4	8.8	9.0	9.2	9.4	9.8	13.0	15.9	17.3	Total
-2.6%	4.5%	6.6%	5.3%	7.3%	-2.6%	1.6%	3.0%	-5.8%	2.2%	2.1%	1.6%	4.7%	32.3%	22.7%	8.6%	% Change Year Ago
																Jewelry
30.5	31.7	32.7	31.2	33.6	36.5	34.6	33.9	31.4	28.9	24.5	23.9	22.0	16.2	14.9	14.2	Developed Countries
44.8	47.3	53.5	56.0	58.4	59.1	58.3	61.0	50.9	44.1	45.0	47.7	51.3	47.4	52.1	58.3	Developing Countries
75.4	78.9	86.3	87.2	92.0	95.6	92.9	94.9	82.4	73.0	69.5	71.6	73.3	63.6	67.0	72.5	Total
6.5%	4.7%	9.3%	1.1%	5.4%	4.0%	-2.8%	2.2%	-13.3%	-11.4%	-4.7%	3.0%	2.4%	-13.3%	5.4%	8.1%	% Change Year Ago
82.7	86.6	94.4	95.8	101.2	104.6	102.0	104.3	91.2	82.0	78.7	81.0	83.1	76.6	82.9	89.8	Total Fabrication Demand
5.6%	4.7%	9.0%	1.5%	5.6%	3.4%	-2.4%	2.3%	-12.6%	-10.1%	-4.0%	2.9%	2.6%	-7.9%	8.3%	8.2%	% Change Year Ago
																Official Transactions
-	-	-	-	-	-	-	-	-	-	-	-	-	-	-	-	Int'l Monetary Fund
-0.1	-	-	-	-	-	-	-	-	-	-	-	-	-	-	-	United States
-3.5	-2.2	-0.5	-0.5	-	-0.6	-0.7	-0.6	-0.1	-0.2	-	-	-	-	-	-	Canada
-18.4	-4.8	-7.5	-9.5	-20.0	-14.0	-13.2	-13.7	-0.9	-10.8	-17.6	-15.7	-20.6	-11.5	-16.0	-14.0	Other
-22.0	-7.0	-8.0	-10.0	-20.0	-14.6	-13.9	-13.9	-9.3	-10.9	-17.6	-15.7	-20.6	-11.5	-16.0	-14.0	Total
81.4%	-68.1%	14.3%	25.0%	100.0%	-27.0%	-4.7%	0.0%	-33.4%	17.3%	61.8%	-11.0%	31.9%	-44.5%	39.4%	-12.3%	% Change Year Ago
																Net Private Investment
3.9	2.2	2.5	2.0	3.3	4.0	4.0	1.7	2.2	2.4	3.2	3.7	4.0	4.5	4.5	4.5	Official Coins
18.2	1.6	-3.7	1.9	7.6	10.4	12.9	11.8	7.3	23.8	32.9	19.8	20.7	11.2	21.0	14.6	Bullion
0.7	0.7	0.6	0.6	0.6	0.6	0.8	1.0	1.0	1.0	1.2	1.5	2.0	3.0	2.8	3.0	Medallions
-	-	-	-	-	-	-	-	11.6	9.8	12.9	16.1	19.3	20.5	15.4	16.0	Indian Demand
22.8	4.5	-0.6	4.5	11.5	15.0	17.7	14.5	22.1	37.0	50.2	41.1	46.0	39.2	43.7	38.1	Total
47.8%	-80.4%	-113.9%	NM	157.2%	30.6%	18.3%	-18.1%	51.8%	67.8%	35.5%	-18.1%	11.9%	-14.8%	11.7%	-12.9%	% Change Year Ago
0.9	-2.5	-8.6	-5.5	-8.5	0.4	3.8	0.6	12.8	26.2	32.6	25.4	25.3	27.7	27.8	24.1	Total Stock Demand
-74.0%	NM	-240.4%	-35.8%	53.9%	NM	861.2%	-83.7%	NM	104.5%	24.6%	-22.0%	-0.3%	9.4%	0.2%	-13.3%	% Change Year Ago
																Total Demand (Fabrication Plus Stock Change)
83.5	84.0	85.8	90.3	92.6	105.0	105.8	104.9	104.0	108.2	111.3	106.4	108.5	104.3	110.7	113.9	
																Price Per Ounce
$407.00	$398.00	$397.80	$417.70	$366.60	$315.80	$326.00	$318.70	$293.40	$349.70	$417.20	$457.80	$531.70	$721.50	$842.70		High
326.30	370.60	372.20	369.20	284.80	275.40	253.70	265.30	256.60	278.40	322.20	374.90	414.30	527.80	606.90		Low
359.89	384.04	384.64	389.11	332.61	295.30	279.76	280.44	271.67	310.94	364.07	410.05	446.42	606.67	700.11		Average
4.7%	6.7%	0.2%	1.2%	-14.5%	-11.2%	-5.3%	0.2%	-3.1%	14.5%	17.1%	12.6%	8.9%	35.9%	15.4%		% Change Year Ago

these issues represent problems to investors. Put another way: While gold prices already are at record levels, they should be expected to stay high and even rise further until such time as investors around the world reduce the level of fears.

One of the trends which emerged in the middle of 2007 was a shift in investor attitudes. Prior to June or July 2007, it was common for investors from Hong Kong to Mumbai, from Dubai to London and New York, to express the view that they expected 2007 and 2008 to be volatile years, economically, politically, and thus for gold prices. The consensus view around the world was that things could calm down beyond 2008, that economic and political problems might subside, taking gold prices lower. This view was predicated in part on the view that international tensions and U.S. economic policies might improve under a new U.S. Administration.

In the middle of 2007 there was a palpable shift in investor attitudes. The realization sank in to the market's collective conscious that regardless of who becomes president of the United States in January 2009 he or she will face enormous economic, budgetary, international, and military problems that will take many years to solve, if they in fact are to be solved. Furthermore, the new thinking went, most of the candidates did not seem to be projecting confidence that they had any strong ideas how to tackle these issues. On top of that, the realization

that the present U.S. Administration is not the only agent of anti-globalization, war, terror, and anti-free market policies in the world. Put together, the thought process led to the conclusion that the world's problems would extend well beyond 2008. This realization was spreading around the world during June and July. In August, the subprime lending and credit availability issues hit the world financial markets and economy, driving home the seriousness and intractability of current problems. All of this combined to lead investors around the world to adopt a gloomier view of economic and political prospects, the dollar, interest rates, inflation, equity markets, bond values, and more.

As a result of this collective re-evaluation of the future, there was, starting in September, an acceleration in the level of investment demand for gold, regardless of how high prices were, which was reflected in an acceleration of the rate of increase in gold prices. This period of accelerated price increases has lasted into the first quarter of 2008.

At some point, investors will exhale, and some of the upward pressures will come off of gold prices. Equity values will fall low enough, and management shifts at corporations will instill renewed confidence sufficient to lure investors back into equity and bond issues. Economic activity will recover. One of the economic facts of life that gold bulls often overlook is that recessions end. They tend always to look toward the collapse of the international economic and financial system. That tends not to happen, even during times of world war and depression. Instead, the paradigm for economic crises that they should use ought to end with economic recovery. This current period of economic weakness too shall pass, and with it will investors' presently seemingly insatiable appetite for gold. It may be 2009 or beyond before that happens, but it should be expected to happen.

In the history of free gold prices, since the 1960s, there were five bull markets prior to the current one. Each one lasted one or two years, followed by four or five years of weaker gold prices. Each period of strong increases in prices reflected a rush of investors into

gold, seeking safety and protection from various economic or political problems. A bull market in gold from the 1960s until this decade was defined as a period of years in which investors bought more than 20 million ounces of gold on an annual basis and gold prices rose substantially as a result. The last bull market occurred in 1993. Investors bought 22.8 million ounces of gold that year. Prices rose 28.0% from a low of $326.30 in 1992 to a peak of $417.70 in 1994.

This last bull market in gold was followed by a protracted period of weak gold prices and low investor demand. Whereas the previous interludes had lasted four or five years, the gold market entered a period of sideways and

Gold Cycles - Trough to Peak

Monthly Average Price.

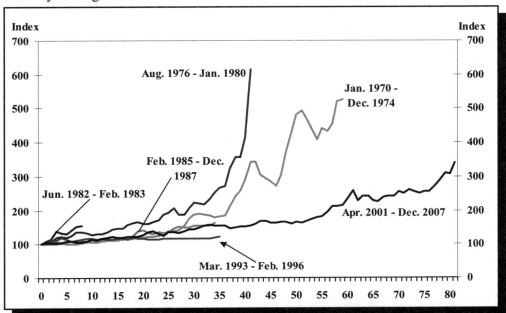

then lower prices in 1994 that lasted seven years, from 1994 through 2000.

This protracted bear market in gold in turn has been followed by an unprecedented gold bull market. The bull market emerged in 2001, when net investor demand for physical gold rose from 14.5 million ounces the year before to 22.1 million ounces. This helped start gold prices moving upward, from a low of $256.60 earlier in the year to a high of $293.00 toward the end of 2001. Investment demand rose sharply, over the next two years, and has remained high ever since. Gold prices have responded accordingly.

Last year was the seventh consecutive year of high levels of gold investment demand and rising prices, in sharp contrast to the one or two year gold rallies of the past four decades. Gold has risen from that 2001 low of $256.60 (it touched $253.70 in 1999) to $927.10 in January 2008, and is showing signs of continuing to rise.

Investment Demand

The bull market in gold has been fueled by strong investment demand, which is continuing this year. More investors have been buying more gold for a longer period of time than ever before, at least since World War Two, and possibly throughout history. The bull market that emerged in 2001 entered its eighth year in 2008.

The buying is coming from more parts of the world than ever before, in part reflecting liberalized financial markets in more countries than existed in the past and in part reflecting an impulse toward portfolio diversification on the part of individual and institutional investors. The demographic composition of gold investors also has changed, with more institutional money managers in industrialized nations participating as gold buyers than ever before.

Since 2001 investors have purchased an estimated 279.2 million ounces on a net basis worldwide. This is just physical demand for gold in bullion and coin form. It includes the 29.3 million ounces purchased through the numerous gold exchange traded funds begun in recent years that buy and hold gold in allocated accounts for their investors. It excludes some portion of the 338.5 million ounces of gold jewelry produced and sold in developing countries during the past seven years that reflects investment demand and savings. It also excludes futures, forwards, options, and other derivative or 'paper' gold securities that do not involved mobilizing physical gold in their purchase and sale.

Most of the demand for physical gold is coming from individual and other investors in India and the Middle East. Last year, as in 2006, India was the site of the largest volumes of gold investment demand. In 2006 around 20.5 million ounces of gold were purchased by investors in India. That was more than half of the 39.2 million ounces purchased in total on a net basis worldwide by investors that year. In 2007 investors in India purchased another 15.4 million ounces. While less than the year before and less than half of the 43.7 million ounces of total net investment demand for physical gold last year, it still was the largest single national market, and represented an enormous amount of gold.

The second largest national market in 2006 was Iran, where citizens have strong reservations about both their own government and the U.S. government, feeling that either government could set off major problems within that country. Demand also is strong throughout the Middle East. While demand has been particularly vibrant in these countries and regions since 2006, it must not be overlooked that the demand for gold investments is spread around the world at present, including strong demand from professional money managers in Europe and the United States.

As just mentioned, investment demand totaled an estimated 43.7 million ounces in 2007. This was up 11.7% from 39.2 million ounces in 2006. Demand had risen from 22.1 million ounces in 2001 to 37.0 million ounces in 2002 and then 50.2 million ounces in 2003, the year the United States invaded Iraq. Investors bought another 41.1 million ounces in 2004 and 46.0 million ounces in 2005, as economic, political, and financial market uncertainties, problems, and worries have kept investors keen on adding to their gold holdings throughout this period.

Central Bank Gold Holding and Investor Gold Holdings

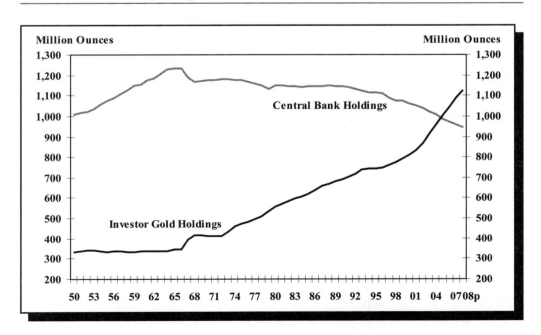

There has been a secular shift upward in the investment demand curve for physical gold, in the words of an economist. This means that more investors want larger volumes of gold at any given price than before. A corollary is that investors have shifted their views of what a 'low' gold price is. Investors that viewed $500 as a high gold price in any year up to 2006 now see that as a low price for gold.

Indeed, one phenomenon that has helped keep gold prices strong during 2007 has been a continue re-valuation of gold price expectations by investors. Many investors thought $740 was too high of a price in early 2007 and were waiting for prices to drop to around $680 before buying. When prices did not fall, they chose to buy around $705 - $710. They later viewed $840 as a low price, but gave up on that view and bought anyway. While investors viewed $840 as a high price as recently as November 2007, within two months, by late January 2008, many investors were waiting to see if prices could fall to around $850 - $860 before jumping back in as buyers. This constant upward revision in price expectations is characteristic of bull markets and also speculative bubbles.

The Past As Precedent

In many ways, the conditions that have pushed gold prices so sharply higher over the past seven years are reminiscent of the events that originally propelled gold to $834 in 1980. There were massive economic, political, and financial market problems facing the world, and precious metals seemed one of the few safe places to put one's money.

In late 1979 and January 1980 the world economy was in a mess. U.S. inflation was running around 14%, monetary policy had gone from being wildly accommodating to massively restrictive, interest rates had shot up to 22%, the U.S. and world economies had been thrown into their deepest recession since World War Two. Oil prices had quadrupled, from around $10 to $40 per ounce, and there were gasoline shortages and lines in the United States, Europe, and elsewhere. The stock market was incredibly anemic. There were banks and other financial institutions running into trouble, closing, and arranging emergency takeovers to stay in business. There were few ways for investors to protect themselves from these economic and financial market problems. There were no stock index futures and options, no currency options, inflation-indexed Treasury notes, or other assets that provided an alternative to gold and silver as a portfolio diversifier and hedge against these problems. Most citizens of most countries of the world could not legally hold assets in foreign currency bank deposits, either.

One important difference between then and now, economically, is that the dollar was strong in late 1979, rising from the second half of 1978 into the first half of 1980. At that time, the dollar and gold were seen as the safe havens, and both of them benefited in terms of rising prices. Gold far outpaced the dollar because, as just stated, most people around the world could not legally buy dollars as a hedge against weakness in their own currencies. This is not the case in the present bull market, with important implications for the sustainability of the current run up in prices in contrast to the experience of the early 1980s.

The problems were not only economic and financial. Political issues were prominent. There were U.S. hostages in Iran, and the Soviet Union had invaded Afghanistan after a protracted period of messy military involvement there. As a result of these two political issues Soviet and Iranian assets had been frozen in Europe, Japan, and the United States. The U.S. was locked into one of the most controversial presidential campaigns in decades.

In that environment, investors turned to gold as a currency hedge, an inflation hedge, a safe haven against political, economic, and financial market problems, a portfolio diversifier, and a form of savings. When prices started to rise, other investors poured in to the gold market, adding to the buying pressure on prices.

Then Things Improved

There were a couple of very important developments in the aftermath of the

run-up to $834 in gold prices that could have significant value to investors who have been buying gold lately.

For one thing, investors shifted away from gold as a safe haven as the recession continued into 1982. Economic and political conditions continued to be bad for a couple of years, but by 1982 investors were focusing on the dollar and not gold as a safe haven.

Second, the Federal Reserve Board and other monetary authorities ultimately rescued the world economy from the brink of collapse, in the second half of 1982. They did so by flooding the world with money, in what was mistakenly seen as a prelude to a sharp round of inflation, which never appeared. Investors jumped in to the gold market again in late 1982, expecting inflation to follow the sharp increase in money supply. The Fed and other central banks sucked the liquidity out of the economy once recovery was clearly underway. There never was an inflationary consequence, and in fact the U.S. economy entered into a quarter-century of consistently low inflation that continues today.

Gold prices did not stay at their historical highs for long, but they stayed high compared to their past levels. Gold prices already had risen to a then-high level of $217.60 in January 1979. Many financial market observers felt gold was over-priced at that level. Over the next twelve months prices rose to that intraday high of $873. Gold fell sharply the next day, with spot gold falling $143 on 22 January 1980. Prices remained above $400 for most of the next two years, averaging $611.98 in 1980 and $459.02 in 1981. A number of the economic and political problems continued to plague the world, as the recession of 1980 gave way to a second, or double-dip recession that lasted into 1982. Some problems were solved, which reduced some of the concerns that had driven investors toward gold, but enough was wrong in the world that investor demand for gold was strong enough to sustain prices at these levels.

As 1982 progressed economic conditions worsened. The recession, high interest rates, persistent inflation, and a strong rise in the U.S. dollar's exchange rates led to financial problems for governments around the world. Initially the problems appeared in Eastern Europe in 1981, where governments were having difficulties servicing their debt. By early 1982 the issues had spread to Latin America. By the middle of the year Mexico, Brazil, Argentina, and other Latin American governments were considering defaulting on their sovereign debt, which could have tightened credit for all borrowers.

By the middle of 1982 the world financial system was teetering on the brink of collapse. Interestingly, the price of gold was declining sharply, falling from around $384 in January of that year to a low of $298 in the middle of

the year. Investors were racing into the U.S. dollar as a safe haven, and were ignoring gold.

When the international debt crises was about to precipitate defaults in Mexico and Brazil, the monetary authorities of the major economies met and decided to reflate the world economy. They poured massive amounts of money into the economy around the world. The world economy responded, with real output and demand rising sharply during the second half of the year. When it was clear that the world economic recovery had taken hold, by the first quarter of 1983, the monetary authorities of the world drained all of the excess liquidity out of the world economy. This effectively precluded any long-term major inflationary consequences of their largess.

Non-inflationary Inflationary Policies

This event is extremely important to understand going forward from 2008. It represented a major change in the way that the Federal Reserve Board and other central banks managed economies. They responded to a crisis by pouring money into the markets. As soon as the crisis was passed and the economy was stabilized, they drained the excess liquidity out of the market, sterilizing the inflationary impact. It worked in 1982, and demonstrated to central bankers how they could behave in future crises. In fact, they have followed this practice repeatedly in subsequent decades, in response to the stock market crash in 1987, the recession of 1990, the Asian currency crisis of 1997, the Russian debt default and Long Term Capital Management collapse in 1998, and the recession and terrorist attacks of 2001.

Financial market commentators, especially gold oriented ones, seem to have been slow to pick up on this change in how central banks approach financial crises, even though the central banks have been quite forthright about how this works ('throwing money out of helicopters' is one often quoted and grossly misunderstood attempt at humor on the part of a monetary authority to describe the process) and the fact that this has been the primary approach to financial crises since 1982, for a quarter of a century. Books have been written about how central banks can and do work during this period, yet many market observers still refer to a central bank management model from the 1970s or 1920s as the model of how they think central banks work. The disconnection between monetary management techniques today and commentary about it is obvious and stark, and equally inexplicable.

This is obviously important in 2008 and beyond, since the world's monetary authorities have responded to the weak and chaotic financial markets of late 2007 and early 2008 by injecting massive amounts of money into the world's economies. If central banks' past behavior over the past quarter century is any indication of how they may

behave this time around, one would expect the central banks to sterilize the inflationary consequences of their recent monetary ease and liquidity injections as soon as they view the world financial markets and economy out of danger.

Many gold investors may miss this point. They may hold the view that the monetary and fiscal largess of late 2007 and early 2008 points inexorably toward higher inflation later. Inflation may rise, but the increase may not be as great as many investors and commentators expect in early 2008. The key will be how central bankers behave as the economy recovers, and whether they will and can effectively counter the inflationary pressures by draining the excess liquidity from the world economy.

Many investors missed this point in 1982. That was understandable back then, since it was the first time the central banks of the world had cooperated in such an exercise. People were used to the policies that had failed in the past. Additionally, the Leading Index of Inflation Indicators had been released a year or two earlier, based primarily on money supply trends. This indicator was being followed by economists and market participants in 1982. It pointed to higher inflation, based on the money supply increases of late 1982. It did not pick up on the withdrawal of that liquidity in early 1983 until later, by which time the markets, including gold, had turned.

Given these conditions, investors saw the monetary ease of 1982 as surely signalling massive inflation later. They bought gold, driving the price from $298 in June 1982 to a peak of $510.10 in January 1983. Inflation never returned, however, and gold prices soon fell back as investors fled the gold market in disillusion. Gold fell back to $372.60 later in 1983, and ultimately to $282, its lowest level since 1979, in the first quarter of 1985. The reason for this is that by the first quarter of 1983 it was clear that the world economy was roaring forward once more. The Fed, Bank of Japan, and European central banks sucked up the excess liquidity in the economy, by selling bonds. Inflation never rose. In fact, inflation in the United States fell from there, into what as of today stands as a quarter-century of inflation largely below 5%.

Twenty Years of Solitude

The period from 1983 through 2000 then became one of relative stability, both in gold prices and in the overall economic and political world. There were political crises and massive developments, including the fall of the Communist Bloc in eastern Europe, the dissolution of the Soviet Union, the rise of emerging economies, the 1987 stock market crash, the Asian currency crisis, the European currency crisis of 1992, and more. They were relatively mild events compared to the events of the 1970s, however, and governments and monetary authorities handled them with greater finesse and expertise. The

period since 1982 has seen fewer, shorter, and shallower recessions than any time since at least the 1950s, as described in a special section at the end of this chapter.

The gold market reflected this relative calm and also was less volatile than it had been. The gold price spent most of the years from 1983 into 1997 between $320 and $400 per ounce, with one more dip below this range, in 1985, and a couple of brief, unsustained runs into the $400 - $500 range. None of these periods were long-lived, however, and prices traded for roughly 15 years in this relatively narrow range. It made miners happy, as the average price was far above the $113 average price received from 1970 through 1978. It disappointed gold bulls, who kept expecting prices to rise back to their brief 1980 peak. Despite the lack of any economic, mathematic, or natural law saying so, many gold bulls continue to this day to believe that if the price of an asset, such as gold, reaches a certain peak, if only for a moment, as some point in history, the price must return to that level on a sustained basis at some point in the future.

In 1997 gold prices fell below this range, trading between $253 and $300 for most of the next five years. These prices were too low to be sustainable in the long run, as they discouraged mine development and encouraged strong growth in gold jewelry demand, which encourages higher prices later

The world economic and political environment was relatively sanguine for most of this time, however. The period of high inflation, deep and protracted recessions; high unemployment; major military conflicts; wild gyrations in stocks, bonds, and currencies; and financial crises seemed to have been left behind. It was very easy to believe tales about a "New Economic Paradigm" that precluded inflation, recession, and other financial crisis, in which stock prices always rose and investors could not lose money no matter how risky the assets they bought.

This Time….

This came to a halt in 2000. In that year, the new economic paradigm of the late 1990s was shown to be a chimera. The stock market bubble burst, and the world began to teeter toward a recession. The recession hit in 2001, along with the terrorist attacks on the United States and the beginnings of a prolonged U.S. military response in the Middle East. The year 2000 also witnessed an embarrassing debacle in the U.S. presidential election vote count, which did not help confidence in the U.S. economy and dollar. That was followed by a series of financial scandals involving companies in the United States and elsewhere, which began to raise investor concerns about the security of stock and bond investments. Economic nationalism began appearing, from the United States and Canada, both of which had governments thwart acquisition

attempts of natural resource companies by Chinese corporations, to Europe, Russia, and Latin America. More bad news followed, with the dollar entering a period of sharp decline after 2001.

This is the period in which the gold market now finds itself. In the release of CPM Group's **Gold Survey** in November 2000, the point was made that the two decades between the wild events of 1980 and 2000 had been characterized by relatively steady economic growth, relatively stable financial market conditions, steady increases in equity prices worldwide, a move toward liberalized and globalized economies worldwide, and low inflation. The dollar had been seen as the bastion of strength for most of that period. In such an economic and political environment, it only was reasonable that gold prices should have spent most of the time in a market clearing range of $320 - $400. There was little reason to put a political or economic risk premium on gold during those years. Standing at the end of 2000, with the economic, financial, and political storm clouds gathering, the **Gold Survey**'s conclusions that year were that for the first time since 1980 the economic and political prospects for the world were deteriorating rapidly, and suggested that gold prices might not only rise as high as they had in 1980, but could surpass that level by a wide margin. That report was released on 7 November 2000, a day the gold price settled at $265.40.

Market Overview

The gold market has undergone many major transformations since November 2000. Gold mine production has continued the slow decline that had begun to emerge that year, as a consequence of the long period of low gold price's reduction of the availability of financing to gold producers. Secondary recovery of gold from scrap, primarily old jewelry, has risen more than 50% meanwhile, more than offsetting the decline in mine production in terms of the number of ounces being refined and sold in to the market. The rise in scrap recovery is a direct result of the rise in gold prices since the beginning of this decade.

Gold use in jewelry meanwhile has fallen sharply. It has been cut in half in developed economies, where gold jewelry primarily is a luxury item. Demand has help up relatively better in developing countries, where much of this jewelry still is purchased as a form of gold investment. Central banks still are selling large volumes of gold. The key fundamental development over the past seven years has been that investors have been buying historically large amounts of gold, and continue to do so. Each of these trends is covered in detail in subsequent chapters of this report. A few comments follow here as highlights.

The Gold Market 1997 - 2006

2007 Through December.

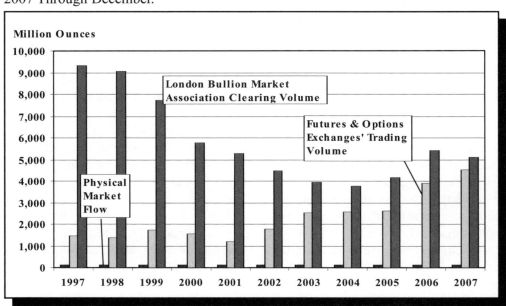

Supply

Total gold supply stood at 110.7 million ounces in 2007. This was up 6.2% from 104.3 million ounces in 2006. It was the second highest level of total newly refined gold supply on record, surpassed only by the 111.3 million ounces of refined gold supply in 2003. Total gold supply rose due to higher scrap refining and sales by the transitional economies, even though mine production continued to decline.

In 2008 total gold supply is projected to continue rising, increasing 2.8% to 113.9 million ounces. Mine production is projected to rise, along with scrap refining and transitional economy exports into the international market.

Mine production in the market economy nations declined 1.1% to 59.3 million ounces last year. Production dropped in all of the five largest gold producing market economy nations, but rose in Indonesia and emerging national producers such as Bolivia, Tanzania, Ghana, Mali, and Burkina Faso. Gold mine production last year was at its lowest level since 1992, having contracted in seven of the past eight years.

Gold mine output may rise in 2008, perhaps as much as 1.1% to 60.0 million ounces. The increase has been expected to begin emerging for the past few years. There is a gold mining exploration and development rush

Annual Total Supply

Projected Through 2008.

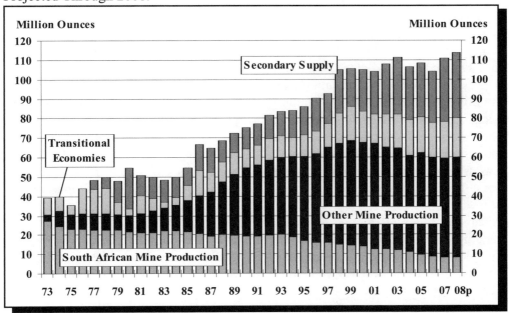

19

underway that far surpasses any previous gold rushes. At some point the massive efforts being put into finding, delineating, designing, financing, building, and starting new mines, as well as re-opening or expanding older ones, will have the intended effect of increasing mine production. Logistical problems and rising costs have delayed these projects, as the mining exploration and development rush underway around the world and across metals and minerals today is taxing the mining industry's infrastructure. The increases in supply will come, however, and they may begin appearing on a net world total gold production basis inn 2008.

It should be noted that after gold prices rose from $200 in 1978 to $611.98 (on an annual average price) in 1980, gold mine production rose. It did not rise dramatically immediately. Mine production rose from 30.5 million ounces in 1980, produced mostly in South Africa, to 35.7 million ounces in 1984. It then increased to 54.5 million ounces in 1990 and a peak of 68.8 million ounces in 1999. Most of this more than doubling in world gold production occurred outside of South Africa, in countries that did not have major gold mining industries in 1980. Most of it was developed by companies that were not gold mining companies in 1980.

A similar mine production response should be expected to the current rise in gold prices. Assuming prices stay above $500 even when the current period of high investment demand dissipates, gold mine production may increase for many years to come as a response to the recent run up in prices. There are many un-developed gold reserves and resources available in the world at present, and more are being discovered. New areas of the world are being opened for exploration and development which never were available in the past.

New mines and expansions with around 15.9 million ounces of annual capacity that are presently in the development stage are itemized in a table in the *Supply* chapter of this report. Other projects should be expected to come along as time progresses. While some older mines will close, offsetting some of the increases to aggregate production from these newer projects, net gold mining capacity nonetheless might increase by one-fifth over the next five years, and by even more in the longer term.

China, which is not included in the market economies mine production data in these reports yet, has surpassed South Africa as the world's largest gold producer. In 2007 China mined around 8.7 million ounces of gold, while South Africa produced an estimated 8.0 million ounces. Chinese production has risen from around 2.0 million ounces per year in the middle of the 1980s.

The data in these reports segregate China, Russia, Uzbekistan, and other countries for which good gold demand statistics are not available, putting production in these transitional economies in a separate category and measuring their net exports into the international market as a source of supply.

The data for mine production and secondary recovery of gold in China have improved dramatically in recent years. Data on domestic fabrication and investment demand are getting better and may be able to be incorporated into the main statistics by 2009's report. Data for the former Soviet nations are less accurate at this point, however. Meanwhile, data on exports from all of these countries, including China, are clouded by large volumes of circular trade, for example between China and Hong Kong, and China and Taiwan. In January 2008 the Chinese government announced plans to try to control the import and export of gold and silver better, requiring permits from the People's Bank of China in order to clear Customs effect 31 January 2008. This applies to gold and silver bullion and products, including material in bonded warehouses. The new regulations are aimed at trying to reduce abuses to the import and export system.

Secondary recovery of gold from old scrap rose sharply in 2007, primarily due to a sharp increase in the amount of gold being sold back into the market in India in the form of jewelry, statues, and decorative objects. Total scrap rose from 26.3 million ounces in 2006 to 32.4 million ounces in 2007, a 23.3% increase. A further 4.6% increase to 33.9 million ounces is projected for 2008.

India remains the largest gold scrap market, recovering an estimated 12.9 million ounces of gold last year. The flow of gold into the market from domestic scrap was so high in India, especially during the second half of the year, that the domestic Indian market gold price fell below the landed price of imported gold - the cost of buying gold overseas, shipping it into India, and paying the various customs duties and import tariffs. Thus, the flow of gold into India ground to a virtual halt during the last part of 2007.

Scrap recovery elsewhere was relatively modest in its price response. There was not a strong increase in gold jewelry sales for scrap in the Middle East, for example. Investors there are using freshly received petrodollars to buy more gold in 2007 and 2008, hanging on to their older gold jewelry and adding to their holdings, rather than trading in old jewelry for new pieces. Scrap recovery is estimated to have declined in the United States, as more old jewelry and electronics were shipped overseas to Europe and Asia for actual refining.

Fabrication Demand

Gold use in fabricated products rose 8.3% in 2007. The largest increase came in gold use in jewelry in developing countries, where much of the gold jewelry is a form of investment or savings. Gold use in developing countries jewelry totaled 52.1 million ounces in 2007, up from 47.4 million ounces in 2006. This was in sharp contrast to the continued contraction of gold use in jewelry in developed countries, where gold use fell from 16.2 million ounces in 2006 to 14.9 million ounces in 2007. Combined, jewelry use of gold rose 5.4%, from 63.6 million ounces in 2006 to 67.0 million ounces in 2007.

Gold use in electronics, dental, medical, and other fabricated products also rose sharply in 2007. Gold use may have increased 22.7% from 13.0 million ounces in 2006 to 15.9 million ounces in 2007. The use of gold in many such applications is highly price inelastic, so the high prices for gold appears to have had a modest impact

on gold demand trends. Gold use in electronics rose from 7.5 million ounces in 2006 to 8.9 million ounces in 2007. Gold use in other fabricated products rose from 3.1 million ounces in 2006 to 4.6 million ounces in 2007. Most of the growth in gold use in these products is occurring in India, Japan, and other Asian nations, where the manufacture of these products is growing at the expense of manufacturers in North America and Europe.

The exception to this is the use of gold in dental alloys, where gold use has been flat. Dental alloy manufacturers can shift their alloys to use more palladium when the price differential between gold and palladium makes this

Annual Total Demand

Projected Through 2008.

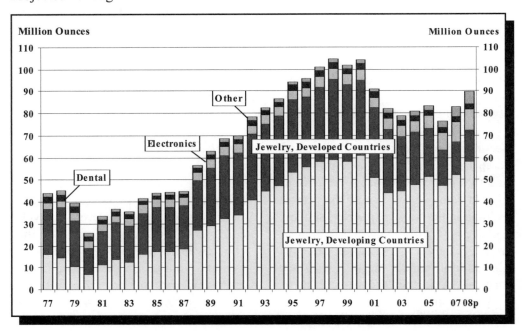

financially prudent. This is what has been happening.

Gold use is projected to rise another 8.2% in 2008. Again, the bulk of the increase is expected to be in jewelry in developing countries. Gold use in these countries may rise to 58.3 million ounces this year, up from 52.1 million ounces in 2007. Gold use in jewelry in industrialized nations meanwhile is projected to continue contracting, falling to 14.2 million ounces this year from 14.9 million ounces last year. Gold use in other fabricated products is projected to rise another 8.6% this year, to around 17.3 million ounces.

Official Transactions

Central banks are estimated to have sold around 16.0 million ounces of gold in 2007. This was up from 12.5 million ounces sold in 2006. It also was 7.0 million ounces greater than the 9.0 million ounces of gold that central banks had been expected at the beginning of last year to sell on a net basis in 2007.

The rise in gold prices and decline in the dollar has caused the percentage of monetary reserves held in gold in European central banks to swell to high numbers. Because of this, and fiscal issues in Spain, Spain sold more gold in 2007 than had been anticipated at

Official Transactions

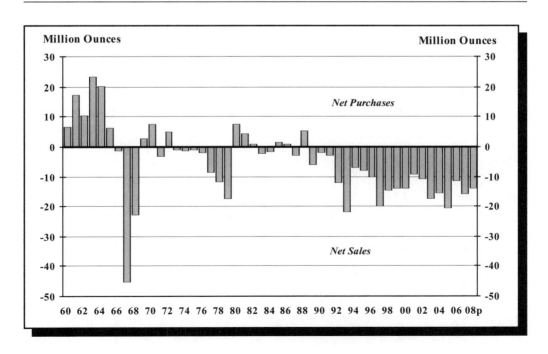

the start of the year. Also, Switzerland decided to further reduce its gold holdings, reversing an earlier position that the Swiss National Bank had sold as much gold as it wanted to between 2000 and 2005, and did not desire to sell any more of its gold. In total, central bank gold sales were about 7.0 million ounces higher than they otherwise would have been, due to these two sales.

Central bank sales may continue to be higher than otherwise would have been expected in 2008 and beyond, reflecting the facts that gold prices are at historic highs, the dollar remains under long-term pressure, and governments need money. Net official monetary gold reserve sales may total 14.0 million ounces this year, around 6.0 million ounces higher than projected a year ago.

Spain sold 4.4 million ounces of gold in 2007. This was up from 1.7 million ounces it sold in 2006. The sales proceeds were not deposited as foreign currency reserves with the Bank of Spain, but were transferred to the Treasury for use in general government expenses.

In 2000 Switzerland began selling half of the 83.3 million ounces of gold it held at that time, seeking to reduce its gold holdings to 41.5 million ounces. It completed those sales in 2005, and stated at that time that it was content to continue holding 41.5 million ounces of gold. In 2007 Switzerland

announced plans to sell another 8.8 million ounces of gold. It sold 4.4 million of this in 2007, and is expected to sell another 4.4 million ounces this year.

The other large seller of gold last year was the Banque de France, which sold 3.1 million ounces. The *Official Transactions* chapter later in this book discusses the 12 countries and official institutions that sold gold last year in greater detail. It also discusses the 10 countries that bought gold.

The largest buyer of gold among central banks was Russia, which purchased 1.4 million ounces of gold from domestic miners and refiners. Qatar's central bank also purchased around 380,000 ounces of gold during the year.

Gold market observers continued to speculate that Asian central banks would begin buying gold for their monetary reserves at some point, given the weakness of the dollar and the predominance of the dollar as their reserve currency. No Asian central bank has made such moves, and most say that they have no interest in buying gold for their monetary reserves. Most central bank managers do not view gold as a viable candidate as a monetary asset, given the small, illiquid, and transparent nature of the market. Also, insofar as a central bank holds monetary reserves for use in defending its national currency in times of crises, holding monetary reserves in dollars and other currencies is a much more efficient approach to monetary reserve management.

That is not to say that non-central bank government agencies might not be investing in gold. In many countries there is a central bank or monetary authority responsible for monetary policy, but also one or more separate agencies such as investment authorities, sovereign funds, and strategic materials managers. Some such government agencies might be purchasing gold as an investment or a strategic material, but these purchases would not be related to monetary policy or monetary reserve management.

Russia is one country that historically had enormous non-monetary gold reserves. Prior to the dissolution of the Soviet Union in 1991, Soviet gold reserves were estimated at more than 65 million ounces. Soviet gold reserves were classified as state secrets, but were estimated to have peaked at 80 million ounces in 1984. As the Soviet Union fell into financial disarray, it is believed to have sold 15 million ounces of these reserves, between 1985 and 1991, leaving around 65 million ounces of gold at the end of 1991. Of this total, only around 12 million ounces were in monetary reserves. The remaining 53 million ounces were considered 'trading reserves' or strategic reserves. Upon the dissolution of the Soviet Union there was a discussion and debate among the former republics as to the dispersion of these invento-

ries. Initially the Russian government took the position that only the monetary reserves ought to be divided among the former republics. Some of the gold ultimately was transferred to the other countries emerging from the former Soviet Union, but the amount of gold so transferred, at least from monetary reserves, was only around 1.3 - 2.0 million ounces. The disposition of the 53 million ounces of non-monetary reserves held by the former Soviet government was never made clear. Some of it appears to have been sold off by the Russian Army to support itself during the chaos immediately following the end of the Soviet Union, with other groups within the Russian government also apparently 'mobilizing' some of this gold for their own use.

There were strong indications by the middle of the 1990s that much of this gold no longer could be accounted for by the Russian government. Government officials began to say that they would like to rebuild the national patrimony of gold and other assets dispersed in the immediate post-Soviet disorder. During the late 1990s and early part of this decade the Russian central bank was not really in a good position to purchase gold, however. Oil and gas prices, the country's major sources of foreign exchange earnings, were very low, and taxes and other remittances to the government were not being paid on much of the materials being sold for export. Foreign exchanges reserves were below $10 billion.

As this decade has advanced, with oil and gas prices rising sharply, and the Russian government able to collect taxes on corporate earnings since 2001, the country has managed to build its foreign exchange reserves to around $450 billion. As a result, the Russian government now is in a position to rebuild its gold reserves to some extent.

It is interesting that given the improved financial position, the Russian central bank added only 1.4 million ounces of gold to its monetary reserves, in 2007, boosting these stocks to 14.3 million ounces. It may well be that additional amounts of gold have been purchased by other government agencies, and have not been added to reported official monetary reserves. In the Soviet era such stocks were controlled by the same entities within the government, but were distinguished from monetary reserves and went unreported.

The same policy was in place in China, although in China the non-monetary gold reserves were estimated to be much smaller. When the People's Bank of China extricated itself from being the national market maker in gold, in 2001, it transferred 3.4 million ounces of gold from non-monetary reserves to its monetary reserves, boosting its reported stocks from 12.7 million ounces to 16.1 million ounces. Some gold market commentators saw the increase in Chinese monetary reserves and began to trumpet in 2001 that the Chinese central bank was adding gold

to its reserves. In fact, it did not purchase any of this gold, but merely transferred the metal from working inventories used in the daily management of the domestic gold market, prior to 2001, to its monetary reserves once the central bank no longer was involved in the daily gold market activity.

Some central banks treat their working gold inventories in this way, so that their official monetary reserves do not fluctuate regularly due to the central banks' roles as national buyers and sellers of metal. Others do not segregate gold in this way. The U.S. Treasury, for example, reports small fluctuations in its monetary reserves when it loans gold to the U.S. Mint, an agency within the Treasury, for use as working inventories for the U.S. Mint's gold coin programs. The Mint borrows gold from the Treasury and uses this gold to strike gold Buffalo and Eagle bullion coins. As it sells the coins, it purchases the same amount of gold on a daily basis. Thus, the amount of gold held within the Treasury remains unchanged. For reporting purposes, however, the Treasury reports that the gold that it has in monetary reserves fluctuates slightly, on the order of a few thousand ounces at a time, reflecting the ebb and flow of metal from official stocks and the inventories on loan to the U.S. Mint for the coin program. These are the gold loans and swaps referred to in the U.S. Treasury's reports showing its monetary reserves, which some gold conspiracy theorists assume must be loans to private bullion banks or other central banks, rather than loans within the Treasury to its own Mint agency.

Incidentally, gold conspiracy theorists also like to say, with no basis in fact, that they are convinced the U.S. government has sold off its gold stocks and that the gold no longer is in Fort Knox, the famous Treasury depository in Kentucky. They are partly right: Most of the U.S. government's gold is held at the U.S. Army's West Point facilities, and not at Fort Knox. There is gold at Fort Knox, as well as at the U.S. Mints in Philadelphia and San Francisco, but most of the gold is at West Point. The conspiracy theorists who say it has been sold or leased are wrong on that account. They also are wrong when they say it has not been audited in decades. The Treasury regularly audits its gold and keeps track of this metal down to the thousandths of an ounce. It does not make its internal audits available to the public, for security reasons among other issues, as do most other central banks, government treasuries, and private corporations.

The Economic Environment For Gold

The discussion up to now has focused on the role of investor demand in setting the tone of the gold market, whether prices rise or fall, and how fast and fall they move. Investment demand in turn is set by a complex and far-reaching set of issues that affect investors' attitudes toward the world in which they live. Some of these are specific to gold: Whether investors' views of gold supply and demand trends are such that they think gold prices may rise or fall based on gold's fundamental balance. Most of the issues are broader economic and political views, including investor perceptions of the state of the economy both worldwide and as it affects them, their opinions regarding the stability of financial institutions that handle their money, whether they perceive political or military risks as being great or small, and much more. The complexity of these issues and how they interact to create investor sentiments is one of the most difficult barriers to analysts accurately projecting or predicting the future trends of all financial assets, including gold.

This section will discuss the economic outlook that informs the supply and demand projections of this report. How these economic variables interact with gold will be discussed in greater detail in the *Investment Demand* chapter of

World GDP

Annual, through 2007p.

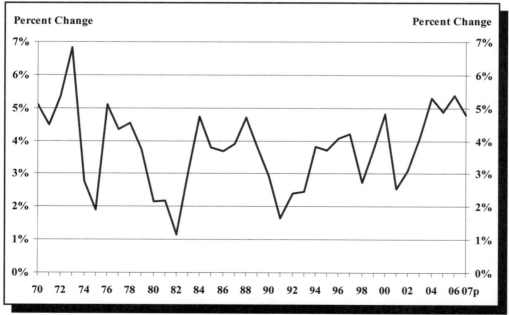

this book, which includes a discussion of the statistical relationships between gold and such macro-economic variables as inflation, the dollar's exchange rate, and trends in stocks, bonds, and bills.

One of the interesting aspects of the recent rise in gold prices, since 2001, is the degree to which it has occurred in a time of almost unprecedented wealth generation around the world. As the chart of world gross domestic product shows, real GDP on a global basis has been stronger over the past few years than it has been for most of the past 35 years. The world's economy has moved into a period of stronger growth, based on the liberalization of economies from China and Russia to Brazil and India. Globalization and movements toward increased trade have helped boost this period of relatively better prosperity, as have a range of economic deregulation efforts, productivity gains, and improved business management practices.

Economic activity in the United States also has been relatively benign for most of the past several years. The U.S. economy appears to be moving into a period of extremely weak, perhaps even recessionary, conditions as of the fourth quarter of 2007 and early 2008. Even within the context of that weakness, however, economic conditions have been relatively healthy. Stock market trends were good, until the second half of 2007, and interest rates

were relatively low, even with the increases in U.S. and other interest rates over the past two years. The U.S. dollar was falling, giving up roughly one-quarter of its value on a trade-weighted basis since 2002.

Certainly the stock markets have given investors cause for alarm over the past eight years. After the tech stock and stock market bubble burst in 2000, stocks fell sharply, with added downward pressure from the recession of 2001, the financial market scandals of 2001 and 2002, and the terrorist attack on the World Trade Center in 2001. Stocks rebounded handsomely after that, for a year or two. The markets have shown some variability since 2004, but have moved broadly upward throughout the past six years.

It was in the context of these relatively decent economic conditions that investors have been loading up on gold. Even as the economy was doing well, investors and investment advisors were concerned about economic conditions.

There appears to be a great deal of fear abroad among investors. Some of this fear is based on the worsening economic conditions, but much of it appears inflated. That is dangerous, as it suggests that if and when a more reasoned view toward various economic conditions gains hold, there could be sharp reactions to earlier over-reactions to economic conditions.

The Economy

	1994	1995	1996	1997	1998	1999	2000	2001	2002	2003	2004	2005	2006	2007e	2008p
Real GDP (a)															
(Percent Change)															
United States	4.0	2.5	3.7	4.5	4.2	4.4	3.8	0.8	1.6	2.5	3.6	3.1	2.9	2.2	2.0
Japan	0.6	1.5	5.0	1.6	-2.5	0.3	1.7	0.7	-0.7	0.5	4.0	2.4	2.8	1.9	1.6
Eurozone	2.5	2.6	1.5	2.6	2.8	3.0	3.9	1.9	0.9	0.8	2.0	1.4	2.6	2.3	2.3
China	13.1	10.9	10	9.3	7.8	7.6	8.4	8.3	9.1	10.0	10.1	10.4	11.1	11.5	10.0
India	6.8	7.6	7.5	4.9	5.9	6.9	5.4	3.9	4.5	6.9	7.9	9.0	9.7	8.9	8.4
Total OECD	2.9	2.2	2.6	3.1	2.3	2.8	3.7	2.4	1.0	1.7	3.6	2.7	3.2	2.6	1.9
Consumer Price															
Inflation (a)															
(Percent Change)															
United States	2.6	2.8	2.9	2.3	1.6	2.2	3.4	2.8	1.6	2.3	2.7	3.4	2.7	2.8	2.4
Japan	0.7	-0.1	0.1	1.7	0.6	-0.3	-1.7	-0.7	-0.9	-0.7	-2.3	0.3	0.3	0.0	0.3
Eurozone	2.7	2.4	2.2	1.6	1.1	1.1	2.1	2.4	2.3	2.1	2.1	2.2	2.2	2.0	2.0
China	25.5	10.1	7.0	0.4	-1.0	-0.9	0.9	-0.1	-0.6	2.7	3.2	1.4	2.0	5.7	3.5
India	8.8	11.3	10.1	5.3	16.3	0.0	3.2	5.2	4.0	2.9	4.6	5.3	6.7	4.9	4.0
Total OECD	2.4	2.5	2.3	1.7	1.3	2.6	1.4	2.8	2.0	1.7	1.8	2.1	2.2	2.2	2.1
Industrial Output (a)															
(Percent Change)															
United States	5.3	3.3	3.2	5.0	4.9	3.5	5.6	-3.7	1.5	1.8	2.2	2.2	3.0	2.1	
Japan	0.8	3.5	2.6	4.4	0.1	1.7	6.3	-13.5	1.3	1.3	1.5	1.5	4.7	3.0	
Eurozone	-	-	-	-	-	-	-	0.4	-0.5	0.3	1.8	1.8	3.9	2.9	
China	21.4	16.1	15.1	13.2	9.6	9.8	11.2	9.9	12.7	16.7	16.3	15.9	15.4	18.2	
India	-	12.6	8.6	5.4	3.3	7.6	7.4	2.1	5.1	6.4	8.3	7.9	10.3	na	
Total OECD	3.9	3.0	2.8	4.3	3.5	2.1	5.7	-3.6	2.5	1.3	1.6	1.6	2.0	2.5	
Interest Rates															
(Percent)															
United States	4.3	5.5	5.0	5.1	4.8	4.6	5.8	3.4	1.6	1.1	1.5	2.8	4.7	4.4	
Japan	3.7	2.5	2.2	1.7	1.1	1.8	1.7	1.3	1.3	1.0	1.5	1.4	1.7	1.7	
Eurozone	-	-	-	-	3.7	3.0	4.4	4.3	3.3	2.3	2.1	2.2	3.1	3.8	
China	10.1	10.4	9.0	8.6	4.6	3.2	3.2	3.2	2.7	2.7	3.3	3.3	3.3	3.3	
India	12.0	12.0	12.0	9.0	9.0	8.0	8.0	6.5	6.3	6.0	6.0	6.0	6.0	6.0	
United Kingdom	5.2	6.3	5.8	6.5	6.8	5.0	5.8	4.8	3.9	3.6	4.4	4.6	4.7	5.6	

Notes: (a) Seasonally adjusted annual rates of change from previous period. Projections are based on those of the OECD and IMF, modified by CPM Group. (b) U.S. interest rates are annual average rates on three-month Treasury bills. Japanese interest rates are annual average rates on government bonds. U.K. interest rates are average rates on treasury bills. China and India interest rates are bank rates. Projections are CPM Group's, based on OECD's. p -- projections. e -- estimates.
Sources: OECD, IMF, U.S. Dept. of Commerce, CPM Group.
January 31, 2008

For example, there presently are fears of a recession in the United States. Moving in to 2008, the U.S. economy is showing signs of recessionary conditions. A formal recession may be avoided, but real economic growth is slowing markedly, and the weakness is spread across numerous sectors of the economy. Additionally, the degree to which the rest of the world still is heavily related to U.S. economic trends and conditions has been driven home in early 2008.

That said, economic conditions are not so dire, either in the United States or worldwide. The chart earlier showed world GDP. Even with a significant mark down for 2007 and 2008 growth, on a global basis economic conditions still are fairly solid.

The same is true of the United States. A chart showing U.S. real GDP from World War Two through the third quarter 2007 shows a much healthier U.S. economy than one might suspect from current market chatter. The fourth quarter saw lower real GDP, although it still was 0.6%. Real GDP is projected to be low again in the first quarter of 2008, perhaps on the order of 0.5%, before strengthening in the second half of this year. While an actual contraction in real GDP may be avoided, recessionary economic conditions, if not outright recession, are present in the economy during the first half of 2008.

United States Real GDP

Quarterly, through Third Quarter 2007.

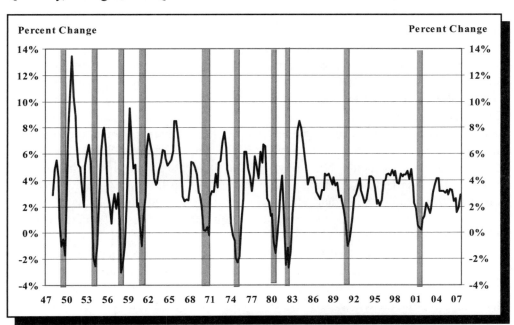

The same is true across the economy. Inflationary pressures are building in the U.S. and world economies. Inflation is worsening from where it has been for most of the time from 1984 through 2006. Inflation creeped up to 4.1% year on year in December 2007. This rise has been causing increased concern about future expectations over inflation. However, overall inflation still is relatively contained, especially compared to the double-digit levels that drove investors toward gold in the 1970s and early 1980s.

Inflation will become increasingly problematic around the world in the years ahead. Inflationary pressures will come from a number of sectors. Certainly the rise and sustained high levels of many natural resource prices, from oil and gas to metals and agricultural products, will generate higher general prices. The move toward increased food and product safety also will exert inflationary pressures. Consumer price inflation has been kept under control over the past 22 years by a number of trends, including increased productivity and globalization of manufacturing processes which may not be reversed. Other trends most likely will be reversed. The move toward industrialization of food production, from cattle, hogs, and chickens, to vegetables, has led to a reduction in the quality and safety of foodstuffs. A consumer backlash to this is beginning to emerge, and politicians from the United States and Europe to China, India, and Africa are starting to move to impose tighter health restrictions. Not only does the food produced in these factories raise health and safety issues for consumers, but also the waste generated by these factories is presenting serious environmental problems. Any move away from the animal farms that have grown so dramatically over the past two decades will lead to higher prices, compounded by rising demand for more food amid the diversion of food crops to biofuels. The same is true with non-food consumer and industrial products: There has been a measurable reduction in the safety of such products, and an emerging backlash probably will lead to higher production costs and sales prices for a wide range of industrial and consumer goods.

That said, while inflation is worsening, it is not a serious problem yet, and it may not grow back to the drastic levels of the 1970s.

Investor perceptions of inflation may be quite less sanguine that the current statistical realities suggest, however. And, it is investor perceptions that matter first to markets, including gold. The risk for investors is that they will react to perceptions of rising inflation, as they did in late 1982, buying up even more gold, only to find that the inflation they fear does not emerge later.

The disconnection between economic realities and investor perceptions of economic conditions is not aided by market commentary. One prominent newsletter writer, for example, has been writing about how U.S. stock prices are wildly over-valued by any measure, and thus a collapse of stock prices is inevitable. A chart showing the price to earnings ratio for the S&P 500 stocks shows that this simply is not the case. In fact, P/E ratios are at their lowest levels since the late 1980s, suggesting that there is plenty of upside remaining in stock markets. This ties in with the earlier comment that investors are lamenting the returns available in the stock market and stock price volatility, even as stock markets have moved higher over the past few years, albeit in a volatile fashion.

Another source of investor concern,

related in part to the inflation concerns, also has been exacerbated by inaccurate market commentaries. Gold newsletter writers and others repeatedly have discussed how the U.S. Federal Reserve Bank has flooded the world with money. Money supply data shows a quite different reality, however. While money supply growth rates, measured by M2 money supply, have risen sharply in recent quarters as the Fed and other central banks have tried to provide liquidity for a credit-starved economy, the monetary largess has been nothing compared to that of the 1960s, 1970s, and 1980s.

In summary, there are economic problems facing the world, but they may

S&P 500 Price to Earnings Ratio
Daily, through 30 January 2008

not be as great as investors perceive them to be. The history of the past 25 years also suggests a more facile monetary policy management style, since 1982, which has limited the economic destruction of recent recessions and other economic problems. This history suggests that, assuming the lessons learned and applied over the past quarter century are applied today and in the future, the economic consequences of current economic problems may be limited and relatively contained.

The world meanwhile is awash in cash. Those analyses that describe the current financial market conundrum as a credit crunch are misplaced by a degree or more. At present there is

more money in cash and cash equivalents worldwide than ever before, searching for good investments. The current problems in the financial and capital markets is not that there is not credit available. It is that those people who have money and are looking for investments do not feel that the equity and debt prices of many investment opportunities are low enough yet to be attractive to them. Additionally, they have concerns over the management of many investment targets. It will take increased confidence that management can effectively use any future infusions of capital, as well as lower asset prices and higher yields on debt instruments, to re-connect those with capital and those who seek it. Until that happens,

M1 Money Stock

Monthly, Percent Change From Year Ago.

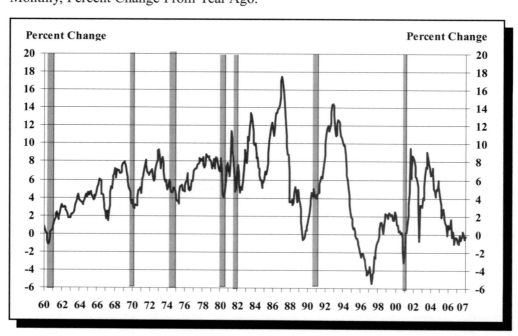

the market will remain in disarray and volatile.

Another issue that is being blown way out of proportion by market commentators, and government officials, is the rise of sovereign wealth funds. These government investment authorities are not much different from those which have existed for decades. And, they are small compared to the total pool of investment capital in the world today. That they have been willing to make investments in financial institutions that have been mismanaged and are starved for capital from their traditional, private sector sources of financing, is not so much a factor to be feared. Rather, it is an indication that perhaps

they are willing to accept greater risks in order to begin establishing investment positions in these companies than are longer established, better capitalized private equity and financing sources. It may also represent a difference in oversight and management, with managers at sovereign wealth funds being able to take on riskier investments than are managers at private money management funds, which may face greater investor scrutiny and higher standards of risk/reward ratios.

M2 Money Stock

Monthly, Percent Change From Year Ago.

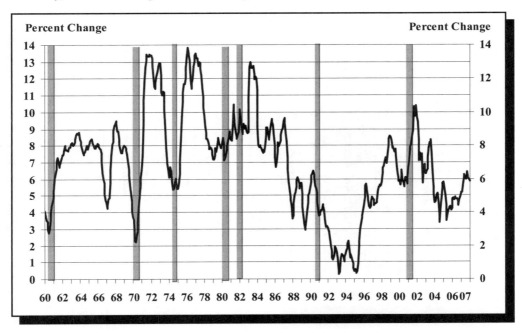

The Good Old Days That Never Were

The issue of gold's role in a monetary system has been resurrected in U.S. political discussions this year, after having lay dormant for more than two decades. Two developments have led to this. One has been the seemingly relentless decline of the dollar's exchange rate in currency markets. The other has been the candidacy of Ron Paul as a Republican candidate for president of the United States. While Paul is seen as having little chance of garnering the candidacy let alone the presidency, he has tapped into a well-spring of conservative discontent over financial management of the U.S. economy. This is the first time that

gold has played a role in U.S. presidential politics since the Republican platform on which Ronald Reagan ran in 1980 carried a platform calling for a return to a watered-down gold standard for the dollar. That cynical proposal did not become a major issue during the campaign, and silently disappeared after the election.

The position of many advocates of a gold standard is that the Federal Reserve system ought to be abolished, that the U.S. government should allow private banks to issue currency as they see fit, and that the U.S. government should extract itself from the control of money supply in the United States. Gold standard advocates believe these

United States Real GDP Since 1850

Annual, through 2007.

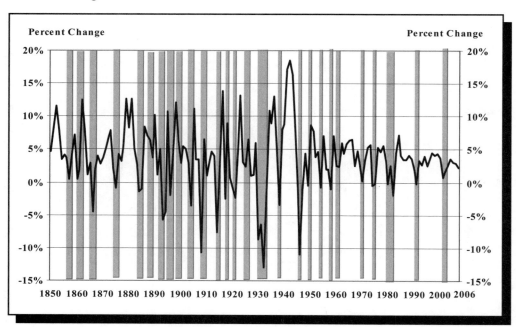

were the "good old days" of monetary stability.

The problem is that the good old days never existed. In the 65 years between the U.S. Civil War and World War One there were 16 recessions in the United States. Several of them were particularly devastating depressions that made the Great Depression pale in comparison. The average duration of these recessions in this period was 22 months. The accompanying table and chart show the degree to which economic conditions were much more volatile and much worse during the era of free banking than they have been since World War Two.

In contrast to these glory days, in the 62 years since World War Two ended there have been 10 recessions, 37% fewer than in the earlier era. The average duration of these recessions has been 10 months, less than half the length of the recessions during the good old days. The last recession, in 2000, was the first recession on record that did not see any actual contraction in U.S. real GDP. Real GDP bottomed out at 0.2% in the third quarter of 2001, but never actually contracted. Most people are familiar with a definition of a recession as two consecutive quarters of contracting real GDP. That is not an 'official' definition, at least not anymore. A recession is a period of extended broad-based economic weakness identified as a recession by a committee at the National Bureau of Economic Research. The NBER says it takes into

consideration such factors as real GDP, real income, employment, industrial production, and wholesale and retail sales. That new definition may have appeared after the 2000 recession. The NBER committee looked at the period of weakness between March and November 2001 and concluded that even though real GDP stayed positive, there was in essence a recession at that time. During the post-war period, there have been no depressions.

Not only has the economic performance, and government management of the economy, been much better over the 62 years since World War Two, compared to the period between the Civil War and World War One, but within the more recent period, the period since 1982 has been incredibly superior. There have been only two recessions in the quarter century since 1982, and they have been among the shortest and shallowest of recessions. As just mentioned, the second one did not even register contracting real gross domestic product.

The concept and history of money and monetary policy in the United States always has been a point of strong opinions. When people have strong opinions about a topic, they often feel that it is acceptable to distort history and reality in order to justify their point. Thus, advocates of private banks issuing private money sometimes misquote Thomas Jefferson. Jefferson famously said:

"I believe that banking institutions are more dangerous to our liberties than standing armies. If the American people ever allow private banks to control the issue of their currency, first by inflation and then by deflation, the banks and the corporations that will grow up around them will deprive the people of all property until their children wake up homeless on the continent their fathers conquered."

In order to try to distort history and misrepresent one of the most knowledgeable American forefathers, people omit the word "private" from the preceding quotation, attempting to convince would-be supporters that Mr. Jefferson was opposed to the concept of a federally organized banking system, as outlined in the U.S. Constitution and envisioned by the founders of the nation. In fact, he was opposed to private banks having unrestrained capacity to issue money and build up debt, the very thing that caused much economic destruction in the period before the Civil War.

Anyone suggesting a return to the old ways of organizing and regulating a banking system and financial markets owes it to themselves and to those to whom they speak to know better the historical record of economic dislocations generated during such systems' operations. The free banking period in U.S. history was an era of massive swings in economic volatility, far greater than those experienced since the 1940s, incorporating periods of massive depressions and recessions; hyper-inflation and massive deflations; economic destruction that destroyed humans, companies, and communities; and lightly to totally unregulated financial markets that make the villainy of recent banking scoundrels seem like misdemeanors.

Further Readings

Readers who are interested in knowing more about the history of money in the United States might read any of the following books. Milton Friedman and Anna Schwartz's **A Monetary History of the United States, 1867 - 1960** offers a detailed and thoroughly analytical review of the positive and negative aspects of various monetary systems tried out over the course of the United States since the Civil War.

Readers seeking a less analytical book might read **The Panic of 1907**, a recent book by Robert F. Bruner and Sean D. Carr. This is a historical narrative by two University of Virginia professors, who, among other resources, had access to transatlantic cables to and from J. P. Morgan's bank during a major banking panic and stock market rout in 1907. The economic dislocations caused by this event were so painful to the U.S. and world economies that they served as the final event that helped push the U.S. government to overcome opposition from various banking interests and create a national monetary system supervised by the Federal Reserve System in 1913.

BUSINESS CYCLE REFERENCE DATES		DURATION IN MONTHS			
Peak *Quarterly dates are in parentheses*	**Trough**	**Contraction** *Peak to Trough*	**Expansion** *Previous trough to this peak*	**Cycle** *Trough from Previous Trough*	*Peak from Previous Peak*
	December 1854 (IV)	--	--	--	--
June 1857(II)	December 1858 (IV)	18	30	48	--
October 1860(III)	June 1861 (III)	8	22	30	40
April 1865(I)	December 1867 (I)	32	46	78	54
June 1869(II)	December 1870 (IV)	18	18	36	50
October 1873(III)	March 1879 (I)	65	34	99	52
March 1882(I)	May 1885 (II)	38	36	74	101
March 1887(II)	April 1888 (I)	13	22	35	60
July 1890(III)	May 1891 (II)	10	27	37	40
January 1893(I)	June 1894 (II)	17	20	37	30
December 1895(IV)	June 1897 (II)	18	18	36	35
June 1899(III)	December 1900 (IV)	18	24	42	42
September 1902(IV)	August 1904 (III)	23	21	44	39
May 1907(II)	June 1908 (II)	13	33	46	56
January 1910(I)	January 1912 (IV)	24	19	43	32
January 1913(I)	December 1914 (IV)	23	12	35	36
August 1918(III)	March 1919 (I)	7	44	51	67
January 1920(I)	July 1921 (III)	18	10	28	17
May 1923(II)	July 1924 (III)	14	22	36	40
October 1926(III)	November 1927 (IV)	13	27	40	41
August 1929(III)	March 1933 (I)	43	21	64	34
May 1937(II)	June 1938 (II)	13	50	63	93
February 1945(I)	October 1945 (IV)	8	80	88	93
November 1948(IV)	October 1949 (IV)	11	37	48	45
July 1953(II)	May 1954 (II)	10	45	55	56
August 1957(III)	April 1958 (II)	8	39	47	49
April 1960(II)	February 1961 (I)	10	24	34	32
December 1969(IV)	November 1970 (IV)	11	106	117	116
November 1973(IV)	March 1975 (I)	16	36	52	47
January 1980(I)	July 1980 (III)	6	58	64	74
July 1981(III)	November 1982 (IV)	16	12	28	18
July 1990(III)	March 1991(I)	8	92	100	108
March 2001(I)	November 2001 (IV)	8	120	128	128

Average, all cycles:					
1854-2001 (32 cycles)		17	38	55	56*
1854-1919 (16 cycles)		22	27	48	49**
1919-1945 (6 cycles)		18	35	53	53
1945-2001 (10 cycles)		10	57	67	67

* 31 cycles
** 15 cycles
Source: NBER

39

The events of 1907 also are a focus of many conspiracy theorists, who say they believe the panic was inspired by J.P. Morgan and others to create an opportunity to grab assets. The documentation provided in this excellent history shows the opposite was the reality. As the banking crisis unfolded, the government of Theodore Roosevelt initially was largely oblivious to what was developing in the nation's financial markets. Numerous entities in the banking community, and ultimately in the government, depended on Morgan personally to salvage the financial system from collapse.

A third good book on the subject of early U.S. monetary systems is the new book, **A Nation of Counterfeiters**, by Stephen Mihm. This also is a historical narrative, covering the disastrous economic and financial results of the private or free banking system that existed between the War for Independence and the Civil War.

These three books, and others, have many things in common. One is that they were written by historians and economists who did not bring biases and a desire to prove a conspiracy theory to their efforts. These are dispassionate, analytical reviews and analyses of what actually happened during the era of private banks, free of the compulsion of mock-libertarians to twist historical reality to try to make a point.

Fear Not The Treasury Agent

As world economic and financial market conditions have deteriorated, another topic related to gold's history has come back into market discussions. Gold coin marketing groups have begun trying to sell numismatic gold coins to investors by saying they should worry about the potential that the U.S. government and other governments might try to confiscate pure gold investment products in the future. This is a perennial topic among serious conspiracy theorists and gold bugs.

It is highly unlikely that the U.S. government ever would seek to confiscate gold. It did in the 1930s, when gold was a central component of the U.S. monetary system and the size of the pool of investable gold was large relative to the overall economy. Those days are long gone, however, and unlikely to return. Today the gold market is very small and inconsequential compared to the total financial and monetary markets. A rush to gold by investors would have a tremendous effect on the gold price, but it would not have a seriously detrimental effect on world monetary markets or governments' attempts to contain any crises of confidence. Therefore, most monetary authorities in major countries such as the United States feel that the gold market would not need to be a point of focus or concern during a future monetary crisis.

As a result of this, the U.S. Treasury

and other monetary authorities have no interest or reason to consider confiscating gold or outlawing its private ownership in a future financial crisis. In the 1930s the value of the gold investment stock, mostly in U.S. Treasury issued coins, circulating in the United States was almost as large as the volume of U.S. currency in circulation. As the Depression tightened its grip on America, people were concerned the dollar would become worthless, and that equities, bonds, and bank accounts were vulnerable to further losses. As a result, people began putting their assets into gold. This reduced the amount of money in circulation, the amounts of money banks could lend, and the investable stock of money in the economy, further choking the real economy. In this environment, the U.S. government outlawed gold ownership, in order to try to get more money into circulation to help the economy revive.

Today, and in the future, the amount of money that could pour into gold is tiny compared to the overall economy and the value of various monetary and financial assets. Even if there were a general panic and investors pushed gold prices to $2,000, $4,000, or whatever level, the amount of money being diverted into gold in this way would not be a major negative impediment to fiscal and monetary policy. As a result, the U.S. Treasury and other monetary authorities today assume there would be no useful purpose for them to try to ban private ownership or purchases of gold.

In April 1933, at the depth of the Depression the U.S. government directed Americans to turn in their gold, gold coins, and gold certificates. Even before the executive order, there was a sharp reduction in the amount of gold coins in circulation in the U.S. economy. At the end of February 1933, there were $571 million in gold coins, or 27.6 million ounces at the then official price of $20.67 per ounce. By the end of March 1933, before the first executive order requiring the transfer of gold coins, the stock of circulating gold coins had fallen to 17.8 million ounces, reflecting an enormous 9.8 million ounces of gold coins, 35.5%, that had been sold back into the banking system. The Treasury officially began the gold coin recall in April 1933, giving citizens until the end of March 1934 to turn in their gold coins and certificates. By the end of March 1934 the amount of gold coins still in circulation was valued at $287 million. This represented 13.9 million ounces of gold, at the early 1933 price of $20.67 per ounce. In other words, 9.8 million ounces of gold coins were turned in to the Treasury prior to the start of the gold recall, and a much smaller amount, 3.9 million ounces, were turned in during the official recall period.

Of the remaining 13.9 million ounces of gold remaining in private hands in the form of U.S. gold coins, it has been calculated that at most 3.9 million ounces of these coins had been transferred abroad in unreported shipments.

In other words, between 10.0 and 13.9 million ounces of gold coins are believed to have been retained by U.S. citizens in defiance of U.S. laws in 1933 and 1934. Another 330,000 ounces of gold coins were sold back to the Treasury, from June 1934 through June 1960. Most of the remainder continues to be held by investors and others.

Long-Term Supply and Demand
Million Troy Ounces

| | Source of Supply | | | | | Distribution of Supply | | | |
Year	Mine Production in Market Economies	Flow from Transitional Economies	Secondary Recovery	Net Official Purchases (-) or Sales (+)	Available Supply	Jewelry and Industrial	Coins and Medallions	Net Private Bullion Purchases (+) or Sales (-)	Investment Bullion, Coins and Medallions
1950	24.3	-	NA	-9.2	15.1	12.0	*	3.1	3.1
1951	23.7	-	NA	-7.5	16.2	13.0	*	3.2	3.2
1952	24.2	-	NA	-6.5	17.7	13.0	*	4.7	4.7
1953	24.2	2.2	NA	-12.9	13.5	12.5	*	1.0	1.0
1954	25.5	2.2	NA	-19.1	8.6	13.0	*	-4.4	-4.4
1955	26.8	2.2	NA	-19.0	10.0	13.5	*	-3.5	-3.5
1956	27.8	4.3	NA	-13.9	18.2	15.0	*	3.2	3.2
1957	29.0	7.4	NA	-19.7	16.7	17.0	*	-0.3	-0.3
1958	29.9	6.3	NA	-19.4	16.8	19.0	*	-2.2	-2.2
1959	32.1	8.6	NA	-21.5	19.2	22.0	*	-2.8	-2.8
1960	33.5	5.7	NA	-8.4	30.8	25.0	*	5.8	5.8
1961	34.7	8.6	NA	-17.2	26.1	28.0	*	-1.9	-1.9
1962	37.3	5.7	NA	-10.5	32.5	30.0	*	2.5	2.5
1963	38.6	15.7	NA	-23.4	30.9	32.5	*	-1.6	-1.6
1964	40.0	12.9	NA	-20.2	32.7	34.5	*	-1.8	-1.8
1965	41.0	11.4	NA	-6.3	46.1	36.0	*	10.1	10.1
1966	41.0	-2.1	NA	1.2	40.1	37.5	*	2.6	2.6
1967	39.8	-0.1	NA	45.1	84.8	38.0	*	46.8	46.8
1968	40.0	-0.9	NA	19.9	59.0	35.8	3.5	19.7	23.2
1969	40.3	-0.5	NA	-2.9	36.9	36.3	2.3	-1.7	0.6
1970	40.9	-0.1	NA	-7.6	33.2	41.1	3.2	-11.1	-7.9
1971	39.7	1.7	NA	3.1	44.5	41.3	3.4	-0.2	3.2
1972	37.8	6.8	NA	-4.9	39.7	39.9	3.3	-3.5	-0.2
1973	35.8	8.8	NA	0.2	44.8	25.2	2.4	17.2	19.6
1974	32.8	7.1	NA	0.6	40.5	14.3	9.0	17.2	26.2
1975	30.9	4.8	NA	0.3	36.0	22.8	8.8	4.4	13.2
1976	31.2	13.2	NA	1.9	46.3	37.2	7.5	1.6	9.1
1977	31.0	12.9	4.5	8.7	57.1	43.9	6.3	6.9	13.2
1978	31.1	13.2	5.7	11.7	61.7	45.2	10.8	5.7	16.5
1979	30.7	6.4	10.9	17.5	65.5	39.7	10.4	15.4	25.8
1980	30.5	2.9	21.2	-7.4	47.2	25.7	8.9	12.5	21.4
1981	31.2	9.0	10.5	-4.5	46.2	33.4	8.2	4.6	12.8
1982	32.4	6.5	11.1	-1.0	49.0	36.7	6.5	5.8	12.3
1983	34.2	2.7	11.7	2.4	51.0	35.6	5.2	10.2	15.4
1984	35.7	3.9	10.4	1.5	51.5	41.6	11.4	-1.5	9.9
1985	37.9	7.6	9.0	-1.5	53.0	44.1	7.5	1.4	8.9
1986	40.3	13.2	13.0	-1.0	65.5	44.5	5.2	15.8	21.0
1987	42.1	10.1	12.8	2.9	67.9	45.0	5.7	17.3	23.0
1988	47.5	10.1	11.1	-5.3	63.4	56.6	4.6	2.2	6.8
1989	51.6	11.0	9.7	6.2	78.5	63.1	5.8	9.6	15.4
1990	54.5	10.0	10.7	2.0	77.2	68.6	3.5	5.1	8.6
1991	56.0	10.0	11.3	2.8	80.1	70.2	4.6	5.4	10.0
1992	58.6	11.0	12.0	12.1	93.7	78.3	2.6	12.8	15.4
1993	59.9	11.0	12.6	22.0	105.5	82.7	3.9	18.9	22.8
1994	60.2	10.0	13.8	7.0	91.0	86.6	4.6	-0.1	4.5
1995	60.3	11.0	14.5	8.0	93.8	94.4	4.8	-5.4	-0.6
1996	61.8	11.5	17.0	10.0	100.3	95.8	2.7	1.8	4.5
1997	65.1	12.0	15.5	20.0	112.6	101.2	3.9	7.6	11.5
1998	67.4	15.0	22.6	14.6	119.6	104.6	4.6	10.4	15.0
1999	68.8	17.0	20.0	13.9	119.7	102.0	4.8	12.9	17.7
2000	67.7	16.0	21.2	13.9	118.8	104.3	2.7	11.8	14.5
2001	67.0	15.0	22.0	9.3	113.3	91.2	3.2	18.9	22.1
2002	65.2	17.0	26.0	10.9	119.0	82.0	3.4	33.6	37.0
2003	64.9	17.0	29.4	17.6	128.9	78.7	4.4	45.8	50.2
2004	61.1	18.0	27.4	15.7	122.1	81.0	5.2	35.9	41.1
2005	62.4	18.0	28.0	20.6	129.1	83.1	6.0	40.0	46.0
2006	60.0	18.0	26.3	11.5	115.7	76.6	7.5	31.7	39.2
2007e	59.3	19.0	32.4	16.0	126.7	82.9	7.3	36.4	43.7
2008p	60.0	20.0	33.9	14.0	127.9	89.8	7.5	30.6	38.1

Notes: Totals may not equal the sum of components due to rounding. NA -- data on secondary supply is not available for years prior to 1977. Demand statstics for years prior to 1977 represent use of gold from mine production, transitional economy sales, and official sector sources, and exclude use of gold from scrap, while demand statistics beginning with 1977 reflect total gold use, including metal recovered from scrap. *Coins and medallions prior to 1968 are included in the jewelry and industrial column. e-estimates, p-projections.
Source: CPM Group.
Janaury 31, 2008

Real and Nominal Gold Prices

Prices, Base=2007

Year	Real	Percent Change	Nominal	Percent Change	U.S. CPI Percent Change
1950	$290	-	$35	-	-
1955	$259	-	$35	-	-
1960	$234	-	$35	-	-
1965	$220	-	$35	-	-
1970	$220	-	$41	-	-
1975	$620	-	$161	-	-
1976	$445	-28.3%	$125	-22.5%	5.8%
1977	$497	11.8%	$148	18.3%	6.5%
1978	$613	23.2%	$193	30.8%	7.6%
1979	$903	47.5%	$307	58.7%	11.3%
1980	$1,680	86.0%	$612	99.5%	13.5%
1981	$1,089	-35.2%	$460	-24.9%	10.3%
1982	$823	-24.4%	$376	-18.3%	6.1%
1983	$903	9.6%	$424	12.9%	3.2%
1984	$728	-19.4%	$360	-15.1%	4.3%
1985	$615	-15.5%	$317	-12.0%	3.5%
1986	$701	13.9%	$368	15.8%	1.9%
1987	$826	17.8%	$446	21.5%	3.7%
1988	$775	-6.2%	$437	-2.1%	4.1%
1989	$640	-17.3%	$382	-12.5%	4.8%
1990	$608	-5.0%	$384	0.4%	5.4%
1991	$549	-9.8%	$362	-5.6%	4.2%
1992	$504	-8.2%	$344	-5.2%	3.0%
1993	$512	1.7%	$360	4.7%	3.0%
1994	$533	4.1%	$384	6.7%	2.6%
1995	$519	-2.6%	$385	0.2%	2.8%
1996	$510	-1.8%	$389	1.2%	2.9%
1997	$424	-16.9%	$333	-14.5%	2.3%
1998	$370	-12.8%	$295	-11.2%	1.6%
1999	$342	-7.4%	$280	-5.3%	2.2%
2000	$332	-3.1%	$280	0.2%	3.4%
2001	$312	-6.0%	$272	-3.1%	2.8%
2002	$352	12.9%	$311	14.5%	1.6%
2003	$404	14.8%	$364	17.1%	2.3%
2004	$445	10.0%	$410	12.6%	2.7%
2005	$469	5.5%	$446	8.9%	3.4%
2006	$622	32.7%	$607	35.9%	3.2%
2007	$700	12.5%	$700	15.4%	2.9%

Averages
Actuals

	Real		Nominal		
1950 - 1975	$276		$49		
1950 - 2007	$464		$226		
1977 - 2007	$623		$379		
1990 - 2007	$473		$384		

Longer term projections are available in CPM Group's Gold Supply, Demand, and Price: 10-Year Projections report.
Source: CPM Group
January 31, 2008

Cumulative World Production and Distribution

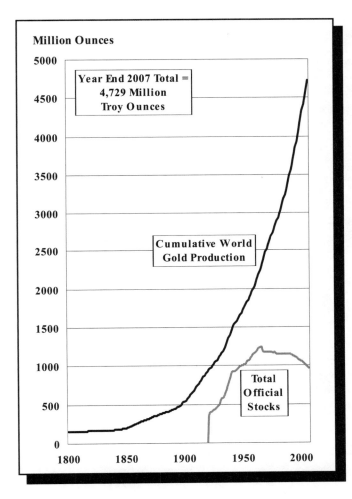

Million Ounces

Year End 2007 Total = 4,729 Million Troy Ounces

Cumulative World Gold Production

Total Official Stocks

Estimated Data as of end 2007 Disposition (Million Troy Ounces)

Industrial Use, Undetermined, or Lost 521

Jewelry, Decorative, and Religious Items 2,098

Private Stocks 1087

Official Reserves: 1,023
      FSU: 63
      Central Banks: 852
      IMF and BIS: 108

Notes: Official stocks include holdings of central banks, the International Monetary Fund, European Central Bank, and the Bank for International Settlements. Total disposition may not equal cumulative production due to rounding and other discrepancies in the historical data. The distribution of 154 million ounces of pre-1800 production is not able to be discerned. Additionally, the assumptions have been made that most of the gold recovered from scrap since 1977 has been from jewelry and decorative objects and the metal thus recovered largely was used in the manufacture of new jewelry. FSU reserves are estimated trading stocks held by governments of countries formerly were part of the Soviet Union. They are not included as official holdings by the International Monetary Fund and are not publicly reported.

Fundamentals

Investment Demand

Investment Demand

Investors have been buying enormous amounts gold over the past seven years. They continued to buy large volumes in 2007. They have purchased an estimated 279.2 million ounces on a net basis since 2001. Last year they are estimated to have bought 43.7 million ounces of gold. That was up from 39.2 million ounces in 2006, but in line with the historically large volumes of gold buying from investors since 2001 - 2002.

Last year was the seventh consecutive year in which investors collectively bought more than 20 million ounces of gold, which used to be a fair measure of a bull market in gold. The volumes of gold investors have been buying have far exceeded the volumes that investors

bought in previous bull markets from the 1960s through the 1990s. The chart showing the relationship between gold prices and investment demand illustrates the degree to which the levels of investor demand for gold tend to influence gold prices.

Since gold prices were freed from a fixed currency exchange rate, beginning in the 1960s, there have been six bull markets in gold. In each bull market a wave of investor anxiety caused by economic and political issues drove investors to buy a lot of gold. A lot of gold is defined as more than 20 million ounces per year, roughly, on a net annual basis around the world. This is all physical gold, and excludes forwards,

Investment Demand's Effect on Gold Prices

Price Change Through December 2007.

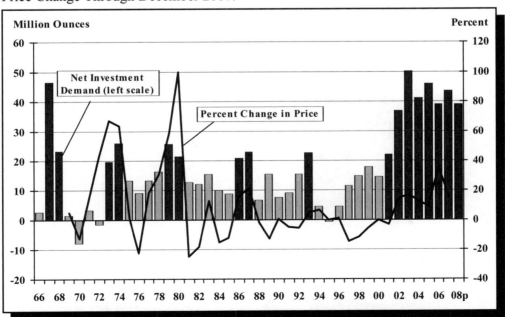

futures, options, and other derivative securities linked to gold that do not require physical gold in their transactions. There is no magic to the 20 million ounce level; this is not an immutable figure carved in stone, dictated by nature, or provided mankind by a higher intelligence. It is just that there is a clear gulf between how much gold investors are buying on a net basis in years of strong or rising prices, and how much they are buying in periods of relatively weak gold prices.

Another aspect of the gold market illustrated by the previous chart is that the difference between a bull and a bear market in gold is that investors almost always are net buyers of gold on an annual net global basis. Investors as a group hardly ever are net sellers of gold. They have been net sellers in only three of the past 42 years. In a bear market investors buy less gold than they do in a bull market; they tend not to appear as net sellers.

In the first five bull markets, the wave of economic and political problems led to heavy investor demand, in excess of 20 million ounces per year, for one or two years. By that time economic and political conditions seemed to investors to be improving, the wave of gold purchases subsided, and gold prices either stopped rising, or fell.

The current period has deviated mighti-

Investment Demand's Share of the Gold Market
Price Change Through December 2007.

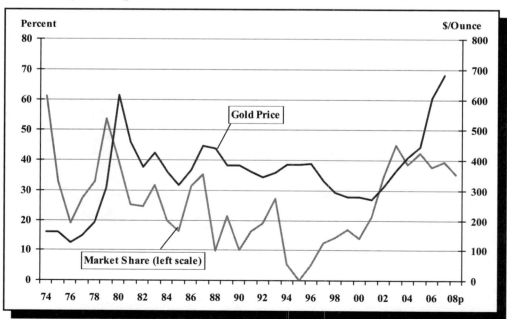

ly from this previous pattern. Whereas previous bear markets were four or five years long, the most recent bear market for gold was seven years, from 1994 through 2000. The current bull market now is into its eighth year. As described in the first chapter, more investors have bought more gold for a longer period of time than ever before, at least since World War Two. As mentioned above, investors have bought 279.2 million ounces of gold over the past seven years, since 2000. This boosted their holdings to an estimated 1,124.9 million ounces. They have added 34.6% to the 807.5 million ounces of gold they held at the end of 2000, before the current bull market began.

This is in contrast to the sale of 100.3 million ounces sold by central banks during this seven year period, representing 9.5% of the 1,060.5 million ounces they held at the end of 2000. By the end of 2007 central banks and other monetary authorities held an estimated 946.1 million ounces. Private investor holdings of gold surpassed central bank holdings in 2005.

Intra 2007

The net purchases by investors of 43.7 million ounces was about 11.7% more than the 39.2 million ounces of net investor demand for gold calculated to have occurred in 2006. The volume of gold demand was flagging a bit in the

Changes in Combined Gold ETF Holdings

Monthly, Through 28 January 2008.

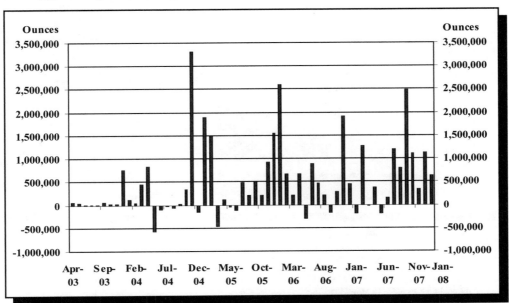

second quarter of last year, as some investors were questioning the sustainability of the upward move in gold prices. Prices had been rising for six years and had reached near-record levels. In this environment, some investors began taking profits, and other observers began to wonder aloud in the market if perhaps the gold bull market that had begun in 2001 was ending.

The gold exchange traded funds which represent less than one-fifth of annual investor demand for gold at present provides the only daily quantitative measure of investor interest. It is not a good barometer of world gold investment demand, as the types of investors involved in the gold ETFs are quite distinct in their attitudes and investing habits from most other physical gold investors. Nonetheless, in a market starved for quantitative, credible information, the daily fluctuations in the gold holdings of the ETFs have become a focus on gold traders, commentators, investors, and others. The amount of gold held in ETFs declined 197,771

Exchange Traded Fund's Physical Gold Holdings

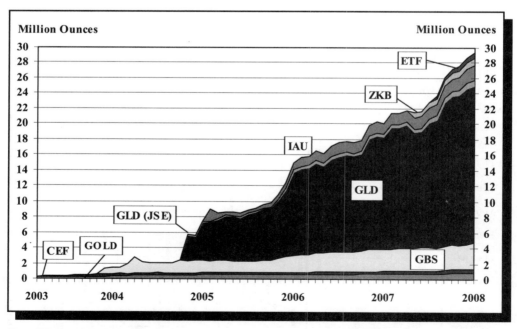

Note: CEF-Central Fund of Canada traded on the Toronto Stock Exchange. GBS-Gold Bullion Securities traded on the Australian Stock Exchange, GOLD-Gold Bullion Securities traded on the London Stock Exchange, GLD-Streettracks Gold Shares traded on the New York Stock Exchange, GLD (JSE)-Gold Bullion Debentures traded on the Johannesburg Securities Exchange, IAU-IShares Comex Gold Trust traded on the American Stock Exchange. IAU, GLD (JSE), GLD, GOLD, and GBS as of 25 January 2008. CEF as of 31 October 2006. ETF Securities' gold ETF included in April 2007 and ZKB -Zurich Cantonal's gold ETF included in May 2007.

Exchange Traded Fund's Physical Gold Holdings
Troy Ounces, Month-end

	CEF TSX	GOLD ASX	GBS LSE	GLD NYSE	GLD JSE	IAU AMEX	ZKB Zurich	ETF Securities	Total
2003 March	261,445	996	-	-	-	-	-	-	262,441
April	297,045	28,007	-	-	-	-	-	-	325,052
May	297,045	78,664	-	-	-	-	-	-	375,709
June	297,045	93,233	-	-	-	-	-	-	390,278
July	297,045	112,468	-	-	-	-	-	-	409,513
August	297,045	130,933	-	-	-	-	-	-	427,978
September	297,045	195,631	-	-	-	-	-	-	492,676
October	297,045	233,342	-	-	-	-	-	-	530,387
November	297,045	257,695	-	-	-	-	-	-	554,740
December	297,045	270,644	755,058	-	-	-	-	-	1,322,747
2004 January	395,431	272,089	779,878	-	-	-	-	-	1,447,398
February	395,431	278,035	829,691	-	-	-	-	-	1,503,157
March	395,431	263,479	1,289,463	-	-	-	-	-	1,948,373
April	523,591	261,687	1,999,778	-	-	-	-	-	2,785,056
May	523,591	259,636	1,421,198	-	-	-	-	-	2,204,425
June	523,591	259,584	1,320,997	-	-	-	-	-	2,104,172
July	523,591	329,018	1,230,827	-	-	-	-	-	2,083,436
August	523,591	257,570	1,231,458	-	-	-	-	-	2,012,619
September	523,591	259,018	1,256,209	-	-	-	-	-	2,038,818
October	523,591	239,670	1,615,712	-	-	-	-	-	2,378,973
November	523,591	239,622	1,521,060	3,329,910	88,334	-	-	-	5,702,517
December	523,591	241,990	1,642,756	3,049,722	96,299	-	-	-	5,554,358
2005 January	619,591	241,942	1,582,651	4,887,966	96,266	34,996	-	-	7,463,412
February	619,591	241,893	1,424,964	5,076,083	96,237	1,509,369	-	-	8,968,137
March	619,591	241,844	1,569,563	5,274,388	92,210	699,469	-	-	8,497,065
April	619,591	253,657	1,503,337	5,751,743	92,181	399,569	-	-	8,620,078
May	619,591	253,607	1,448,172	5,760,002	92,149	399,428	-	-	8,572,950
June	619,591	253,539	1,443,043	5,638,445	92,118	399,297	-	-	8,446,033
July	619,591	253,458	1,482,573	6,035,257	92,089	444,076	-	-	8,927,043
August	619,591	253,366	1,482,034	6,252,647	92,056	443,919	-	-	9,143,613
September	619,591	254,138	1,509,244	6,669,250	92,025	508,594	-	-	9,652,841
October	619,591	258,168	1,602,313	6,696,843	91,994	598,142	-	-	9,867,051
November	619,591	262,213	1,811,743	7,371,741	95,946	627,843	-	-	10,789,077
December	619,591	270,261	2,026,120	8,464,821	247,209	712,318	-	-	12,340,319
2006 January	619,591	274,575	2,100,388	10,731,852	302,842	916,509	-	-	14,945,757
February	619,591	281,787	2,252,242	11,027,349	330,601	1,110,404	-	-	15,621,973
March	619,591	283,036	2,271,467	11,182,894	338,443	1,139,961	-	-	15,835,392
April	637,066	291,460	2,444,921	11,527,474	346,292	1,254,042	-	-	16,501,255
May	637,066	299,469	2,444,030	11,166,258	350,141	1,303,427	-	-	16,200,391
June	637,066	309,139	2,515,382	11,957,329	350,026	1,322,842	-	-	17,091,784
July	637,066	311,524	2,514,520	12,371,022	373,739	1,352,254	-	-	17,560,125
August	637,066	314,365	2,513,658	12,605,374	318,021	1,386,595	-	-	17,775,079
September	637,066	320,018	2,512,852	12,422,497	317,913	1,386,124	-	-	17,596,470
October	680,026	324,040	2,689,927	12,497,746	317,808	1,365,790	-	-	17,875,336
November	680,026	335,760	2,903,975	14,200,312	317,704	1,365,342	-	-	19,803,119
December	680,026	338,575	2,903,043	14,572,124	329,488	1,429,417	-	-	20,252,673
2007 January	732,716	343,022	2,780,254	14,477,672	329,380	1,404,141	-	-	20,067,185
Feb	732,716	363,309	2,799,384	15,672,700	345,126	1,423,506	-	-	21,336,741
March	732,716	367,322	2,856,442	15,558,894	364,816	1,437,944	-	-	21,318,134
April	732,716	371,283	2,920,938	15,860,940	364,700	1,437,468	-	10,038	21,698,084
May	732,716	383,144	2,919,934	14,905,362	412,082	1,476,628	641,400	29,046	21,500,312
June	732,716	394,821	2,993,990	14,930,016	423,815	1,476,134	641,400	60,659	21,653,551
July	732,716	401,248	3,042,923	15,964,095	459,286	1,495,452	681,477	72,466	22,849,662
August	732,716	408,733	2,833,151	16,571,995	526,364	1,519,696	721,511	331,835	23,646,001
September	732,716	459,658	3,069,041	18,584,096	569,699	1,608,255	767,949	346,580	26,137,994
October	805,169	484,264	3,146,635	19,211,042	589,241	1,681,961	783,717	545,052	27,247,081
November	805,169	509,909	3,116,011	19,343,578	616,717	1,740,770	831,673	617,503	27,581,330
December	805,169	526,582	3,180,361	20,186,914	719,286	1,774,786	879,093	633,547	28,705,739
2008 January	805,169	557,393	3,322,506	20,279,144	833,501	1,897,762	952,305	689,085	29,336,865

Note: CEF-Central Fund of Canada traded on the Toronto Stock Exchange. GOLD-Gold Bullion Securities traded on the Australian Stock Exchange, GBS-Gold Bullion Securities traded on the London Stock Exchange, GLD-Streettracks Gold Shares traded on the New York Stock Exchange, GLD (JSE)-Gold Bullion Debentures traded on the Johannesburg Securities Exchange, IAU-IShares Comex Gold Trust traded on the American Stock Exchange. IAU, GLD (JSE), GLD, GOLD, and GBS as of 25 January 2008. CEF as of 31 October 2007. ETF Securities' gold ETF included in April 2007 and ZKB -Zurich Cantonal's gold ETF included in May 2007.
CPM Group
January 28, 2008

ounces in May 2007. Over the course of six weeks from early May through the first week of June there were five days in which more than 230,000 ounces of gold ETF shares were sold. (Offsetting purchases on other days reduced the total outflow for the month of May to the lower figure.) This was taken in the market as a sign of bearishness toward gold by investors. It was not an accurate measure, however, as investors in other parts of the world and in other bullion markets, with investor profiles distinct from those of the gold ETF investors, were buying during this time. However, the gold ETF inventory declines were seen as a sign of flagging interest in gold by investors.

A notable shift in investor attitudes emerged between June and September. This was reflected in an accelerated pace of demand from September onward, which consequently led to a faster rate of increase in gold prices. Investors became more concerned about deteriorating economic conditions and financial market instability, as well as political concerns. This was reflected in a revival of investor demand for gold, from the Middle East to North America.

More than half of the 43.7 million ounces of gold purchased by investors was bought in the form of bullion, in bars ranging from less than one kilogram in size to 100-ounce bars. Bullion bars are estimated to have accounted for roughly 21.0 million ounces of gold last year, excluded any amounts bought in India. Indian market sources report that

investors bought 15.4 million ounces of gold in that country in various forms, including bars, coins, and medallions. They do not provide a breakdown by form or shape of the bullion. It is said that bullion bars are gaining favor in some sociographic segments of the Indian market. Outside of India, and apart from bullion bars, investors are estimated to have bought another 4.5 million ounces of gold in the form of official bullion coins issued by various government mints, and another 3.0 million ounces of gold in the form of medallions. Medallions are small, typically one-ounce in North America and Europe, rounds of silver that look like coins but are not official government issued coins.

The 8,453,066 million ounces of gold purchased by investors through the numerous gold exchange traded funds appear in these statistics as gold bullion purchases. This is because the administrators of these ETFs are required to purchase gold bullion in 100-ounce bars of good delivery status and to arrange for this gold to be stored for them in allocated accounts. Thus, the gold ETFs appear here as bullion demand.

Investment demand also was very strong throughout the Middle East in 2007, once again. Demand was said to be particularly strong for small bars, with demand for gold investment jewelry also strong. There had been a point in the third quarter of 2006 in which bullion stocks in the Dubai market ran dry for a few days, reflecting very strong demand throughout the Gulf region and India, which is supplied by Dubai. In order to avoid such an event this year, dealers held more inventories in the Gulf region.

Demand also was strong in most other parts of the world. Investors continued to buy gold in North America, Europe, and other parts of Asia. One area of noted weakness was in Japan, where investors were said to have been heavy net sellers of gold into the rising price in Japan over the past two years. Japanese investors were net buyers of an estimated 2.6 million ounces per year in 2004 and 2005. In 2006 they are estimated to have been net sellers of 1.4 million ounces, selling another 1.5 million ounces in 2007 on a net basis.

2008

Investment demand is projected to remain high this year. Demand is projected to total 38.1 million ounces. The final figure could vary greatly, depending on investor attitudes toward gold. The estimate here is predicated on the view that investors are going to want to continue buying historically large volumes of gold, but that they may pull back some from the volumes purchased in the second half of 2007. One or more serious economic, political, or other events could radically alter investor sentiments toward gold. One major negative event could drive investors to purchase more than 45 million ounces of gold. For example, in 2003, the year in which the United States invaded Iraq, investment demand soared from 37.0

million ounces the year before to a record 50.2 million ounces. Another major terrorist attack within the United States, a U.S. attack on Iran, or other major development could increase gold investment demand 15% or more from that projected here. Conversely, should investors become less concerned about the political or economic state of affairs in the world, they could pull back even more and buy less than the 38.1 million ounces projected here. Investor sentiment can be fickle and hard to project, and their purchasing and sales patterns in gold and other financial assets are hard to anticipate.

One of the keys to remember in trying to assess future investor demand trends, and thus prices, is that it is investor attitudes toward events that matter more than the events themselves. While the events are important, if investors chose not to view them as such they can develop without affecting gold prices. Similarly, investors will interpret events in different ways. The previous chapter discussed how investors in the first half of 1982 did not view the imminent collapse of the government debt markets as warranting the purchase of gold. Gold fell to its lowest level since 1979 in the midst of this international debt crisis. It was not that investors chose to ignore the event. They were aware of what was happening, but chose for some reason to focus on the U.S. dollar as their safe haven of choice during that crisis, even though the dollar and gold had shared that role just two years earlier.

The Relative Size of the Gold Investment Market

A second point to bear in mind is that the capital flows around the world are enormous at present, and may have more to say about trends in the prices for gold and other assets than the underlying economic and financial market conditions. At present there is more money parked in cash and cash equivalents than ever before in history. Every day more money flows in to the bank accounts of oil exporters, and exporters of other products. Most of these products trading internationally, as well as cross-border services, are denominated in U.S. dollars. Thus, exporters and providers of services face a steady, massive inflow of U.S. dollars. They need to sterilize or reduce their exposure to the dollar, encouraged to focus on this by the steady decline in the dollar over the past few years.

These capital flows suggest that the world economy perhaps is not in as bad of shape as the market consensus seems to make it out to be. It is not that there is not enough money to fund the world's economic needs at present, but rather that those who own these funds are searching for better terms before they invest and lend the funds. This is important for gold, and other commodities, as investors are seeking attractive investments, and some of these funds are being used to buy gold. Also, an ever-

Private Bank Deposits and Gold Holdings

Annual Data, Excludes Stocks, Bonds, and Other Financial Assets.

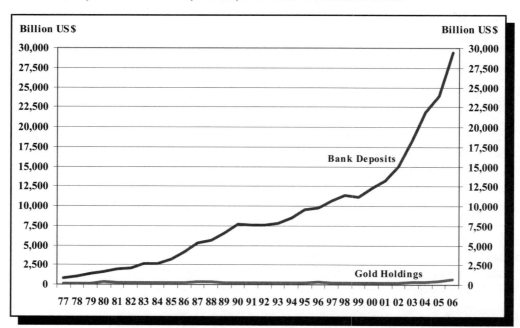

increasing proportion of the money seeking investments is managed by professional fund managers. These managers are paid to beat the market, and cannot afford to let too large of portions of their assets under management lie in cash equivalents. They need to invest, and typically are more willing to take on riskier investments than are the actual underlying investors. Thus, there is a large body of money afloat in the international markets seeking suitable investments. Some of this money will continue to move in to physical gold, in 2008 and beyond.

This leads to a third key point to remember is that the gold market is extremely small compared to the international financial markets. Complete data on the full extent of international wealth is hard

to come by. There is much information available in pieces, but full accounting of the amount of money in equity markets, bond markets, and bank deposits around the world are hard to come by, especially on a historical basis.

The table, "World Financial Assets" provides rough estimates of the amount of wealth in some assets, as of 2006 - 2007. Obviously the value of holdings fluctuate sharply with market changes. However, the amount of money in equities, bonds, and bank deposits totaled around 74.5 trillion dollars as of last year. This excludes real estate and other assets. The value of gold held by investors and central banks was around 1.1 trillion at that time, miniscule compared to the overall pool of investable funds.

World Financial Assets

US$ Trillion

	US$T	Percent of This Total
Equities markets	34.0	45.0%
Bond markets	11.0	14.6%
Bank deposits	29.5	39.0%
Gold	1.1	1.4%
Total	75.6	

Notes: Data from end 2006 for equity markets, bank deposits and gold; September 2007 for bonds. Not complete. Excludes property values and other assets.
Sources: Bank for International Settlements, International Capital Market Association, Dow Jones, CPM Group.
January 16, 2008

Gold's Relationship To Economic Factors

Investment demand for gold is difficult to assess, for reasons discussed earlier. First, there are many factors that investors watch in deciding on whether or not to buy gold, or whether to buy more or less gold in any given time. Some investors are quite monomaniacal about their gold investing, insisting that gold only responds to the U.S. dollar exchange rate, inflation, or some other variable. Other investors take a multivariate approach to gold, analyzing a host of political, economic, and financial market trends in trying to fathom whether gold prices are likely to rise or fall. Others respond primarily to local events and conditions, such as local inflation, invasion, or economic dislocations. Others take a more global view of the markets. Further complicating any analysis of prospective investor activities in gold is the fact that it is investor perceptions, and not necessarily the quantitative reality, that decides whether investors buy or sell gold.

On the following pages are various charts illustrating the quantitative relationships gold has with various economic factors: the U.S. dollar, inflation, stock prices, Treasury bonds and bills, and oil prices. The relationships are loose, and defy many simplistic attitudes toward gold.

Factors Determining Investment Demand For Gold

CPM Group projections are in boxes

	1979	1986	1997	1998	1999	2000	2001	2002	2003	2004	2005	2006	2007	2008p
Alternative Asset	+	+	-	+/-	+	+/-	+/-	+	+	+	+	+/-	+/-	+
Currency Hedge	+	+	-	+	+	+/-	+/-	+	+	+	+/-	+/-	+/-	+
Inflation Hedge	+	-	-	-	-	+/-	+/-	-	+/-	+/-	+/-	+/-	+/-	+
Safe Haven	+	-	-	+/-	+	+/-	+/-	+	+	+	+	+	+	+
Commodity	+	+	-	+/-	+	+/-	+	+	+	+	+/-	-	-	+
Savings	+	+	+	+	+	+	+	+	+	+	+/-	+/-	+/-	+
Positivity Factor	100%	67%	17%	58%	83%	58%	67%	83%	92%	92%	67%	58%	58%	100%

Annual Price Change The Following Year

	1980	1987	1998	1999	2000	2001	2002	2003	2004	2005	2006	2007
	99.5%	21.5%	-11.2%	-5.3%	0.2%	-3.1%	14.5%	17.1%	12.6%	8.9%	35.9%	15.4%

Note: CPM estimates of market concensus.
Source: CPM Group
January 20, 2008

For example, gold tends to trade against currency markets, more than just the U.S. dollar. There are times, such as during the bull market in 1979, when both gold and the dollar were rising in value at the same time. Over the long course of history, since the dollar was freed to float against other currencies in 1971, the statistical correlation between gold and the dollar has been around -0.27. That means that if one thought that gold traded solely against the dollar and invested accordingly, one would lose 73% of the time. This is because while there are times when gold and the dollar are moving in opposite directions, the way some investors and commentators tend to view gold, there also are times when gold and the dollar are both rising or falling together, and there are times when they move independently of each other. There are times, such as for a while in 2005, when the statistical correlation is as high as -0.85. Those times tend not to last, however. From 2003 through 2007, the period of strong declines in the dollar and strong gains in

gold prices, witnessed a -0.46 correlation between these two trends. Gold prices clearly have a relationship with the dollar; it is just that it is not the simplistic one some investors believe.

The same is true of gold and inflation. Using U.S. consumer price inflation as a proxy for world inflation is not a bad idea, given the large portion of world assets denominated in U.S. dollars. There is a 10% correlation between long-term U.S. CPI and gold. This probably would be unbelievable to those people who view gold as the ultimate inflation hedge. The reality is that gold does well in protecting people's wealth from catastrophic inflation, wild bouts of extremely high inflation that tend to coincide with major political or economic dislocations. Gold does not do well in protecting wealth or buying power against the gnawing day-to-day inflation that wears down purchasing power.

That 10% correlation extends back to 1971. Going prior to 1971, or 1968,

Correlations

Gold	Inflation	TWD	DJIA	S&P	T-Bill	T-Bond
1971 - 2007	0.10	-0.27	-0.02	-0.04	-0.06	-0.11
2003 - 2007	0.05	-0.46	-0.16	-0.10	-0.08	-0.24

Note: TWD - Trade Weighted Dollar
Source: CPM Group
January 30, 2008

Gold and the U.S. Dollar

Through January 2008.

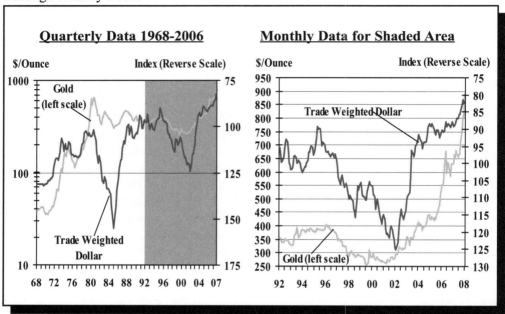

Gold and U.S. Inflation

Quarterly, Through Fourth Quarter 2007.

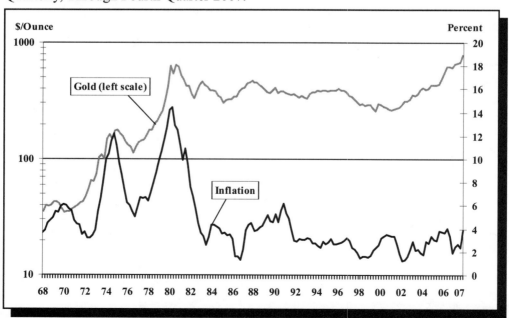

Real and Nominal T-Bill Rates and Gold Prices

Quarterly, Through Fourth Quarter 2007.

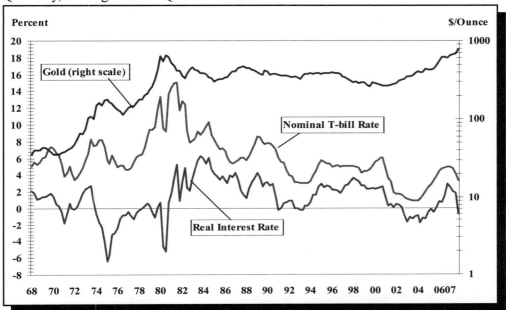

Gold and U.S. T-Bonds

Through December 2007.

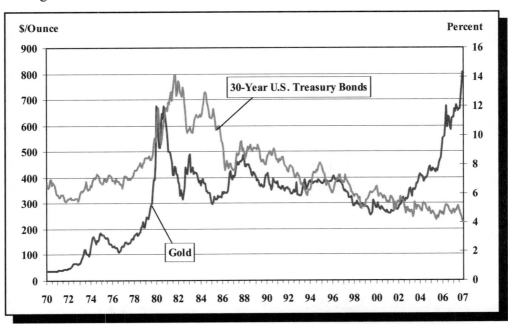

when gold prices were freed, is meaningless, since gold prices were fixed by government mandate for most of the time from 1717 until 1968. Since 2003 the correlation has been even lower, at 5%.

Investors will hear talk about how gold maintains purchasing power over time. Quantitatively this is not true. Gold will play catch up after extended periods in which its purchasing power is whittled away by lower level inflation. Some people will speak about how an ounce of gold could buy the same goods or services today as in past years. The measures they use pick one particular good or service and two points in time when

the gold price was similar when measured against that product. For example, one favorite is the comment that an ounce of gold could buy a good meal for two at the River Room restaurant at London's Savoy Hotel in 1917 and again in 1980. That was true. In between those two times there were times when that same ounce of gold could buy less than one meal, or a banquet for 17 people. The purchasing power of gold, against meals at the Savoy and everything else, fluctuates wildly. Averages are relatively meaningless.

The same is true with the gold/silver ratio and the gold/oil ratio. Some observers will speak of some magical

Gold and Oil Price
Quarterly, Through December 2007

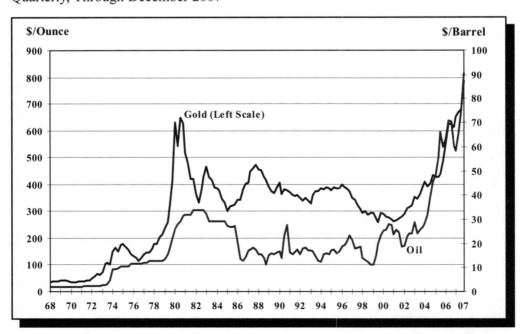

number to which the gold/silver ratio must revert. The numbers vary. One favorite is around 33:1. Another is 16:1, the ratio used by Sir Isaac Newton in setting up the British currency system in 1717. In fact, the ratio of gold to silver has varied between 16:1 and 100:1 in the forty years since gold and silver prices were freed from government dictated levels. The ratio has touched 33:1 at various times, when crossing it to move to an extreme above or below that level. The gold/silver ratio has spent very little time at any given level over the history of free gold and silver prices.

In 2007 many investors were looking at the gold/oil ratio in the same way. The gold/oil ratio has been very low by historical standards recently. From 1968 through 2003 the ratio ranged from 10 barrels per ounce of told to roughly 38 barrels per ounce. Since 2004 the gold/oil ratio has fallen, to around 7 barrels per ounce of gold. Correctly, many investors have viewed this ratio as an indication that gold prices are not rising as sharply as oil prices have been rising, and that gold is under-valued relative to oil at present compared to the historical relationship between these two assets. Some investors have taken this analysis beyond its logical conclusions, however, and have concluded that the gold/oil ratio must return to 15:1 or 20:1, and that gold prices thus have to rise to

The Gold - Oil Ratio

Quarterly, through December 2007

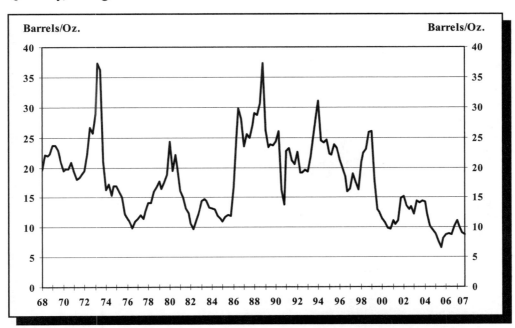

$1,350, $1,800, or some other price. There are no market, mathematic, nor natural laws that support such a conclusion, but that nonetheless is one view prevalent in the gold market today.

Gold prices also trade against equities, bonds, and bills. Historically the relationship is virtually zero. This is one characteristic of gold that makes it extremely attractive as a portfolio diversifier. The price of gold is not directly related to the prices of these other assets, which helps smooth out long-term portfolio variability without negatively reducing long-term returns.

Gold and the S&P 500

Through December 2007.

Gold and the CRB

Through December 2007.

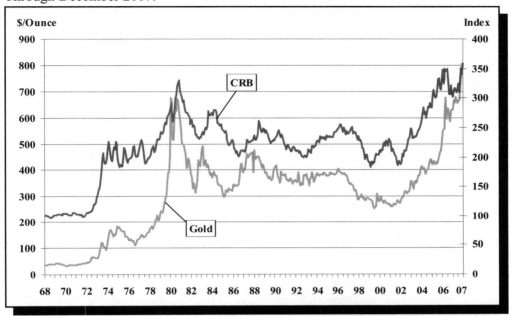

Gold Prices in Different Currencies

Daily, Through Janaury 25, 2007. Indexed to January 4, 1999 = 1.

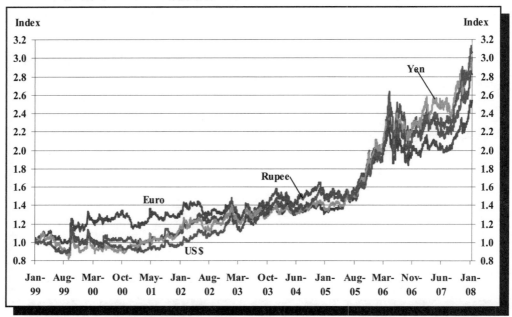

Gold Prices in Different Currencies

Daily, Through January 25, 2008. Indexed to January 4, 1999 = 1.

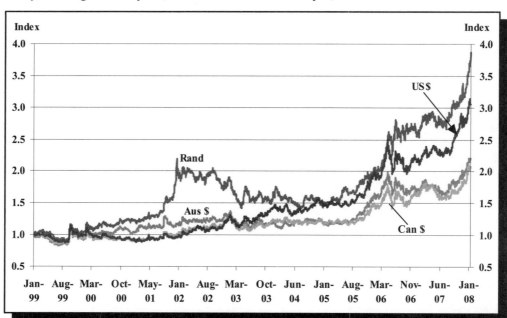

Comparative Investments

	1968-2007		1984-2007		1991-2007	
	Average Return	Average Risk	Average Return	Average Risk	Average Return	Average Risk
DJIA	8.29%	8.54%	12.01%	7.74%	10.68%	6.81%
S&P 500	8.45%	8.68%	11.26%	7.95%	10.01%	7.14%
T-Bills	5.98%	0.46%	4.85%	0.36%	3.86%	0.33%
T-Bonds	7.43%	0.40%	7.09%	0.37%	6.07%	0.33%
Gold	10.91%	10.88%	3.74%	6.30%	4.95%	5.81%
Silver	10.89%	18.53%	4.30%	11.37%	9.54%	11.53%
Platinum	7.91%	12.65%	7.76%	10.08%	9.40%	9.00%
CRB	3.94%	6.12%	1.39%	5.05%	3.13%	5.41%
TWDollar	-0.85%	3.36%	-1.83%	3.48%	-0.62%	3.17%

Note: Calculated on a 12-month moving basis. Risk is defined as the first-order standard deviation of the return over any given 12-month period. Returns based on capital appreciation only.
Source: CPM Group
January 30, 2008

Financial Times Gold Mines and World Stock Indices

Month-End Data, Through December 2007. Indexed to January 1997 = 100.

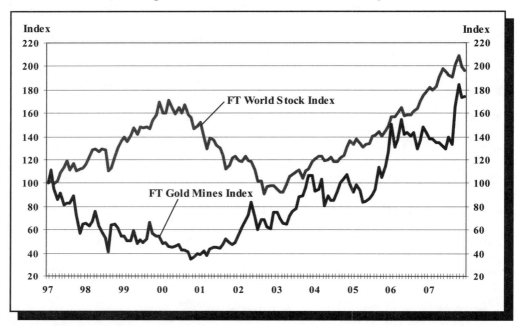

Gold Prices and the XAU

Through December 2007.

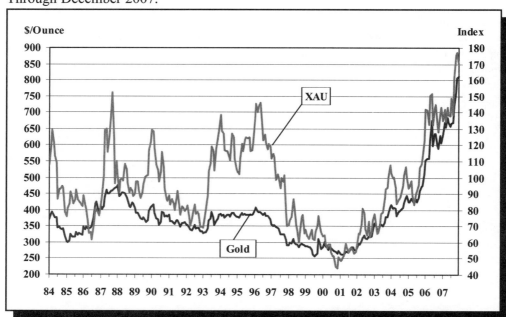

Net Position of Large Speculators in the Gold Market and Gold Prices

Comex gold futures and options. Weekly data, through 15 January 2008.

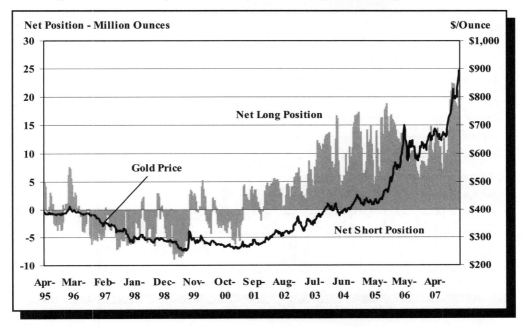

Monthly Gold American Eagle Sales

Through December 2007.

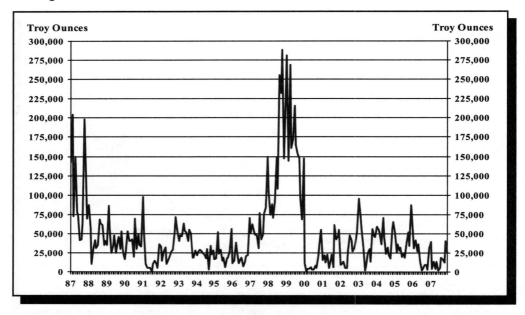

U.S. Eagle Gold Coin Sales

Troy Ounces

Uncirculated	1986	1987	1988	1989	1990	1991	1992	1993	1994	1995
January	-	142,500	87,500	35,000	17,000	98,000	32,800	40,000	22,000	17,000
February	-	205,000	57,000	86,500	26,000	53,500	15,000	47,500	25,500	18,000
March	-	73,000	10,000	56,000	53,000	10,000	26,500	47,000	29,500	51,500
April	-	149,500	30,000	25,000	40,000	5,000	32,000	63,000	27,500	23,750
May	-	78,000	41,500	35,000	40,000	5,000	10,500	54,000	25,000	29,000
June	-	75,000	31,000	47,500	43,000	5,000	15,500	50,500	23,000	14,500
July	-	42,000	35,000	25,000	20,000	0	22,000	41,000	17,500	18,500
August	-	43,000	68,000	40,000	70,000	10,000	26,000	55,000	30,000	6,000
September	-	63,500	63,500	45,500	30,000	15,000	29,000	50,000	3,500	17,500
October	692,000	198,000	61,000	30,000	50,000	10,000	52,000	18,500	34,000	19,000
November	469,500	113,000	35,500	53,000	35,000	5,000	72,000	19,000	22,500	27,000
December	626,250	70,000	40,000	25,000	32,950	36,500	52,500	28,000	28,000	56,000
Subtotal	1,787,750	1,252,500	560,000	503,500	456,950	253,000	385,800	513,500	288,000	297,750
% Change	-	-29.9%	-55.3%	-10.1%	-9.2%	-44.6%	52.5%	33.1%	-43.9%	3.4%
Proof/Commemoratives	446,290	425,500	411,000	196,500	113,823	129,000	128,548	137,000	128,000	130,000
% Change	-	-4.7%	-3.4%	-52.2%	-42.1%	13.3%	-0.4%	6.6%	-6.6%	1.6%
Total	1,952,000	1,678,000	971,000	700,000	512,000	382,000	514,348	650,500	416,000	427,750
% Change	-	-14.0%	-42.1%	-27.9%	-26.9%	-25.4%	34.6%	26.5%	-36.0%	2.8%

Uncirculated	1996	1997	1998	1999	2000	2001	2002	2003	2004	2005
January	11,000	51,250	105,500	281,000	11,000	16,000	9,500	96,000	59,500	51,000
February	14,500	62,500	75,000	144,000	0	21,500	11,000	72,000	55,500	26,000
March	38,500	51,500	88,000	269,000	4,500	12,000	13,500	56,500	50,500	36,500
April	28,500	48,500	71,000	161,000	4,500	22,500	5,500	33,000	36,000	28,000
May	11,500	47,500	91,500	172,000	6,000	5,500	5,500	2,000	70,500	32,000
June	17,000	31,500	148,500	216,000	3,000	10,500	26,500	7,000	46,000	20,000
July	18,500	77,000	107,500	165,500	3,000	22,500	48,000	24,500	23,500	24,500
August	7,500	43,000	255,000	154,000	8,000	6,500	42,000	30,500	32,500	19,000
September	14,000	49,000	233,000	147,000	5,500	61,500	26,500	14,000	22,500	38,000
October	21,000	76,000	288,500	98,000	19,500	42,200	31,000	56,000	17,500	51,500
November	22,000	84,000	147,000	68,000	44,500	46,500	43,500	47,000	56,500	34,000
December	71,000	149,500	229,000	147,500	55,000	55,000	52,500	46,000	65,500	87,000
Subtotal	275,000	771,250	1,839,500	2,023,000	164,500	322,200	315,000	484,500	536,000	447,500
% Change	-7.6%	180.5%	138.5%	10.0%	-91.9%	95.9%	-2.2%	53.8%	10.6%	-16.5%
Proof/Commemoratives	130,000	62,500	52,054	73,430	63,028	77,303	122,308	82,572	52,604	49,341
% Change		-51.9%	-16.7%	41.1%	-14.2%	22.6%	58.2%	-32.5%	-36.3%	-6.2%
Total	405,000	833,750	1,891,554	2,096,430	227,528	399,503	437,308	567,072	588,604	496,841
% Change	-5.3%	105.9%	126.9%	10.8%	-89.1%	75.6%	9.5%	29.7%	3.8%	-15.6%

Uncirculated	2006	2007
January	51,000	39,500
February	31,500	4,000
March	42,000	13,000
April	27,000	4,500
May	36,500	13,500
June	13,500	2,000
July	2,000	5,500
August	4,000	19,000
September	9,500	17,000
October	9,000	12,000
November	3,000	41,000
December	31,000	24,500
Subtotal	260,000	195,500
% Change	-41.9%	-5.8%

Note: 2007 percent change from year earlier period.
Commemorative year-end through 2005.
Source: U.S. Mint.
January 18, 2008

Official Gold Coin Fabrication

Thousand Troy Ounces

	1973	1974	1975	1976	1977	1978	1979	1980	1981	1982	1983
Market Economies											
South Africa	968	3,205	5,581	2,923	2,858	6,224	4,675	3,443	3,607	3,289	3,495
Canada	32	3	10	357	96	148	1,138	1,569	666	878	1,077
United States	-	-	87	45	32	32	32	16	23	10	161
Australia	-	-	-	-	-	-	-	-	-	-	-
United Kingdom	23	473	942	260	733	1,579	1,852	1,897	913	923	363
Mexico	386	2,144	318	466	26	730	1,466	739	1,591	-	-
Turkey	109	193	434	460	354	177	-	51	55	-	347
Austria	141	2,411	305	913	251	164	19	6	42	77	96
Switzerland	-	-	26	13	16	39	32	19	10	23	16
Japan	-	-	-	-	-	-	-	-	-	-	-
Chile	-	64	48	116	19	-	55	42	3	-	-
Hungary	-	547	-	-	-	-	-	-	-	-	-
Other	87	190	322	306	174	150	58	-58	385	53	103
Subtotal	1,746	9,230	8,073	5,859	4,559	9,243	9,327	7,724	7,295	5,253	5,658
Transitional Economies											
C.I.S.	-	-	63	250	500	220	350	195	-	-	-
China	-	-	-	-	-	-	164	11	3	42	54
Other	-	-	-	5	22	-	3	2	3	2	-
Subtotal	-	-	63	255	522	220	517	208	6	44	54
WORLD TOTAL	1,746	9,230	8,136	6,114	5,081	9,463	9,844	7,932	7,301	5,297	5,712

1984	1985	1986	1987	1988	1989	1990	1991	1992	1993	1994	
											Market Economies
2,382	1,103	-	325	317	314	413	300	7	150	170	South Africa
1,161	2,103	1,325	1,506	1,231	1,100	1,013	425	530	460	320	Canada
293	79	1,952	1,678	971	700	512	382	514	650	416	United States
-	-	-	509	284	280	381	694	469	340	440	Australia
64	36	67	300	267	106	65	20	32	50	60	United Kingdom
-	325	600	334	378	1,000	318	218	200	225	100	Mexico
-	300	-	400	245	300	-	10	13	135	70	Turkey
61	63	88	-	16	413	639	429	629	334	361	Austria
3	-	3	-	29	23	7	185	-	-	3	Switzerland
-	-	6,400	643	-	-	-	1,900	-	1,150	-	Japan
-	-	-	-	-	-	-	-	-	-	-	Chile
-	-	-	-	-	-	-	2	2	-	-	Hungary
61	596	150	1,003	651	500	380	400	241	200	170	Other
4,025	4,605	10,585	6,698	4,389	4,736	3,728	4,965	2,637	3,694	2,110	Subtotal
											Transitional Economies
-	-	-	-	13	25	12	14	5	15	7	C.I.S.
54	234	250	303	292	300	135	114	106	170	100	China
-	3	-	-	-	-	-	-	4	-	-	Other
54	237	250	303	305	325	147	128	115	185	107	Subtotal
4,079	4,842	10,835	7,001	4,694	5,061	3,875	5,093	2,752	3,879	2,217	WORLD TOTAL

Official Gold Coin Fabrication
Thousand Troy Ounces

	1995	1996	1997	1998	1999	2000	2001	2002	2003	2004	2005	2006
Market Economies												
South Africa	74	34	65	84	11	NA	NA	NA	NA	NA	NA	NA
Canada	340	235	672	724	732	113	168	375	216	259	302	275
United States	428	405	834	1,892	2,096	165	322	315	485	536	448	260
Australia	325	200	328	322	216	147	111	99	120	162	154	170
United Kingdom	36	27	30	30	30	202	97	102	67	48	60	80
Mexico	50	60	60	30	54	136	81	111	32	41	47	NA
Turkey	61	60	60	60	NA	NA	NA	NA	NA	NA	NA	NA
Austria	933	578	636	421	288	266	77	202	207	291	160	135
Switzerland	3	3	3	3	3	2	2	2	1	1	1	1
Japan	-	3	86	-	129	-	-	-	-	-	-	-
Chile	-	-	-	-	-	-	-	-	-	-	-	-
Hungary	-	-	-	-	-	-	-	-	-	-	-	-
Other	130	300	350	300	500	650	1,400	1,200	2,100	2,450	3,280	3,550
Subtotal	2,380	1,905	3,124	3,866	4,059	1,681	2,258	2,406	3,228	3,788	4,452	4,471
Transitional Economies												
C.I.S.	7	12	15	3	-	-	-	-	-	-	-	-
China	80	90	158	100	-	-	-	-	-	-	-	-
Other	-	-	-	-	-	-	-	-	-	-	-	-
Subtotal	87	102	173	103	NA	NA	NA	NA	NA	NA	NA	NA
WORLD TOTAL	2,467	2,007	3,297	3,969	4,059	1,681	2,258	2,406	3,228	3,788	4,452	4,471

Notes: This table represents gold coin fabrication statistics; production of coins
varies from sales in individual years. Data for 2005 include CPM Group estimates.
U.S. figures exclude commemoratives after 2000, perhaps around 60,000 ounces per year.
 *Included in Other. NA -- not available. e -- estimates.
Sources: Industry and mint sources; CPM Group.
30 January 2008

World Gold Investment
Million Troy Ounces

	1974	1975	1976	1977	1978	1979	1980	1981	1982	1983	1984
Official Coins	8.7	8.1	5.9	4.6	9.2	9.3	7.7	7.3	5.3	5.7	4.1
Bullion	17.2	4.4	1.6	8.5	5.7	15.4	12.5	4.6	5.8	8.6	4.4
Medallions	0.3	0.7	1.6	1.7	1.6	1.1	1.2	0.9	1.2	1.1	1.4
Total	26.2	13.2	9.1	14.8	16.5	25.8	21.4	12.8	12.3	15.4	9.9
Value ($Bil.)	4.2	2.1	1.1	2.2	3.2	7.9	13.1	5.9	4.6	6.5	3.6
Investment Demand's Share of Total Market	61%	33%	19%	31%	33%	54%	39%	25%	25%	32%	20%
Coinage's Share of Investment Demand	33%	61%	65%	31%	56%	36%	36%	57%	43%	37%	42%

	1985	1986	1987	1988	1989	1990	1991	1992	1993	1994	1995
Official Coins	4.8	10.8	7.0	4.7	5.0	3.9	5.1	2.8	3.9	2.2	2.5
Bullion	3.7	9.6	15.5	1.6	9.7	4.0	4.2	11.9	18.2	1.6	-3.7
Medallions	0.4	0.6	0.5	0.5	0.7	0.7	0.7	0.7	0.7	0.7	0.6
Total	8.9	21.0	23.0	6.8	15.4	8.6	10.0	15.4	22.8	4.5	-0.6
Value ($Bil.)	2.8	7.7	10.3	3.0	5.9	3.3	3.6	5.3	8.2	1.7	NM
Investment Demand's Share of Total Market	16%	32%	35%	10%	21%	11%	13%	19%	27%	5%	NM
Coinage's Share of Investment Demand	54%	51%	30%	69%	32%	45%	51%	18%	17%	49%	NM

	1996	1997	1998	1999	2000	2001	2002	2003	2004	2005	2006
Official Coins	2.0	3.3	4.0	4.0	1.7	2.2	2.4	3.2	3.7	4.0	4.5
Bullion	1.9	7.6	10.4	12.9	11.8	7.3	23.8	32.9	19.8	20.7	11.2
Medallions	0.6	0.6	0.6	0.8	1.0	1.0	1.0	1.2	1.5	2.0	3.0
Indian Demand	1.5	1.5	1.5	1.5	1.5	11.6	9.8	12.9	16.1	19.3	20.5
Total	4.5	11.5	15.0	17.7	14.5	22.1	37.0	50.2	41.1	46.0	39.2
Value ($Bil.)	1.7	3.8	4.4	5.0	4.1	6.0	11.5	18.3	16.8	20.5	23.8
Investment Demand's Share of Total Market	5%	12%	14%	17%	14%	21%	34%	45%	39%	42%	38%
Coinage's Share of Investment Demand	45%	29%	27%	23%	12%	10%	6%	6%	9%	9%	11%

	2007e	2008p
Official Coins	4.5	4.5
Bullion	19.3	20.3
Medallions	2.8	3.0
Indian Demand	15.4	16.0
Total	42.1	43.8
Value ($Bil.)	29.4	
Investment Demand's Share of Total Market	38%	40%
Coinage's Share of Investment Demand	11%	10%

Notes: Demand statistics for 1977-1983 have been adjusted to reflect the absorption of metal recovered from secondary supply sources; data for 1974-1976 are unadjusted. Value of holdings calculated using annual average London afternoon gold price. Market share is the percent of total annual gold supply absorbed by private investors. Longer term projections are available in CPM Group's Gold Supply, Demand, and Price: 10-Year Projections report.
Sources: Gold Institute, national mints, Consolidated Gold Fields, CPM Group.
January 30, 2008

Supply

Supply

The total supply of newly refined gold from all sources rose in 2007, even as mine production continued to be constrained by logistical delays in expanding new operations. Total new supply rose sharply, by 6.2% to 110.7 million ounces in 2007. Annual total supply reached the second highest level in history last year, surpassed only by 2003. The increase in total new supplies reflected a sharp rise in gold recovered from old jewelry and other quasi-investment decorative objects, especially in India. Mine production declined slightly meanwhile. The flow of gold from Russia, China, Uzbekistan, and other transitional economies also continued to rise last year, reflecting higher mine output rates in these countries.

Of this total, mine production is estimated to have declined 1.1% to 59.3 million ounces. Production was off in five of the six largest mining countries, among the market economies. It was rising in other countries where gold mining is emerging as a more vibrant industry. As discussed below, gold production also is rising in China, which has surpassed South Africa as the world's largest producing nation, and Russia, although production in these transitional economies is excluded from the market economy production figures here.

There was an enormous, 23.3% increase in gold recovered from scrap, mostly in India, last year. Gold scrap refining totaled an estimated 32.4 million

Annual Total Supply

Projected Through 2008.

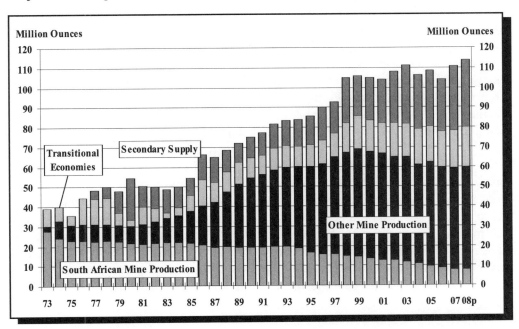

ounces, 6.1 million ounces more than in 2006. Most of this surge was in India. Middle Eastern scrap markets reported that in those countries many jewelry investors continued to hold their old jewelry, using dollars to buy new gold jewelry rather than trading in old jewelry.

Total new supply stood at 104.3 million ounces in 2006. This was down 3.9% from 108.5 million ounces the year before, and off from the peak of 111.3 million ounces in 2003. Total supply has ranged between 104 and 111 million ounces since 1998, reflecting the decline in gold mine production since the late 1990s, stimulated by low prices at that time which triggered a reduction in mine expansions and developments. While mine production has slid since 1999, the amount of gold being recovered from old scrap has risen sharply. This reflects not only the effects of higher gold prices in recent years stimulating sales of gold jewelry and decorative objects for their gold content, but also a shift away from using jewelry, statues, and other gold objects as a form of savings by some segments of society in India and the Middle East.

Last year, mine production declined once more. A small increase in global gold production had been expected, but it did not emerge. It should be noted that the mine production figures here represent mine production in market economy nations, and exclude production in China, Russia, and other countries mak-

ing the transition from centrally planned economies to market economies. This will be discussed shortly.

Related to these countries, it appears that China has surpassed South Africa as the largest gold mining country in the world. South African production declined from 8.8 million ounces in 2006 to 8.0 million ounces last year, while Chinese production rose from around 7.7 million ounces to 8.7 million ounces. For several years the trends toward lower South African and higher Chinese gold output have clearly pointed to a time in the near future when China would surpass South Africa. Three years ago it seemed this would happen by 2009 or 2010. Chinese output is rising more sharply than had been expected, however, and the cross occurred in 2007.

2008 and Beyond

Total gold supply may rise a further 2.8% in 2008, to 113.9 million ounces. That would be a record, surpassing the previous 111.3 million ounce peak in 2003. This increase, should it emerge, would reflect a combination of both continued rising secondary recovery, and rising mine production.

Mine production is projected to rise 1.1% back to 60.0 million ounces this year. Secondary recovery from scrap is projected to rise another 1.5 million ounces, to 33.9 million ounces. Perhaps another 20.0 million ounces will be exported into the market by China, Russia, Uzbekistan, and other transitional economies.

The net increase in mine output projected for this year is relatively modest: 1.1% or 700,000 ounces to 60.0 million ounces. A similar rise was projected a year ago for 2007, but, as mentioned above, did not occur. Actually, in early 2007 it seemed as if an even larger increase in mine production in the market economies would occur last year, but a range of technical, labor, and logistical problems conspired against the numerous mine expansions and new mine developments, as well as existing operations, to cause a small decline in production.

These problems are persisting in early 2008, and could cause mine production to decline slightly once more this year. In the middle of January a power shortage led all of the gold mines in South Africa to close down, as they could not rise workers far underground with power outages. As this was being written the closure was only a few days old, and it was unclear how dramatic a negative impact it would have on South Africa production. The view was that the country could lose at least 300,000 ounces of production due to the problems, and possibly much more. Given that world gold mine production is projected to rise only 700,000 ounces this year in this report, this one problem may be sufficient to extend the period of

Mine Output in Major Gold Producing Market Economies, 1992-2008p

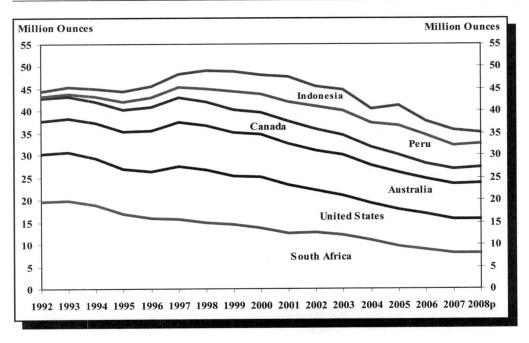

Major Market Economy Gold Producers
Thousand Troy Ounces

	1983	1984	1985	1986	1987	1988	1989	1990	1991	1992	1993	1994	1995
South Africa	21,847	21,905	21,598	20,518	19,437	19,927	19,492	19,380	19,224	19,562	19,926	18,772	16,795
United States	1,956	2,059	2,475	3,739	4,947	6,460	8,537	9,452	9,452	10,610	10,642	10,513	10,192
Australia	1,035	1,257	1,833	2,508	3,533	5,048	6,752	7,877	7,555	7,591	7,739	8,029	8,400
Canada	2,223	2,491	2,815	3,308	3,724	4,334	5,128	5,284	5,635	5,155	4,850	4,708	4,888
Indonesia	77	79	300	320	440	500	525	600	828	1,154	1,490	1,891	2,377
Peru	166	137	135	145	150	150	139	111	121	320	739	1,125	1,817
Brazil	1,640	1,726	2,025	2,375	2,694	3,222	3,305	2,807	2,667	2,400	2,251	2,138	2,026
Papua New Guinea	584	835	1,067	1,157	1,190	1,286	1,085	1,093	1,980	2,289	2,003	1,886	1,662
Chile	571	541	554	588	548	663	713	735	922	1,029	1,100	1,250	1,433
Ghana	304	287	299	287	324	390	428	487	845	1,190	1,325	1,430	1,650
Philippines	812	773	810	1,139	1,048	1,044	964	790	830	820	800	875	870
Zimbabwe	453	478	472	475	473	481	515	543	573	585	608	660	722
Mexico	223	244	257	267	289	344	385	322	286	358	393	450	672
Colombia	439	800	1,143	1,286	853	973	871	956	946	961	868	877	800
Bolivia	49	41	30	28	90	157	157	166	160	160	335	412	453
Ecuador	68	280	300	317	305	256	300	322	261	219	200	250	340
Venezuela	33	51	73	81	3	113	124	240	223	273	280	320	245
New Zealand	10	22	45	50	55	64	95	149	190	328	361	331	391
Guyana	5	11	10	14	21	19	17	39	59	80	298	350	288
Japan	116	129	159	195	200	235	196	235	267	286	301	308	318
South Korea	72	79	77	149	244	250	250	250	250	250	250	219	238
Tanzania	1	1	3	3	3	3	3	100	120	160	225	270	250
Mali	13	16	16	16	16	23	32	167	158	183	200	205	220
Sweden	108	142	149	130	150	150	129	136	140	193	209	148	210
Spain	162	123	125	132	177	180	179	175	176	212	200	193	188
Burkino Faso	-	-	-	-	-	-	-	240	180	174	160	190	180
Dominican Republic	361	338	337	246	246	186	177	139	130	96	80	65	106
Yugoslavia*	130	125	110	115	115	120	121	263	263	235	107	129	122
Others	771	727	687	724	847	909	947	1,443	1,606	1,729	2,003	2,248	2,434
Total	34,229	35,696	37,906	40,313	42,123	47,485	51,566	54,501	56,047	58,601	59,942	60,242	60,286

Notes: Totals may not equal the sums of the columns due to rounding. * Yugoslavia is comprimised of
Serbia and Montenegro from 1993. e - estimate.
Sources: Chamber of Mines of South Africa; U.S. Bureau of Mines;
American Bureau of Metals Statistics; Gold Institute; Statistics Canada;
industry sources; United States Geological Service. Raw Materials Group. CPM Group.
January 15, 2008

1996	1997	1998	1999	2000	2001	2002	2003	2004	2005	2006	2007e	
15,902	15,800	14,931	14,451	13,770	12,652	12,705	12,082	11,019	9,559	8,845	7,961	South Africa
10,481	11,639	11,767	10,963	11,349	10,771	9,581	8,906	8,295	8,359	8,000	7,750	United States
9,200	10,005	9,995	9,705	9,560	9,150	8,777	9,100	8,325	8,250	7,950	7,900	Australia
5,268	5,513	5,298	5,068	4,944	5,059	4,889	4,529	4,203	3,833	3,350	3,300	Canada
2,571	2,821	4,025	4,450	4,200	5,600	4,650	4,600	3,050	4,525	2,950	3,500	Indonesia
2,081	2,468	3,013	4,176	4,240	4,461	5,050	5,550	5,569	6,687	6,521	5,350	Peru
1,833	1,802	1,708	1,700	1,600	1,425	1,250	1,200	1,350	1,275	1,325	1,400	Brazil
1,658	1,559	1,983	2,110	2,350	2,160	2,030	2,160	2,350	2,200	1,800	1,750	Papua New Guinea
1,634	1,522	1,420	1,525	1,720	1,350	1,250	1,250	1,285	1,300	1,350	1,350	Chile
1,620	1,700	2,360	2,601	2,450	2,300	2,220	2,250	2,000	2,100	2,300	2,650	Ghana
970	1,050	1,090	995	1,170	1,085	1,125	1,125	1,125	1,175	1,175	1,200	Philippines
827	867	898	964	680	579	500	400	650	450	355	355	Zimbabwe
774	837	836	800	800	828	748	713	804	1,025	1,175	1,400	Mexico
760	648	500	1,100	1,200	701	670	1,495	1,210	1,150	1,250	1,300	Colombia
421	432	472	384	353	396	360	275	220	290	400	500	Bolivia
400	344	260	160	130	130	130	130	160	170	180	190	Ecuador
396	600	480	480	320	300	300	300	300	325	380	400	Venezuela
380	370	250	276	321	320	320	300	335	335	335	335	New Zealand
391	448	451	450	450	450	418	385	375	365	375	375	Guyana
297	281	288	284	264	254	257	262	255	265	265	270	Japan
250	263	250	250	250	250	250	250	250	250	250	250	South Korea
230	217	230	328	500	1,050	1,250	1,400	1,550	1,500	1,500	1,500	Tanzania
227	556	720	803	900	1,340	1,801	1,500	1,250	1,450	1,624	1,673	Mali
206	226	204	193	193	154	177	183	185	197	215	215	Sweden
171	174	209	240	230	161	160	165	165	165	165	165	Spain
119	83	104	104	64	10	10	25	40	57	62	67	Burkino Faso
118	76	46	46	21	21	10	5	5	5	5	5	Dominican Republic
110	102	122	122	36	35	30	30	30	30	30	30	Yugoslavia*
2,455	2,734	3,449	4,105	3,641	4,012	4,232	4,353	4,711	5,152	5,850	6,172	Others
61,751	65,136	67,357	68,834	67,707	67,003	65,150	64,923	61,066	62,445	59,983	59,313	*Total*

declining global gold output through 2008.

Longer term expansions still are underway around the world. In fact, a global mine rush, not only in gold but in a wide range of other metals, is occurring. More money is being pumped into exploring for and developing new mines and expansions than ever before in history. The amount of funds being spent on exploration and development dwarf even the gold rush from 1980 through 1999. Additionally, vast reaches of the world formerly off limits to exploration and development are being explored and developed. As mentioned above, China now is the largest producer of gold in the world, after producing very little as recently as a decade ago. The mining boom is stretching from all parts of Asia through all parts of Africa, Latin America, and the former Soviet nations.

The results of this gold rush already are starting to appear. The table later in this chapter itemizes a list of 64 expansions or new mines under development now, slated to come onstream between now and 2012. The combined gross additions to capacity of these projects would be 15.9 million ounces, or slightly more than one quarter of current annual output. Most of this is front-loaded into 2008 - 2010, as projects slated to come onstream in these years are more advanced and better defined. Of the total, 23 projects with 4.2 million ounces of capacity are scheduled to start production this year, 21 projects with 3.8

Total Worldwide Metal Exploration Expenditures

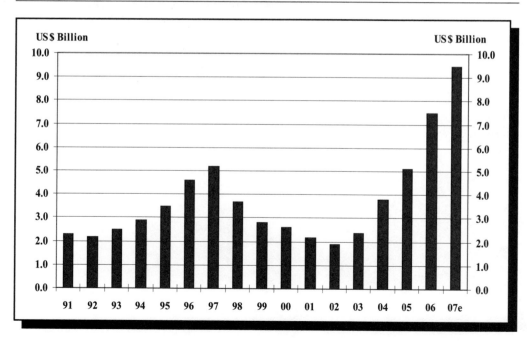

million ounces of capacity are scheduled for 2009 and 11 projects with 4.6 million ounces of capacity are lined up for 2010. Fewer projects are on the list for 2011 and 2012, but as time progresses more projects will be announced and advanced to the stage that they will appear on this list.

These are gross additions to capacity. While these 64 operations will come onstream, along with others not listed or maybe even known at present, other, older mines will close down. Even accounting for such closures, it appears that net additions to mine capacity could rise sharply in the longer term, perhaps on the order of 20% or more.

Mining costs are sky-rocketing, mean-

while. In 2006 the average cash cost was around $331.This average is estimated to have risen to more than $370 last year. The average total production cost in 2006 meanwhile was $406 and is estimated to have climbed to more than $480 in 2007. There are two broad sets of reasons for the sharp increase in gold mining costs. First, the mining and exploration boom is straining the supply channels for everything from geologists and mining engineers to concrete and structural steel. Second, as the gold price has more than doubled, mining companies are re-activating and developing gold mining properties that were not economic to mine at previous lower prices. Just as gold mining costs followed gold prices higher in the early 1980s, so today mining costs are rising

Estimated Gold Production Additions

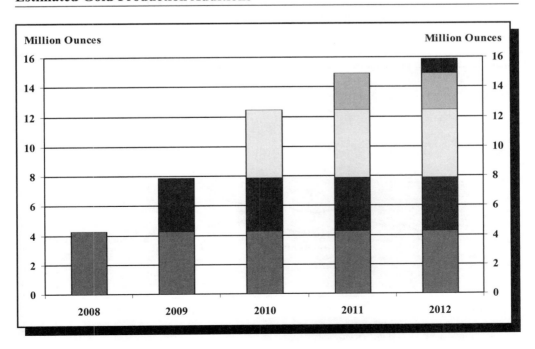

in no small part because miners are working higher cost deposits than they could afford to mine before. Properties with costs in the $400 - $500 range, which were passed by in the 1980s and 1990s, are being developed and mined now.

Refined gold from scrapped jewelry also is projected to rise in 2008. Scrap recovery rose very sharply in 2007, primarily as investors holding jewelry, statues, and other objects in India turned them in for their gold content. Scrap recovery is estimated to have risen 23.3% to 32.4 million ounces, up from 26.3 million ounces in 2006. A further 4.6% increase is projected for this year, to around 33.9 million ounces.

Mine Production

South African gold mine production declined for the fifth consecutive year in 2007. Mine output totaled 8.0 million ounces last year, down 10% from 8.8 million ounces produced in 2006. Over the past several years, production has been affected by lower ore grades than in previous years, coupled with rising working costs. This along with safety related shaft closures at mines and labor strikes at several operations added to the existing problems being faced by mining companies. The safety related closures were partly due to fatalities at these mines.

The lack of investment at many mining operations during the period from 1997

The Price of Gold and Cash Operating Costs of Production
Quarterly, Price Through Fourth Quarter 2007.

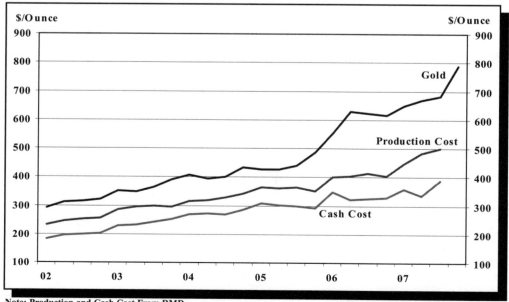

Note: Production and Cash Cost From RMD

through 2002, when gold traded below $300 for the most part, may have attributed to the degradation of these properties. Many mining companies with gold producing operations did not see it beneficial to upgrade or expand these mining operations. Costs were too high and rising, and gold prices were too low. Many companies already suffering the pinch from low profit margins delayed or scaled back projects. As gold prices have risen over the past several years, investment in these operations has risen as well. However, these investments will probably not be seen in increased mine output at least until the end of this year or next.

The other factors that have recently weighed on gold production are safety related problems and fatalities at several platinum group metal and gold mining operations. With gold prices at current levels and attention on the gold market high, labor unions and government institutions have reacted negatively toward mining companies. There have been legal and illegal work stoppages by employees, and the government has increased its scrutiny over mining operations. Early in 2008, power outages at several major mining operations caused a halt to gold production.

At its peak South Africa produced 32.2 million ounces in 1970. In 2008 South African mine output is projected to total 8.0 million ounces, similar to what it produced in 2007. Many of the issues experienced in 2007 in the South

The Price of Gold and Cash Operating Costs of Production

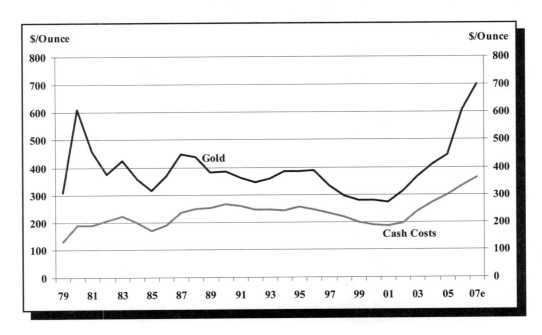

African gold mining industry are expected to spill over into 2008. Production may not begin to pick up for at least several quarters. Great Basin Gold's Burnstone project is expected to commence production in the third quarter of this year. It could produce up to 254,000 ounces annually.

Gold production in the **United States** is estimated to have totaled 7.8 million ounces in 2007. This is off from 8.0 million ounces produced in 2006 and off from the peak of 11.8 million ounces produced in 1998. In 2006 Barrick's majority held Cortez gold mine produced approximately 443,700 ounces, down more than half of the 904,300 ounces produced in 2005. That year total mine production in the United States totaled 8.4 million ounces. In early 2006 Barrick acquired Placer Dome and has since been increasing exploration and development at the Cortez property. When Barrick's program is complete, which may be two years away, it expects annual gold production to be between 966,000 and 991,000 ounces over the first five years.

This year U.S. gold output could rise to 7.9 million ounces, from the 7.8 million ounces estimated to have been produced last year. Mixed to lower production levels from various mines caused the decline in output last year. Some of these mining operations contributed less gold due to lower ore grades, operational upgrades, expansion projects, and accidents. This year the decline in mine output should taper off. Kinross' Buckhorn mine is expected to come on stream in the second quarter and could contribute 160,000 ounces annually

Australia contributed approximately 7.9 million ounces of gold to total supply last year. This was down from 8.0 million ounces produced in 2006 and 8.3 million ounces produced in 2005. In 2006 Barrick's and Newmont's Super Pit gold mine produced 664,200 ounces, down from 832,700 ounces produced in 2005. Newcrest's Telfer mine offset some of this decline in 2006, producing 663,900 ounces that year, up from 487,400 ounces produced in 2005. This year gold production is projected to rise to 8.0 million ounces. Oxiana's Prominent Hill mine could begin production in the fourth quarter of this year, contributing 115,000 ounces annually when in full production. St. Barbara Limited also is expected begin production in the third quarter at its Gwalia Deep mine. Gold output could average 100,000 ounces annually. La Mancha's Frog's Leg mine is expected to contribute 44,000 ounces annually when it begins production in the second half of this year.

In **Peru**, gold production is estimated to have fallen sharply in 2007 to 5.4 million ounces. Gold production fell from 6.5 million ounces produced in 2006. The bulk of the decline was due to a sharp reduction in output from Minera Yanacocha. This project, majority owned by Newmont and Buenaventura,

Near-term Mine Development Projects
Annual Production, Due within five years

Project	Company	Country	Reserves Mil. Oz.	Production Thou. Oz.	Commencement	Additions
Dolores	Minefinders	Mexico	2.5	127	2008 Q3	
Paciencia	Jaguar Mining	Brazil	0.4	50	2008 Q2	
Toka Tindung	Archipelago	Indonesia	1.0	160	2008 Q3	
Kittila	Agnico-Eagle	Finland	2.6	150	2008 Q3	
Bonikro	Equigold	Ivory Coast	0.9	130	2008 Q3	
Penasquito	Goldcorp	Mexico	13.0	350	2008 Q4	
Camp Caiman	Iamgold	French Guiana	1.1	115	2008	
Skouries	European Goldfields	Greece	3.9	220	2008	
Gualcamayo	Yamana	Argentina	2.2	200	2008 Q3	
Prominent Hill	Oxiana	Australia	1.3	115	2008 Q4	
Goldex	Agnico-Eagle	Canada	1.6	170	2008	
Los Filos	Goldcorp	Mexico	4.5	300	2008 Q1	
Buckhorn	Kinross	United States	1.0	160	2008 Q2	
Palmerejo	Bolnisi	Mexico	2.6	300	2008 Q1	
Hollister	Great Basin Gold	United States	1.8	150	2008 Q3	
Molejon	Petaquilla	Panama	1.5	120	2008	
Cerro Corona	Gold Fields	Peru	3.2	140	2008 Q3	
Sukari Gold Deposit	Centamin Egypt	Egypt	3.7	200	2008 Q4	
Frog's Leg	La Mancha	Australia	0.6	44	2008 Q3	
Gwalia Deep	St. Barbara	Australia	1.7	100	2008 Q3	
El Aguila	Gold Resource	Mexico	1.0	100	2008 Q3	
Paracatu	Kinross	Brazil	16.3	500	2008 Q3	
Burnstone	Great Basin Gold	South Africa	3.5	254	2008 Q3	
						4,155
Casposo	Interpid Mines	Argentina	0.3	70	2009 Q1	
Boddington Expansion	Newmont, et al.	Australia	13.0	850	2009	
Las Lagunas	Enviro Gold	Dominican Republic	0.5	80	2009	
Santa Luz	Yamana	Brazil	0.6	100	2009	
Las Cristinas	Crystallex	Venezuela	16.9	256	2009 Q3	
Martabe	Oxiana	Australia	6.0	250	2009 Q4	
Buzwagi	Barrick	Tanzania	2.6	255	2009	
Dinkidi	OceanaGold	Philippines	1.6	142	2009	
Lapa	Agnico-Eagle	Canada	1.2	125	2009 Q3	
Hidden Valley	Harmony	Papua New Guinea	2.7	285	2009 Q2	
Modder East	Uranium One	South Africa	1.4	110	2009 Q3	
Copler	Anatolia	Turkey	2.8	180	2009 Q3	
Mirador	Corriente	Ecuador	4.5	60	2009	
Sao Vicente	Yamana	Brazil	1.0	60	2009	
Andorinhas	Troy Resources	Brazil	0.3	50	2009	
Pinos Altos	Agnico Eagle	Mexico	2.2	150	2009 Q2	
Caete	Jaguar Mining	Brazil	0.5	40	2009 Q2	
Kemess North	Northgate	Canada	4.1	200	2009	
Trident	Avoca Resources	Australia	0.8	170	2009	
Hope Bay	Miramar	Canada	2.0	125	2009	
Wiluna	Apex minerals	Australia	1.0	200	2009	
						3,758
Oyu Tolgoi	Ivanhoe	Mongolia	31.6	800	2010	
Pueblo Viejo	Barrick	Dominican Republic	18.1	600	2010	
Pascua Lama	Barrick	Chile	17.0	765	2010	
Quimsacocha	Iamgold	Ecuador	2.0	281	2010	
Nico	Fortune Minerals	Canada	3.3	65	2010	
Meadow Bank	Agnico Eagle/Cumberland	Canada	2.9	350	2010	
Brisas	Gold Reserve	Venezuela	10.4	456	2010	
Young Davidson	Northgate	Canada	2.5	175	2010	
Rosia Montana	Gabriel Resources	Romania	10.1	635	2010	
Corimayo	Newmont	Peru	3.0	250	2010	
Esperanza	Antofagasta	Chile	3.5	197	2010	
						4,574
LaRonde	Agnico-Eagle	Canada	3.8	320	2011	
Tampakan	Indophil	Philippines	4.3	218	2011	
Cerro Casale	Kinross, Barrick	Chile	23.0	975	2011	
Akyem	Newmont	Ghana	7.7	400	2011	
Agua Rica	Nrtn Orion/Yamana	Argentina	4.0	135	2011	
Aphrodite	Apex Minerals	Australia	0.4	100	2011	
Éleonore	Goldcorp	Canada	2.8	350	2011	
						2,498
Donlin Creek	NovaGold/Barrick	United States	3.5	600	2012	
Galore Creek	NovaGold/Tech Cominco	Canada	5.3	340	2012	
						940
Total			296.9	15,925		

Notes: Some dates are approximate. These statistics were collected prior to January 2008. Some projects plans have
changed since that time. Sources: Company reports, RMD, CPM Group.
January 15, 2008

produced approximately 2.6 million ounces in 2006. In 2007 Minera Yanacocha is estimated to have produced 1.5 million ounces. Through the third quarter Minera Yanacocha had produced 1.1 million ounces. Last year less ore was mined while there was in increase in waste material processed. There also was a reduction in ore grade. These factors contributed to less gold being produced. This year mine output from Yanacocha could increase slightly as operational upgrades are expected to be completed soon. Gold Fields' Cerro Corona project is expected to begin gold production in the third quarter of this year, adding 140,000 ounces annually. Mine production from Peru this year could total 5.5 million ounces.

Gold production in **Indonesia** is estimated to have totaled 3.5 million ounces in 2007. This is up sharply from 3.0 million ounces produced in 2006. The largest gold mine in Indonesia is Freeport McMoRan's Grasberg project. It produced 1.9 million ounces of gold in 2006 and is estimated to have produced 2.4 million ounces last year. Over the past several years mine output from this mine has been mixed. There was a major landslide in late 2003, which affected gold production the following year. In 2005 gold output increased sharply, but in 2006 mine output fell due to lower ore grades. Last year's mining of Grasberg found better ore grades and therefore increased gold production. This year because of the sequencing of mining areas with again lower ore

grades, gold production from the Grasberg mine could amount to 1.3 million ounces. Archipelago's Toka Tindung mine could begin annual production of 160,000 ounces of gold beginning in the second half of 2008. This will not be enough to offset the large decline in production from Grasberg, however. Gold production in Indonesia is projected to total 2.5 million ounces this year, but is expected to increase in 2009.

Canada is estimated to have produced 3.3 million ounces of gold last year, down from 3.4 million ounces in 2006. This year gold production could increase back to 3.4 million ounces. Agnico-Eagle's Lapa mine is expected to begin production in the fourth quarter of this year and could produce 125,000 ounces of gold annually. Agnico-Eagle's Goldex project could begin to add another 170,000 ounce of gold annually.

Other Countries

African gold production including South Africa totaled 15.7 million ounces in 2007, down from 16.1 million ounces produced in the previous year. Gold mine output in Africa, not including South Africa, rose last year to 7.7 million ounces, from 7.3 million ounces in 2006. Newmont's Ahafo mine in **Ghana** is estimated to have provided the bulk of the increase last year. The Ahafo mine began production in the second half of 2006, producing 200,000 ounces that year. Last year production is estimated

Gold Mine Production by Company
Troy Ounces

Company	2006
Barrick Gold Corp	8,643,000
Newmont Mining Corp	5,982,298
Anglogold Ashanti Ltd	5,635,000
Gold Fields Ltd	4,348,605
Harmony Gold Mining Co Ltd	2,343,885
Freeport McMoran Copper & Gold Inc	1,782,436
Goldcorp Inc	1,693,300
Cia de Minas Buenaventura SA	1,546,000
Newcrest Mining Ltd	1,531,110
Kinross Gold Corp	1,476,329
Rio Tinto plc	1,003,000
Iamgold Corp	814,526
Lihir Gold Ltd	650,795
Northgate Minerals Corp	502,741
Randgold Resources Ltd	499,912
Xstrata plc	467,021
DRDGold Ltd	448,503
Yamana Gold Inc	346,842
Bema Gold Corp	340,315
Meridian Gold Inc	304,307
Industrias Penoles SA de CV	291,752
Resolute Mining Ltd	271,738
Teck Cominco Ltd	263,636
Inmet Mining Corp	254,949
Agnico Eagle Mines Ltd	245,824
Oxiana Ltd	223,704
Aruntani SA	207,340
Golden Star Resources Ltd	201,392
Hochschild Mining plc	195,734
BHP Billiton Group	191,895
Oceana Gold Ltd	182,295
Hecla Mining Co	179,276
St Barbara Ltd	169,434
Consorcio Minero Horizonte	162,071
Minera Aurifera Retamas SA	159,146
Cia Minera Aurifera Santa Rosa SA	157,828
Monarch Gold Mining Company Ltd	157,506
Lionore Mining International Ltd	155,912
Queenstake Resources Ltd	154,195
High River Gold Mines Ltd	153,680
Thistle Mining Inc	152,716
Equigold NL	147,604
Boliden AB	145,032
Companhia Vale do Rio Doce	141,463
Eldorado Gold Corp	135,644
Sub-Total	45,061,691
Totoal Market Economy Mine Production	59,982,919
Percentage of Production Accounted:	75.1%

Note: Production totals estimated for some companies.
Source: CPM Group, RMD, Company Reports
December 28,2007

to have reached 480,000 ounces. Production also increased in **Mali** and **Guinea**. In late 2008, Centamin's Sukari Gold Deposit in **Egypt** could begin producing 200,000 ounces annually. Equigold's Bonikro mine in the **Ivory Coast** could add another 130,000 ounces.

In 2007 Asia and the Middle East mine output also rose. **Mongolia**, **Turkey**, and the **Philippines** combined added an additional 70,000 ounces of gold. This was in addition to the increase in production from Indonesia.

Gold output in **Mexico** totaled 1.4 million ounces last year, up from 1.18 million ounces produced in 2006. The sharp increase came from several mines with increases of several thousand ounces of production from each. Metallica's Cerro San Pedro mine produced 27,000 ounces last year. This year Mexican gold production could surge much higher. Goldcorp's Penasquito mine is expected to begin production later this year, with annual production of 350,000 ounces. Goldcorp's Los Filos mine commenced commercial production in January of this year and could produce 300,000 ounces. Minefinders' Dolores mine is expected to begin gold production in the third quarter and could contribute 127,000 annually. Bolnisi's Palmerejo mine and Gold Resource's El Aguila mine could add another 300,000 and 100,000 ounces, respectively.

In **Guatemala** gold production rose to 230,000 ounces in 2007, from 162,000

ounces produced in the previous year. Goldcorp's Marlin mine contributed the bulk of the increase last year, producing 227,200 ounces. In **Panama**, Petaquilla's Molejon mine is expected to begin producing 120,000 ounces of gold annually.

Although Peruvian gold output is estimated to have declined last year, gold production from its neighboring countries is estimated to have increased. Gold output in **Argentina**, **Bolivia**, **Brazil**, and **Colombia** rose. Excluding Peru, South American gold production increased approximately 425,000 to 7.7 million ounces in 2007, from 7.3 million ounces produced in 2006. This year Kinross' Paracuta mine in Brazil is expected to begin production of 500,000 ounces of gold.

Transitional Economy Supply

China, Russia, the other nations of the former Soviet Union, and other countries still transitioning from centrally planned economies are separated in these reports. It is not that mine production figures have not gotten better for these countries. They have improved dramatically. Also, these countries have increased their production sharply. China appears to have surpassed South Africa as the largest gold mining nation in 2007.

The problem with integrating the supply from these countries into the global supply and demand statistics in this report is that very poor data exists for demand for

gold within China, Russia, and some of these other countries. Clearly there is sizeable and rising demand for gold, as jewelry, for use in electronics and other applications, and as an investment, in these countries. The data simply are not available to allow for an accurate measure of how much gold is being used and bought by investors in these countries. To add figures for these countries to the global statistics for mine production, and refined production from scrap, without accurately measuring domestic demand, would be to skew and distort the balance in the market.

Work continues to develop reasonable estimates of demand in China, Russia, and other countries, but until these fig-

Transitional Economy Mine Production

Annual, Through 2007.

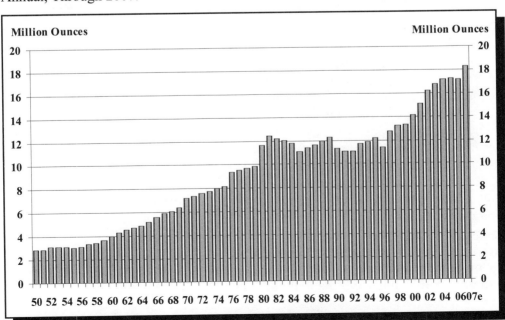

ures have a higher degree of statistical integrity, it is best to segregate these countries' supply from the total global figures, and instead to try to measure the net flow of gold into the international market from these countries.

China became the world's largest gold producing country last year, with gold output reaching 8.7 million ounces. This was up from 7.65 million ounces produced in 2006. In 2008 Chinese gold production is expected to increase, perhaps at a similar double-digit rate of growth. The economic expansion going on there has been seen in the mining industry as companies have been increasing proven and probable reserve levels.

Russian gold output also increased, rising to 5.34 million ounce in 2007, from 5.21 million ounces in 2006.

Secondary Recovery

As discussed earlier, a tremendous surge occurred in the sale of gold jewelry and decorative objects in India, which pushed secondary recovery sharply higher in 2007. Most of this surge occurred in India. Indian gold refining from scrap is estimated on a preliminary basis to have risen from around 7.0 million ounces in 2006 to around 12.9 million ounces in 2007. A further increase, to around 13.5 million ounces, is projected for 2008. This reflects the combination of rising gold prices, falling U.S. dollar, volatile financial markets in

India, and a shift on the part of some households in India away from viewing gold and silver as the prime form of savings and investment. Investors continue to hold gold and silver, but some are shifting from traditional jewelry and decorative objects to buying and holding bars, coins, and medallions. In this environment, Indians took advantage of the rise in gold prices and sold a great amount of gold jewelry last year.

This pattern was not repeated elsewhere. In the Middle East, investors held on to their old jewelry, and used dollars to buy more gold jewelry. This made sense, given the heavy inflows of depreciating dollars into the oil-exporting region. As a result, gold recovery from old jewelry and scrap rose only slightly in the Middle East and Turkey last year. A more pronounced increase is projected for 2008, reflecting expectations of higher gold prices.

Annual Gold Recovery and Average London Gold Price

Price Through December 2007.

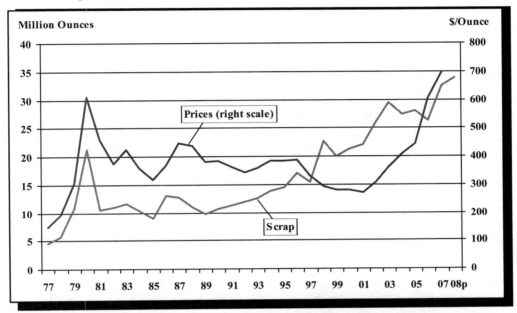

Secondary Supply

Thousand Troy Ounces

	1984	1985	1986	1987	1988	1989	1990	1991	1992	1993	1994	1995
United States	2,167	1,640	1,720	1,694	1,716	2,172	2,076	2,016	2,090	2,275	2,500	2,630
Japan	1,366	1,350	916	965	965	482	588	735	816	860	944	990
Europe	1,270	1,209	948	1,093	1,270	1,350	1,511	1,360	1,521	1,600	1,760	1,850
Indian Subcontinent	1,800	2,090	2,186	1,929	1,768	1,608	1,800	2,160	2,590	2,720	2,990	3,140
Far East (Excluding Japan)	804	707	1,125	1,447	1,286	965	1,000	1,700	1,906	2,100	2,310	2,430
Middle East	643	611	4,823	4,180	2,572	1,929	2,200	1,800	1,580	1,500	1,645	1,730
Africa	225	177	161	161	177	161	175	158	160	180	200	210
Latin America	2,045	1,122	1,029	1,222	1,286	965	1,320	1,280	1,250	1,225	1,345	1,410
Canada	64	58	58	64	64	64	64	64	64	96	105	110
Other	13	10	10	13	13	13	13	13	13	13	13	13
Total	10,397	8,974	12,976	12,768	11,117	9,709	10,747	11,286	11,990	12,569	13,812	14,513
Percent Change	--	-13.7%	44.6%	-1.6%	-12.9%	-12.7%	10.7%	5.0%	6.2%	4.8%	9.9%	5.1%

Notes: Scrap recovery data for individual countries and regions include metal
refined domestically and gold contained in scrap which is exported for refining.
Totals may not equal sums for individual countries due to rounding.
Sources: Gold Institute; U.S. Bureau of Mines; Consolidated
Gold Fields; industry sources; CPM Group.
January 18, 2008

1996	1997	1998	1999	2000	2001	2002	2003	2004	2005	2006	2007e	2008p	
3,080	3,150	3,000	1,800	1,300	750	775	800	775	825	725	690	720	United States
1,160	980	1,000	800	750	650	680	725	745	762	740	775	800	Japan
2,170	2,200	2,300	2,350	2,450	2,300	2,500	2,500	2,500	2,550	2,800	2,815	2,850	Europe
													Indian
3,680	3,250	3,250	2,450	2,800	3,000	5,800	11,253	10,500	9,600	7,000	12,860	13,500	Subcontinent
													Far East
2,850	2,425	10,000	9,690	10,500	11,500	11,700	9,300	8,500	9,200	8,600	8,750	9,180	(Excluding Japan)
2,028	1,700	1,360	1,300	1,700	2,100	2,750	2,900	2,600	3,100	4,300	4,350	4,575	Middle East
246	230	200	180	250	200	200	200	175	185	200	205	215	Africa
1,653	1,430	1,330	1,310	1,350	1,375	1,500	1,600	1,450	1,675	1,800	1,835	1,925	Latin America
129	134	110	110	120	95	100	120	100	110	110	112	115	Canada
13	13	13	10	11	12	12	12	10	15	20	23	25	Other
17,009	15,512	22,563	20,000	21,231	21,982	26,017	29,410	27,355	28,022	26,295	32,415	33,905	Total
17.2%	-8.8%	45.5%	-11.4%	6.2%	3.5%	18.4%	13.0%	-7.0%	2.4%	-6.2%	23.3%	4.6%	Percent Change

Production Costs in South Africa by Mine

Fourth Quarter 2006

Mine	Working Costs	Refined Production	Cumulative Production
	($/Troy Oz.)	(Troy Oz.)	(Troy Oz.)
South Deep	668.55	63,433	63,433
Evander	489.85	53,920	117,353
Freestate	480.57	116,932	234,285
Elandsrand	457.50	54,553	288,839
Randfontein	432.22	81,190	370,029
ARMgold	415.68	37,909	407,938
Freegold	415.51	165,261	573,199
Kloof	354.93	230,585	803,784
Driefontein	344.58	247,303	1,051,087
Beatrix	339.29	149,504	1,200,591
Target	317.53	31,527	1,232,118
Anglogold Ashanti	264.02	643,615	1,875,733
Subtotal and Average	*$355.71*	*1,875,733*	
Other Member Chambers (Uranium Producers, etc.)		*61,787*	
Non-Chamber Members		*252,519*	
Total		*2,190,039*	

Note: Working costs were converted from rand to dollars using average exchange rate of $0.13686 per rand for the 4Q06. Anglogold Ashanti: Profits from sales of the by-products uranium and acid/or pyrite, is offset against cash costs, in accordance with the Gold Institute definition. Retrenchment costs are included net of other costs. South Deep, previously listed as Placer Dome Western Areas JV was acquired by Goldfields on 1 December 2006.
Source: Chamber of Mines of South Africa.
March 11, 2007

Production Costs in South Africa by Mine

| | First Quarter 2007 | | |
Mine	Working Costs	Refined Production	Cumulative Production
	($/Troy Oz.)	(Troy Oz.)	(Troy Oz.)
ARMgold	628.33	25,688	25,688
South Deep	604.25	66,713	92,401
Elandsrand	566.16	43,497	135,898
Randfontein	454.56	68,012	203,909
Beatrix	425.13	119,231	323,140
Free State	423.10	123,259	446,400
Evander	421.17	60,090	506,489
Freegold	418.96	169,183	675,673
Kloof	383.33	220,010	895,683
Driefontein	352.07	251,226	1,146,909
Anglogold Ashanti	311.82	566,679	1,713,587
Target	284.16	37,552	1,751,139
Subtotal and Average	*$383.28*	*1,751,139*	
Other Member Chambers (Uranium Producers, etc.)		*44,741*	
Non-Chamber Members		*223,400*	
Total		*2,019,280*	

Note: Working costs were converted from rand to dollars using average exchange rate of
$0.13791 per rand for the 1Q07. Anglogold Ashanti: Profits from sales of the by-products
uranium and acid/or pyrite, is offset against cash costs, in accordance with the Gold Institute
definition. Retrenchment costs are included net of other costs.
Source: Chamber of Mines of South Africa.
June 30, 2007

Production Costs in South Africa by Mine

| | Second Quarter 2007 | | |
Mine	Working Costs	Refined Production	Cumulative Production
	($/Troy Oz.)	(Troy Oz.)	(Troy Oz.)
Free State	771.54	124,436	124,436
Target	694.68	38,263	162,699
Freegold	645.27	109,785	272,484
Randfontein	600.14	68,134	340,617
South Deep	590.57	69,548	410,166
ARMgold	589.94	26,441	436,607
Evander	551.51	61,874	498,481
Elandsrand	550.10	51,676	550,156
Beatrix	418.69	125,671	675,827
Kloof	377.64	229,607	905,434
Driefontein	350.95	260,540	1,165,974
Anglogold Ashanti	312.28	581,365	1,747,339
Subtotal and Average	*$438.30*	*1,747,339*	
Other Member Chambers (Uranium Producers, etc.)		*66,912*	
Non-Chamber Members		*227,875*	
Total		*2,042,126*	

Note: Working costs were converted from rand to dollars using average exchange rate of $0.14103 per rand for the 2Q07. Anglogold Ashanti: Profits from sales of the by-products uranium and acid/or pyrite, is offset against cash costs, in accordance with the Gold Institute definition. Retrenchment costs are included net of other costs.
Source: Chamber of Mines of South Africa.
October 30, 2007

Production Costs in South Africa by Mine

Third Quarter 2007

Mine	Working Costs	Refined Production	Cumulative Production
	(\$/Troy Oz.)	(Troy Oz.)	(Troy Oz.)
ARMgold	860.89	23,660	23,660
Free State	647.15	136,464	160,123
Elandsrand	601.66	56,347	216,471
Freegold	580.93	137,457	353,928
Target	577.70	23,419	377,346
South Deep	575.54	74,345	451,692
Randfontein	486.04	86,633	538,325
Evander	485.32	72,159	610,484
Beatrix	459.09	119,173	729,657
Kloof	374.77	235,308	964,965
Driefontein	368.75	260,344	1,225,308
Anglogold Ashanti	336.56	617,856	1,843,164
Subtotal and Average	*\$435.52*	*1,843,164*	
Other Member Chambers (Uranium Producers, etc.)		*49,747*	
Non-Chamber Members		*245,632*	
Total		*2,138,543*	

Note: Working costs were converted from rand to dollars using average exchange rate of
\$0.14078 per rand for the 3Q07. Anglogold Ashanti: Profits from sales of the by-products
uranium and acid/or pyrite, is offset against cash costs, in accordance with the Gold Institute
definition. Retrenchment costs are included net of other costs.
Source: Chamber of Mines of South Africa.
January 5, 2008

Gold Mine Output in South Africa
Projected Through 2008.

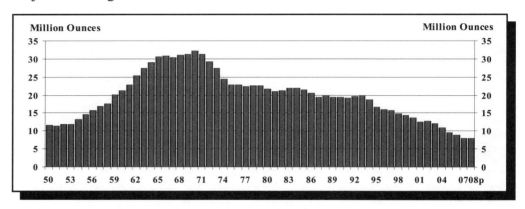

Average Quarterly South African Working Costs and Ore Grade
Through Third Quarter 2007.

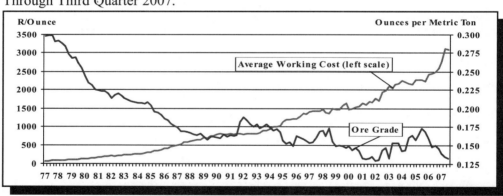

Average Quarterly South African Working Costs in U.S. Dollars
Through Third Quarter 2007.

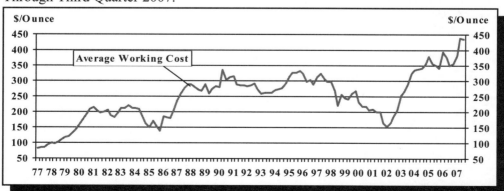

Quarterly South African Gold Production - Ore Milled

Through Third Quarter 2007.

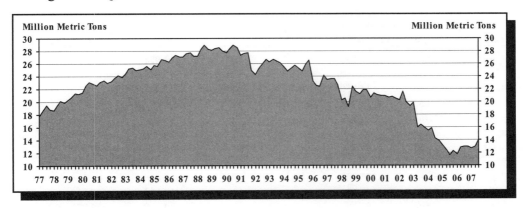

Rand Price and Ore Grade

Through Third Quarter 2007.

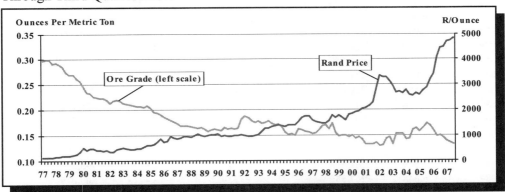

Refined Production

Through Third Quarter 2007.

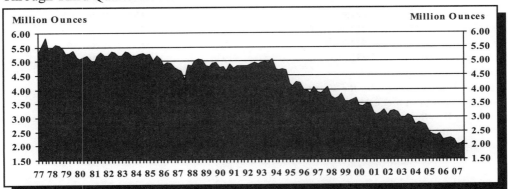

Global Production Since 1800

Thousand Troy Ounces

Year	Thousand Ounces	Cumulative Production	Year	Ounces	Cumulative Production
1800-09*	608	6,080	1897	13,921	347,584
1810-19*	391	9,990	1898	15,073	362,657
1820-29*	486	14,850	1899	12,421	375,078
1830-39*	652	21,370	1900	12,692	387,770
1840-49*	1,760	38,970	1901	12,692	400,462
1850-59*	6,445	103,420	1902	14,494	414,956
1860-69*	6,107	164,490	1903	15,934	430,890
1870	5,030	169,520	1904	16,920	447,810
1871	6,381	175,901	1905	18,488	466,298
1872	5,798	181,699	1906	19,534	485,832
1873	5,504	187,203	1907	20,040	505,872
1874	5,360	192,563	1908	21,484	527,356
1875	5,341	197,904	1909	22,094	549,450
1876	5,430	203,334	1910	22,147	571,597
1877	6,001	209,335	1911	22,475	594,072
1878	5,987	215,322	1912	22,637	616,709
1879	5,416	220,738	1913	22,352	639,061
1880	5,349	226,087	1914	21,218	660,279
1881	5,064	231,151	1915	22,649	682,928
1882	4,886	236,037	1916	22,047	704,975
1883	4,746	240,783	1917	20,216	725,191
1884	5,015	245,798	1918	18,523	743,714
1885	4,945	250,743	1919	17,543	761,257
1886	5,256	255,999	1920	16,304	777,561
1887	5,509	261,508	1921	15,987	793,548
1888	6,048	267,556	1922	15,471	809,019
1889	5,814	273,370	1923	17,781	826,800
1890	6,400	279,770	1924	19,031	845,831
1891	7,060	286,830	1925	19,013	864,844
1892	7,544	294,374	1926	19,343	884,187
1893	8,657	303,031	1927	19,388	903,575
1894	9,518	312,549	1928	19,433	923,008
1895	9,717	322,266	1929	19,589	942,597
1896	11,397	333,663	1930	20,873	963,470

Notes: *Annual averages for the 10-year period.
Sources: American Metal Market Metal Statistics 1974, attributed to Dr. Adolph Soetbeer; U.S. Bureau of Mines; Statistics Canada; Chamber of Mines of South Africa; Central Intelligence Agency; Gold Institute; CPM Group.
January 17, 2008

Year	Ounces	Cumulative Production	Year	Ounces	Cumulative Production
1931	22,341	985,811	1969	46,730	2,273,950
1932	24,255	1,010,066	1970	48,090	2,322,040
1933	25,511	1,035,577	1971	47,095	2,369,135
1934	27,028	1,062,605	1972	45,395	2,414,530
1935	29,460	1,092,065	1973	43,577	2,458,107
1936	33,101	1,125,166	1974	40,829	2,498,936
1937	35,263	1,160,429	1975	39,156	2,538,092
1938	37,598	1,198,027	1976	40,604	2,578,696
1939	39,635	1,237,662	1977	40,601	2,619,297
1940	42,176	1,279,838	1978	40,760	2,660,057
1941	39,030	1,318,868	1979	40,537	2,700,594
1942	35,325	1,354,193	1980	42,135	2,742,729
1943	27,989	1,382,182	1981	43,631	2,786,360
1944	25,346	1,407,528	1982	44,627	2,830,987
1945	24,483	1,432,011	1983	46,249	2,877,236
1946	24,946	1,456,957	1984	47,506	2,924,742
1947	25,347	1,482,304	1985	49,026	2,973,768
1948	26,559	1,508,863	1986	51,703	3,025,471
1949	27,580	1,536,443	1987	53,750	3,079,221
1950	27,237	1,563,680	1988	59,456	3,138,677
1951	26,583	1,590,263	1989	63,893	3,202,570
1952	27,335	1,617,598	1990	65,799	3,268,369
1953	27,287	1,644,885	1991	67,168	3,335,536
1954	28,653	1,673,538	1992	69,646	3,405,182
1955	29,901	1,703,439	1993	71,679	3,476,861
1956	30,974	1,734,413	1994	72,151	3,549,011
1957	32,354	1,766,767	1995	72,478	3,621,489
1958	33,416	1,800,183	1996	73,165	3,694,654
1959	35,832	1,836,015	1997	77,936	3,772,591
1960	37,549	1,873,564	1998	80,629	3,853,220
1961	38,984	1,912,548	1999	82,133	3,935,353
1962	41,860	1,954,408	2000	81,816	4,017,168
1963	43,272	1,997,680	2001	82,136	4,099,304
1964	44,841	2,042,521	2002	81,383	4,180,688
1965	46,225	2,088,746	2003	81,745	4,262,432
1966	46,580	2,135,326	2004	78,226	4,340,658
1967	45,759	2,181,085	2005	79,679	4,420,337
1968	46,135	2,227,220	2006	77,184	4,497,521
			2007	77,654	4,575,175

Mine Production By Country
Troy Ounces

	1984	1985	1986	1987	1988	1989	1990	1991	1992	1993	1994	1995
Africa												
Algeria	-	-	-	-	-	-	-	-	-	-	-	-
Botswana	-	-	-	-	-	-	1,500	1,000	6,000	6,000	6,000	3,000
Burkino Faso	-	-	-	-	-	-	240,000	180,000	174,000	160,000	190,000	180,000
Burundi	1,115	800	1,000	800	500	800	300	800	1,030	650	700	1,000
Cameroon	250	250	250	250	250	250	320	320	320	320	320	320
Central African Republic	6,953	7,000	7,000	7,000	12,000	10,000	8,000	6,000	5,000	5,000	6,000	7,000
Congo	150	200	200	200	200	500	300	400	300	300	300	300
Democratic Republic of Congo	117,115	75,000	62,950	140,560	114,553	112,525	140,000	190,000	190,000	220,000	350,000	320,000
Ethiopia	15,000	13,000	13,000	15,000	20,000	20,000	50,000	98,700	100,000	110,000	90,000	95,000
Gabon	1,325	1,000	1,250	1,250	4,400	4,500	2,600	1,600	2,300	2,900	2,300	2,000
Ghana	287,000	299,363	287,000	324,000	390,000	427,670	487,375	844,674	1,190,000	1,324,609	1,430,000	1,650,000
Guinea	-	-	-	-	-	-	200,000	140,000	63,500	68,000	75,000	100,000
Ivory Coast	-	-	-	-	-	-	-	1,000	56,000	90,000	50,000	69,500
Kenya	600	600	600	600	600	500	800	800	16,000	16,000	16,000	16,000
Liberia	10,500	12,000	12,000	21,100	21,800	23,600	23,000	23,000	23,000	23,000	20,000	15,000
Madagascar	130	130	130	130	130	130	7,000	6,400	6,400	16,000	16,000	18,000
Mali	16,075	16,000	16,000	16,000	22,500	32,150	167,200	157,500	183,300	200,000	205,000	220,000
Mauritania	-	-	-	-	-	-	-	-	22,560	40,710	55,880	38,450
Mozambique	-	-	-	-	-	-	-	-	-	-	-	-
Namibia	-	-	-	-	-	-	48,400	59,700	65,000	63,000	78,800	69,735
Niger	-	-	-	-	-	-	-	-	15,000	15,000	15,000	15,000
Rwanda	240	250	250	250	250	300	300	300	2,000	2,000	3,200	4,500
Sierra Leone	18,233	18,000	18,000	18,000	13,000	13,000	2,000	1,000	4,000	5,000	6,000	6,750
South Africa	21,904,874	21,598,486	20,518,287	19,437,238	19,927,102	19,491,817	19,380,000	19,224,200	19,562,230	19,925,575	18,772,350	16,794,796
Sudan	1,000	1,500	1,500	2,000	16,000	16,000	16,000	16,000	32,200	51,400	100,000	115,000
Tanzania	800	2,680	2,700	2,700	2,700	3,000	100,000	120,000	160,000	225,000	270,000	250,000
Uganda	-	-	-	-	-	-	-	-	-	-	-	64,000
Zambia	12,185	11,600	12,000	12,000	7,000	8,000	8,000	8,000	6,400	9,600	6,800	4,000
Zimbabwe	478,306	472,000	475,000	472,937	481,000	514,503	543,347	573,000	585,368	608,163	660,000	722,000
Other Africa	1,000	1,000	1,000	1,000	1,000	1,000	1,000	1,000	1,000	1,000	1,000	1,000
Total	22,872,851	22,530,859	21,430,117	20,473,015	21,034,985	20,680,245	21,427,442	21,655,394	22,472,908	23,189,227	22,426,650	20,782,351
% Change Year Ago	0.2%	-1.5%	-4.9%	-4.5%	2.7%	-1.7%	3.6%	1.1%	3.8%	3.2%	-3.3%	-7.3%

1996	1997	1998	1999	2000	2001	2002	2003	2004	2005	2006	2007	
												Africa
-	-	-	-	-	9,600	11,900	11,700	19,000	20,000	19,000	19,000	Algeria
2,500	900	320	320	320	300	300	300	300	89,000	91,000	94,000	Botswana
118,800	83,160	104,200	104,200	64,300	10,000	10,000	25,000	40,000	57,000	62,000	67,000	Burkina Faso
900	700	700	700	700	13,500	13,500	90,000	104,000	125,000	126,000	127,000	Burundi
320	320	320	320	320	20,000	32,000	32,000	50,000	50,000	50,000	50,000	Cameroon
												Central African
5,650	5,650	5,970	5,970	600	600	600	650	650	650	650	650	Republic
300	300	300	300	300	300	300	300	300	300	300	300	Congo
												Democratic
250,000	160,000	160,000	160,000	160,000	160,000	200,000	150,000	160,000	160,000	160,000	160,000	Republic of Congo
74,100	88,920	88,920	160,754	144,700	160,800	160,800	161,000	161,000	161,000	161,000	161,000	Ethiopia
2,000	2,000	2,000	2,000	2,300	2,300	2,300	2,300	10,000	10,000	10,000	10,000	Gabon
1,620,000	1,700,000	2,360,000	2,600,720	2,450,000	2,300,000	2,220,000	2,250,000	2,000,000	2,100,000	2,300,000	2,650,000	Ghana
110,000	128,000	356,100	383,520	400,000	450,000	450,000	514,000	400,000	400,000	400,000	425,000	Guinea
71,250	85,000	60,000	90,000	100,000	110,000	112,500	45,000	50,000	50,000	50,000	50,000	Ivory Coast
16,000	16,000	16,000	30,000	40,000	39,900	50,000	50,000	20,000	20,000	20,000	20,000	Kenya
21,000	21,000	21,000	21,000	32,200	32,200	23,000	15,000	10,000	5,000	5,000	5,000	Liberia
25,720	30,000	30,000	32,000	32,000	20,000	500	500	500	500	500	500	Madagascar
226,660	556,232	720,000	802,800	900,000	1,340,000	1,801,000	1,500,000	1,250,000	1,450,000	1,624,000	1,672,720	Mali
5,000	5,000	5,000	5,000	-	-	-	-	-	-	-	-	Mauritania
-	-	-	-	-	5,000	5,000	10,000	10,000	10,000	10,000	10,000	Mozambique
70,409	79,626	68,000	73,000	73,000	90,700	90,000	80,000	70,700	85,000	92,000	92,000	Namibia
15,000	15,000	15,000	15,000	15,000	15,000	15,000	15,000	35,000	95,000	50,000	50,000	Niger
2,250	1,125	900	900	300	300	300	300	-	-	-	-	Rwanda
7,000	4,380	2,190	1,686	1,000	1,000	1,000	1,000	1,000	1,000	1,000	1,000	Sierra Leone
15,902,345	15,800,000	14,930,502	14,450,849	13,770,260	12,652,086	12,705,141	12,081,849	11,018,854	9,558,806	8,845,309	7,960,778	South Africa
128,818	143,117	183,000	180,000	185,000	176,800	176,800	170,000	160,800	160,000	115,000	100,000	Sudan
230,000	217,000	229,700	328,012	500,000	1,050,000	1,250,000	1,400,000	1,550,000	1,500,000	1,500,000	1,500,000	Tanzania
64,000	65,000	54,000	54,000	1,800	-	-	-	45,000	50,000	50,000	50,000	Uganda
4,000	4,000	4,000	4,000	19,300	4,200	4,200	-	-	14,000	38,000	38,000	Zambia
827,433	867,150	898,000	964,452	680,000	578,700	500,000	400,000	650,000	450,000	355,000	355,000	Zimbabwe
-	-	-	-	-	-	-	-	-	-	-	-	Other Africa
19,801,455	20,079,580	20,316,122	20,471,502	19,573,400	19,243,286	19,836,141	19,005,899	17,817,104	16,622,256	16,135,759	15,668,948	Total
-4.7%	1.4%	1.2%	0.8%	-4.4%	-1.7%	3.1%	-4.2%	-6.3%	-6.7%	-2.9%	-2.9%	% Change Year Ago

Mine Production By Country -- continued

Troy Ounces

	1984	1985	1986	1987	1988	1989	1990	1991	1992	1993	1994	1995
Asia and Middle East												
India	62,800	55,781	64,800	52,300	62,437	58,734	64,269	59,157	56,324	71,616	76,600	70,732
Indonesia	78,677	300,000	320,000	440,000	500,000	525,000	600,000	828,000	1,154,000	1,490,000	1,891,200	2,377,250
Iran	-	-	-	-	-	-	16,100	16,100	16,100	13,400	24,000	24,000
Japan	128,600	158,567	195,000	200,000	235,000	196,000	234,700	266,851	286,000	301,000	308,000	318,000
Malaysia	89,527	92,400	87,000	113,010	94,137	91,919	83,367	80,000	113,000	140,000	130,000	130,000
Mongolia	-	-	-	-	-	-	-	85,000	85,000	85,000	129,000	151,000
Myanmar	1,000	1,000	1,000	1,000	10,000	13,700	25,000	28,000	30,000	25,000	15,000	15,000
Oman	-	-	-	-	-	-	-	-	-	2,894	4,405	19,001
Philippines	772,931	809,735	1,139,097	1,048,092	1,044,447	964,264	790,000	830,000	820,000	800,000	875,000	870,000
Saudi Arabia	-	-	-	-	-	-	113,700	153,700	197,700	241,700	255,000	265,000
South Korea	79,156	77,258	149,436	244,300	250,000	250,000	250,000	250,000	250,000	250,000	218,631	237,870
Taiwan	37,794	30,600	33,000	34,000	34,000	48,000	44,000	44,000	44,000	40,000	35,000	30,000
Turkey	-	-	-	-	-	-	-	-	-	30,000	30,000	30,000
Total	1,250,485	1,525,341	1,989,333	2,132,702	2,230,021	2,147,617	2,221,136	2,640,808	3,052,124	3,490,609	3,991,836	4,537,853
% Change Year Ago	-3.1%	22.0%	30.4%	7.2%	4.6%	-3.7%	3.4%	18.9%	15.6%	14.4%	14.4%	13.7%
Europe												
Bulgaria	-	-	-	-	-	-	-	-	-	65,000	70,000	65,910
Finland	28,067	19,130	37,680	57,871	64,300	80,400	90,022	100,000	51,441	45,000	38,600	43,700
France	70,279	90,021	75,618	70,731	83,592	96,452	135,033	145,000	92,272	76,679	138,344	150,000
Germany	1,500	1,125	1,190	836	500	500	2,000	2,500	2,500	2,500	2,500	2,500
Hungary	20,000	20,000	20,000	20,000	20,000	20,000	16,000	15,200	16,000	19,300	8,000	5,000
Poland	-	-	-	-	-	-	-	-	-	-	13,000	15,000
Portugal	9,100	9,259	8,000	10,000	12,000	9,000	11,250	12,500	11,000	1,000	1,000	1,000
Romania	65,000	65,000	65,000	65,000	65,000	65,000	65,000	61,700	64,300	65,000	70,000	70,000
Spain	123,330	125,000	131,560	176,989	180,043	179,112	175,000	176,000	211,616	200,000	193,000	188,000
Sweden	141,600	148,900	130,000	150,000	150,000	128,600	136,000	140,000	192,904	209,000	148,000	210,000
Serbia/Montenegro	-	-	-	-	-	-	-	-	235,000	107,000	129,000	122,000
Yugoslavia	125,000	110,000	115,000	115,000	120,000	121,000	263,300	263,300	-	-	-	-
Total	583,876	588,435	584,048	666,427	695,435	700,064	893,605	916,200	877,033	790,479	811,444	873,110
% Change Year Ago	-3.3%	0.8%	-0.7%	14.1%	4.4%	0.7%	27.6%	2.5%	-4.3%	-9.9%	2.7%	7.6%
North & Central America												
Belize	-	-	-	-	-	-	-	-	161	64	161	161
Canada	2,491,438	2,815,184	3,308,272	3,723,616	4,334,330	5,127,859	5,283,828	5,635,443	5,155,398	4,850,337	4,707,784	4,887,936
Costa Rica	30,000	35,000	35,000	35,000	35,000	35,000	30,000	35,000	35,000	19,300	19,675	21,220
Dominican Republic	338,272	337,150	246,400	246,000	186,000	177,000	139,000	130,000	96,000	80,000	65,000	105,699
El Salvador	285	280	275	275	275	275	275	275	275	275	275	2,645
Guatemala	-	-	-	-	-	-	-	-	1,029	965	965	1,000
Honduras	2,784	2,500	2,600	2,958	3,955	2,411	5,000	5,800	5,200	3,600	3,400	3,000
Mexico	244,000	257,000	267,000	289,000	344,000	385,000	322,000	286,000	358,000	393,000	450,000	672,029
Nicaragua	34,000	25,316	28,664	30,500	28,300	35,400	38,581	41,000	43,000	40,000	39,900	45,300
Panama	-	-	-	-	-	-	2,700	6,200	8,000	8,200	7,900	35,360
United States	2,058,784	2,475,436	3,738,998	4,947,028	6,459,526	8,537,329	9,452,335	9,452,335	10,609,764	10,641,915	10,513,312	10,191,804
Total	5,199,563	5,947,866	7,627,209	9,274,377	11,391,386	14,300,274	15,273,719	15,592,053	16,311,826	16,037,656	15,808,371	15,966,153
% Change Year Ago	7.4%	14.4%	28.2%	21.6%	22.8%	25.5%	6.8%	2.1%	4.6%	-1.7%	-1.4%	1.0%

1996	1997	1998	1999	2000	2001	2002	2003	2004	2005	2006	2007	
												Asia and Middle East
78,769	87,611	75,265	78,960	125,000	50,000	95,000	105,000	115,000	100,000	80,000	90,000	India
2,571,352	2,821,059	4,025,000	4,450,000	4,200,000	5,600,000	4,650,000	4,600,000	3,050,000	4,525,000	2,950,000	3,500,000	Indonesia
24,000	24,380	22,850	27,000	27,000	24,800	25,000	25,000	25,000	25,000	25,000	25,000	Iran
296,931	281,000	287,930	284,475	264,475	254,400	257,200	261,804	255,000	265,000	265,000	270,000	Japan
117,000	176,965	137,647	120,000	122,400	127,500	135,000	150,000	127,000	127,000	110,000	110,000	Malaysia
192,904	260,850	225,374	277,887	276,835	289,400	289,400	385,810	600,000	750,000	775,000	800,000	Mongolia
23,000	14,380	13,000	13,000	13,000	13,000	13,000	13,000	13,000	13,000	13,000	13,000	Myanmar
18,519	18,500	18,500	18,500	18,500	19,000	19,000	19,000	19,000	19,000	19,000	19,000	Oman
970,000	1,050,000	1,090,000	995,000	1,170,000	1,085,000	1,125,000	1,125,000	1,125,000	1,175,000	1,175,000	1,200,000	Philippines
240,592	260,000	182,780	179,124	128,000	140,000	170,000	250,000	260,000	270,000	280,000	280,000	Saudi Arabia
250,000	263,400	250,000	250,000	250,000	250,000	250,000	250,000	250,000	250,000	250,000	250,000	South Korea
30,000	24,500	27,300	27,300	300	100	100	100	100	100	100	100	Taiwan
30,000	30,000	30,000	30,000	30,000	65,000	160,000	200,000	150,000	150,000	160,000	180,000	Turkey
4,843,067	5,312,645	6,385,646	6,751,246	6,625,510	7,918,000	7,188,700	7,384,714	5,989,100	7,669,100	6,102,100	6,737,100	Total
6.7%	9.7%	20.2%	5.7%	-1.9%	19.5%	-9.2%	2.7%	-18.9%	28.1%	-20.4%	10.4%	% Change Year Ago
												Europe
62,000	70,000	70,000	70,000	70,000	51,400	50,000	60,000	80,000	110,000	115,000	120,000	Bulgaria
63,870	88,680	104,199	115,661	125,000	160,000	150,000	160,000	150,000	160,000	165,000	165,000	Finland
146,778	148,100	125,145	115,000	95,000	75,000	70,000	48,000	48,000	48,000	48,000	48,000	France
-	-	-	-	-	-	-	-	-	-	-	-	Germany
5,000	5,000	5,000	5,000	5,000	5,000	5,000	5,000	5,000	5,000	5,000	5,000	Hungary
17,039	12,060	12,060	12,060	12,060	10,000	10,000	12,000	15,000	15,000	15,000	15,000	Poland
1,000	1,000	1,000	1,000	1,000	1,000	1,000	1,000	1,000	1,000	1,000	1,000	Portugal
65,000	65,000	65,000	65,000	50,000	35,000	40,000	35,000	35,000	35,000	35,000	35,000	Romania
170,516	174,440	209,300	240,100	230,000	160,800	160,000	165,000	165,000	165,000	165,000	165,000	Spain
205,765	226,159	203,995	192,905	192,905	154,300	177,200	183,300	185,000	197,000	215,000	215,000	Sweden
110,000	101,860	121,723	121,723	36,000	35,000	30,000	30,000	30,000	30,000	30,000	30,000	Serbia /Montenagro
-	-	-	-	-	-	-	-	-	-	-	-	Yugoslavia
846,968	892,299	917,422	938,448	816,965	687,500	693,200	699,300	714,000	766,000	794,000	799,000	Total
-3.0%	5.4%	2.8%	2.3%	-12.9%	-15.8%	0.8%	0.9%	2.1%	7.3%	3.7%	0.6%	% Change Year Ago
												North & Central America
161	161	193	193	193	193	100	100	100	100	100	100	Belize
5,268,405	5,513,188	5,297,594	5,067,515	4,944,182	5,058,900	4,889,000	4,528,783	4,202,982	3,833,184	3,350,000	3,300,000	Canada
21,220	20,200	28,000	16,044	10,000	10,000	10,000	10,000	10,000	16,000	50,000	55,000	Costa Rica
117,629	75,515	45,794	45,794	20,900	20,900	10,000	5,000	5,000	5,000	5,000	5,000	Dominican Republic
5,753	5,753	5,753	5,753	5,753	5,753	2,500	2,500	2,500	2,500	2,500	2,500	El Salvador
1,000	3,200	3,200	1,608	2,000	2,000	2,000	2,000	2,000	24,000	162,000	230,000	Guatemala
4,565	4,821	4,821	35,000	35,000	150,000	160,000	150,000	150,000	150,000	150,000	155,000	Honduras
774,294	836,885	835,900	800,000	800,000	827,800	747,632	713,000	803,800	1,025,000	1,175,000	1,400,000	Mexico
54,734	85,698	122,462	153,078	120,927	125,000	125,000	126,000	135,000	130,000	125,000	125,000	Nicaragua
38,542	63,274	69,556	27,056	10,000	2,000	2,000	2,000	2,000	2,000	2,000	2,000	Panama
10,481,161	11,638,590	11,767,193	10,963,423	11,349,232	10,770,500	9,580,909	8,905,744	8,294,881	8,359,182	8,000,000	7,750,000	United States
16,767,464	18,247,284	18,180,466	17,115,463	17,298,188	16,973,046	15,529,141	14,445,127	13,608,263	13,546,966	13,021,600	13,024,600	Total
5.0%	8.8%	-0.4%	-5.9%	1.1%	-1.9%	-8.5%	-7.0%	-5.8%	-0.5%	-3.9%	0.0%	% Change Year Ago

Mine Production By Country -- continued

Troy Ounces

	1984	1985	1986	1987	1988	1989	1990	1991	1992	1993	1994	1995
Oceania												
Australia	1,257,092	1,832,590	2,507,755	3,533,400	5,047,700	6,751,647	7,876,922	7,555,415	7,590,615	7,738,673	8,029,000	8,400,000
British Solomon Is.	2,500	1,900	3,900	2,649	2,500	2,500	2,500	2,500	2,500	2,500	2,500	2,500
Fiji	53,869	60,707	94,903	95,230	138,344	135,450	132,300	90,000	119,000	122,000	95,000	116,954
New Zealand	21,605	45,011	50,000	55,000	64,300	95,000	149,000	190,000	328,000	361,000	330,746	390,539
Papua New Guinea	835,000	1,067,400	1,157,425	1,189,576	1,286,028	1,085,000	1,093,124	1,980,000	2,288,911	2,002,989	1,885,773	1,662,229
Total	2,170,066	3,007,608	3,813,983	4,875,855	6,538,872	8,069,597	9,253,846	9,817,915	10,329,026	10,227,162	10,343,019	10,572,222
% Change Year Ago	29.9%	38.6%	26.8%	27.8%	34.1%	23.4%	14.7%	6.1%	5.2%	-1.0%	1.1%	2.2%
South America												
Argentina	22,120	23,000	24,000	25,000	31,508	30,000	39,000	45,000	42,000	36,000	36,000	33,060
Bolivia	40,827	30,000	28,000	90,215	157,410	157,410	166,000	160,000	160,000	335,000	412,000	453,000
Brazil	1,726,493	2,025,494	2,375,000	2,694,229	3,221,500	3,305,091	2,806,756	2,666,500	2,400,000	2,250,549	2,138,000	2,025,500
Chile	541,051	554,281	588,000	547,687	662,754	713,103	734,643	921,680	1,028,822	1,100,000	1,250,000	1,433,443
Colombia	799,889	1,142,830	1,285,878	853,472	972,880	870,962	955,840	946,282	961,000	868,000	877,000	800,000
Ecuador	280,000	300,000	317,300	305,400	256,000	300,000	322,000	261,000	219,000	200,000	250,000	340,000
French Guiana	10,127	12,000	10,000	10,000	11,000	11,000	16,000	20,000	65,000	80,400	80,400	82,000
Guyana	11,131	10,323	14,036	21,425	18,800	17,330	39,030	59,300	79,580	298,037	350,000	288,388
Peru	136,534	134,715	145,000	150,000	150,000	139,052	110,856	120,833	320,000	739,466	1,125,275	1,816,500
Suriname	-	-	-	-	-	-	1,000	1,000	9,700	9,700	10,000	10,000
Uruguay	-	-	-	-	-	-	-	-	-	10,000	12,000	27,490
Venezuela	50,885	72,900	80,698	3,416	112,591	124,300	240,000	223,000	273,281	280,000	320,000	245,000
Total	3,619,057	4,305,543	4,867,912	4,700,844	5,594,443	5,668,248	5,431,125	5,424,595	5,558,383	6,207,153	6,860,675	7,554,381
% Change Year Ago	20.6%	19.0%	13.1%	-3.4%	19.0%	1.3%	-4.2%	-0.1%	2.5%	11.7%	10.5%	10.1%
Subtotal	35,695,898	37,905,652	40,312,602	42,123,220	47,485,142	51,566,045	54,500,873	56,046,965	58,601,300	59,942,285	60,241,995	60,286,070
% Change Year Ago	4.3%	6.2%	6.3%	4.5%	12.7%	8.6%	5.7%	2.8%	4.6%	2.3%	0.5%	0.1%
Transitional Economies												
China	2,000,000	2,250,000	2,430,000	2,625,000	2,809,000	3,005,000	3,100,000	3,680,000	3,800,000	3,900,000	4,000,000	4,300,000
Vietnam	-	-	-	-	-	-	-	-	-	50,000	100,000	125,000
North Korea	160,000	160,000	160,000	160,000	160,000	160,000	160,000	160,000	160,000	160,000	160,000	160,000
Russia	-	-	-	-	-	-	-	4,549,325	4,163,516	4,628,100	4,800,000	4,666,000
Uzbekistan	-	-	-	-	-	-	-	1,929,042	2,220,281	2,250,600	2,246,000	2,257,000
Kazakstan	-	-	-	-	-	-	-	482,261	539,315	643,000	517,000	586,000
Armenia	-	-	-	-	-	-	-	160,754	-	6,500	4,000	16,000
Azerbaijan	-	-	-	-	-	-	-	32,151				
Kyrgyzstan	-	-	-	-	-	-	-	34,000	82,000	32,200	27,000	27,330
Georgia	-	-	-	-	-	-	-	61,086	45,011	34,000	21,000	16,100
Tajikistan	-	-	-	-	-	-	-	32,151	34,220	32,200	32,200	32,200
Soviet Union	9,650,000	8,710,000	8,800,000	8,841,443	9,002,196	9,162,950	8,037,675	-	-	-	-	-
Cuba	-	-	-	-	-	-	-	-	-	-	1,447	5,916
Total	11,810,000	11,120,000	11,390,000	11,626,443	11,971,196	12,327,950	11,297,675	11,120,768	11,044,343	11,736,600	11,908,647	12,191,546
% Change Year Ago	-1.7%	-5.8%	2.4%	2.1%	3.0%	3.0%	-8.4%	-1.6%	-0.7%	6.3%	1.5%	2.4%
WORLD TOTAL	47,505,898	49,025,652	51,702,602	53,749,663	59,456,338	63,893,995	65,798,548	67,167,734	69,645,643	71,678,885	72,150,642	72,477,616
% Change Year Ago	2.7%	3.2%	5.5%	4.0%	10.6%	7.5%	3.0%	2.1%	3.7%	2.9%	0.7%	0.5%

Sources: U.S. Bureau of Mines; Statistics Canada; Chamber of Mines South Africa; Gold Institute;
United States Geological Service, Central Intelligence Agency; industry sources; Raw Materials Group; CPM Group.
January 17, 2008

1996	1997	1998	1999	2000	2001	2002	2003	2004	2005	2006	2007	
												Oceania
9,200,000	10,005,298	9,995,293	9,705,430	9,559,848	9,150,000	8,777,141	9,100,000	8,325,000	8,250,000	7,950,000	7,900,000	Australia
2,500	2,500	45,700	111,600	5,000	9,600	3,200	3,200	3,200	3,200	3,200	3,200	British Solomon Is.
152,040	156,753	124,619	149,667	115,000	125,000	120,000	110,000	130,000	90,000	50,000	50,000	Fiji
380,000	370,000	250,000	276,000	321,000	320,000	320,000	300,000	335,000	335,000	335,000	335,000	New Zealand
1,658,113	1,558,626	1,982,573	2,110,000	2,350,000	2,160,000	2,030,000	2,160,000	2,350,000	2,200,000	1,800,000	1,750,000	Papua New Guinea
11,392,653	12,093,177	12,398,184	12,352,697	12,350,848	11,764,600	11,250,341	11,673,200	11,143,200	10,878,200	10,138,200	10,038,200	Total
7.8%	6.1%	2.5%	-0.4%	0.0%	-4.7%	-4.4%	3.8%	-4.5%	-2.4%	-6.8%	-1.0%	% Change Year Ago
												South America
32,000	77,000	680,000	1,050,000	834,400	1,000,000	1,050,000	950,000	900,000	900,000	1,500,000	1,650,000	Argentina
421,000	432,000	471,744	384,471	353,000	395,500	360,000	275,000	220,000	290,000	400,000	500,000	Bolivia
1,832,595	1,801,721	1,708,032	1,700,000	1,600,000	1,425,000	1,250,000	1,200,000	1,350,000	1,275,000	1,325,000	1,400,000	Brazil
1,634,443	1,521,513	1,420,000	1,525,000	1,720,000	1,350,000	1,250,000	1,250,000	1,285,000	1,300,000	1,350,000	1,350,000	Chile
760,000	647,520	500,000	1,100,000	1,200,000	701,000	670,000	1,495,000	1,210,000	1,150,000	1,250,000	1,300,000	Colombia
400,000	344,000	260,000	160,000	130,000	130,000	130,000	130,000	160,000	170,000	180,000	190,000	Ecuador
91,732	91,732	91,732	91,732	111,600	130,000	100,000	110,000	90,000	65,000	70,000	80,000	French Guiana
391,449	448,159	451,042	450,000	450,000	450,000	418,000	385,000	375,000	365,000	375,000	375,000	Guyana
2,081,078	2,467,626	3,012,971	4,175,978	4,240,000	4,460,900	5,050,000	5,549,846	5,569,120	6,687,422	6,521,260	5,350,000	Peru
10,000	10,000	10,000	10,000	10,000	9,600	9,600	9,600	275,000	340,000	340,000	350,000	Suriname
47,232	70,000	74,042	77,226	73,000	64,300	65,000	60,000	60,000	95,000	100,000	100,000	Uruguay
396,000	600,000	480,000	480,000	320,000	300,000	300,000	300,000	300,000	325,000	380,000	400,000	Venezuela
8,097,529	8,511,271	9,159,563	11,204,407	11,042,000	10,416,300	10,652,600	11,714,446	11,794,120	12,962,422	13,791,260	13,045,000	Total
7.2%	5.1%	7.6%	22.3%	-1.4%	-5.7%	2.3%	10.0%	0.7%	9.9%	6.4%	-5.4%	% Change Year Ago
61,749,136	65,136,257	67,357,403	68,833,764	67,706,910	67,002,932	65,150,123	64,922,686	61,065,787	62,444,944	59,982,919	59,312,848	Subtotal
2.4%	5.5%	3.4%	2.2%	-1.6%	-1.0%	-2.8%	-0.3%	-5.9%	2.3%	-3.9%	-1.1%	% Change Year Ago
												Transitional Economies
4,000,000	5,000,000	5,260,000	4,902,320	5,100,680	5,500,000	6,108,600	6,450,000	6,912,000	7,234,000	7,650,000	8,700,000	China
134,250	136,000	136,000	136,000	144,000	80,400	80,400	96,000	100,000	100,000	100,000	100,000	Vietnam
160,000	160,000	160,754	160,754	160,754	170,000	170,000	170,000	170,000	170,000	170,000	170,000	North Korea
4,287,000	4,019,000	3,694,115	4,046,809	4,597,550	4,902,982	5,400,000	5,465,000	5,300,000	5,444,000	5,210,000	5,340,250	Russia
2,314,850	2,411,300	2,572,064	2,572,064	2,572,064	2,732,800	2,829,300	2,890,000	2,890,000	2,890,000	2,890,000	2,800,000	Uzbekistan
401,885	385,810	578,714	642,437	643,016	720,000	760,000	800,000	840,000	600,000	600,000	600,000	Kazakstan
8,000	16,100	11,253	12,860	64,300	64,300	110,000	60,000	67,000	65,000	50,000	50,000	Armenia
-	-	-	-	-	-	-	-	-	-	-	-	Azerbaijan
48,000	559,429	707,318	643,016	643,016	780,000	560,000	720,000	700,000	550,000	350,000	400,000	Kyrgyzstan
16,000	22,500	22,500	64,302	64,302	60,400	92,600	65,000	65,000	65,000	65,000	65,000	Georgia
36,000	82,000	96,452	86,807	86,807	90,000	90,000	90,000	100,000	100,000	100,000	100,000	Tajikistan
-	-	-	-	-	-	-	-	-	-	-	-	Soviet Union
8,038	8,038	32,151	32,151	32,151	32,151	32,151	16,000	16,000	16,000	16,000	16,000	Cuba
11,414,023	12,800,176	13,271,321	13,299,520	14,108,639	15,133,033	16,233,051	16,822,000	17,160,000	17,234,000	17,201,000	18,341,250	Total
-6.4%	12.1%	3.7%	0.2%	6.1%	7.3%	7.3%	3.6%	2.0%	0.4%	-0.2%	6.6%	% Change Year Ago
73,163,158	77,936,433	80,628,724	82,133,284	81,815,550	82,135,964	81,383,174	81,744,686	78,225,787	79,678,944	77,183,919	77,654,098	WORLD TOTAL
0.9%	6.5%	3.5%	1.9%	-0.4%	0.4%	-0.9%	0.4%	-4.3%	1.9%	-3.1%	0.6%	% Change Year Ago

Official Transactions

Official Transactions

Central banks had been expected to reduce the volume of net gold sales in 2007. A year ago, it seemed likely that net central bank gold sales might fall from around 11.4 million ounces in 2006 to around 9.0 million ounces in 2007. In the end, central banks are estimated to have sold 13.1 million ounces in 2006, with sales late in the year, unreported when these reports are written in January, higher than had been projected in January 2007. Net sales in 2007 appear likely to have totaled 16.0 million ounces for the full year, having netted 13.7 million ounces during the first 11 months of the year.

Central banks have been net sellers of gold each year since 1988, and have been net sellers of gold in all but nine years since 1964. Central banks, simply put, have been selling off their gold holdings. This is particularly true of European central banks, along with those of Canada and Australia, which had built up large gold reserves during the decades and centuries in which gold served as the basis for their national currencies.

The opinion has been that most of the gold that central banks have wanted to sell has been sold, and the remaining 961.8 million ounces (as of November 2007) represented gold that the central banks were content to continue holding. Thus, it has been expected that the period of heavy gold destocking by European central banks, from 1988 through 2006, was coming to an end.

Official Transactions

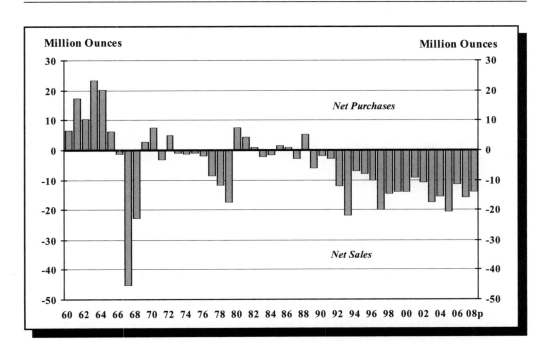

At least two trends intervened in this. First, the U.S. dollar's value has plunged. The dollar constitutes the lion's share of central bank monetary reserves. Second, the value of gold has risen sharply. Third, most European governments are starved for cash. As the dollar's value has fallen 8.8% since the beginning of 2005, gold prices have risen 95.0%. This has led to the temptation to sell additional amounts of gold than had been planned earlier, by some central banks, monetary authorities, and national treasury ministries. In addition to the simple impulse to take advantage of historically high gold prices to make some money, at some monetary authorities central bank managers now face a situation in which gold has risen sharply in term of the percentage of their monetary reserves denominated in gold.

The percentage of total monetary reserves made up by physical gold holdings, valued at market prices, increased in many countries between 2000 and 2007 despite on-going gold sales during these years. International Monetary Fund (IMF) data value gold at SDR 35 per ounce for all countries. At market value in 2007 five countries have gold holdings that are in excess of 50% of total monetary reserves. In 2000 the United States was the only country with gold holdings at market value greater than 50% of total monetary reserves.

Gold as a Percent of Total Monetary Reserves in 2000 and 2007

Selected Countries, Gold Valued at Market

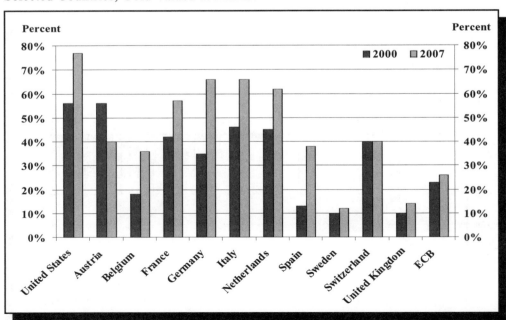

Central Bank Gold As A Percent of Monetary Reserves

Country	2000	2007
Industrial		
United States	56%	77%
Canada	1%	0%
Australia	4%	7%
Japan	2%	2%
Austria	56%	40%
Belgium	18%	36%
Denmark	4%	5%
France	42%	57%
Germany	35%	66%
Greece	8%	81%
Italy	46%	66%
Netherlands	45%	62%
Norway	1%	0%
Portugal	37%	90%
Spain	13%	38%
Sweden	10%	12%
Switzerland	40%	40%
United Kingdom	10%	14%
European Central		
Bank (ECB)	23%	26%
Subtotal	21%	27%
Developing-oil	8%	6%
Developing-Non-oil		
Africa	6%	2%
Asia	2%	2%
Europe	6%	3%
Middle East	4%	0%
Western Hemisphere	2%	1%
Subtotal	2%	2%
Total	11%	10%

Notes: Gold valued at market. Totals do not equal sum
of categories due to rounding. Developing-oil includes
oil exporting countries; developing countries. "Developing
non-oil" consists of other developing countries. Year-end-
data. 2007 through November. Developing-Non-oil, and
BIS through October.
Sources: International Monetary Fund.
January 22, 2008

In 2000 gold comprised 46% of total Italian reserves. By 2007 that had increased to 66%. Approximately 62% of Dutch total reserves were made up of gold in 2007 compared to 45% of total reserves in 2000. In Germany the composition of total reserves accounted for by gold rose from 35% in 2000 to 66% in 2007. The story was similar in France, where gold as a percentage of total reserves rose from 42% to 57%. In Belgium gold as a percentage of total reserves doubled from 18% in 2000 to 36% in 2007.

Austria was one country where the percentage of total reserves accounted for by gold actually decreased from 2000 to 2007. In 2007 gold accounted for 56% of Austrian reserves compared to 40% of reserves in 2000. In Switzerland gold accounted for 40% of total reserves in both 2000 and 2007. During this period Swiss gold holdings fell 52.3% to 37.1 million ounces from 77.8 million ounces.

At least two countries, Spain and Switzerland, sold gold in 2007 as a consequence of a change in policies, taking advantage of rising gold prices with these sales.

Switzerland had disposed of half of its long-held 83.3 million ounces of gold between 1999 and 2006, as part of a long-term plan to reduce its gold holdings. The Swiss National Bank had stated, in 1999, that it wanted to sell half of its gold. It later stated that it was content to continue holding 41.5 million ounces. Last year it sold 4.4 million ounces, to take advantage of the higher gold prices and to reduce gold's percentage of its total monetary reserves.

The Spanish central bank sold 4.4 million ounces of gold last year as well. It did not keep the proceeds of these sales in its monetary reserves, in dollars or other currencies. Instead, it provided the proceeds to the Treasury Ministry, as Spain was facing a sharp deterioration in its government finances. As a result of the fact that the sales proceeds, denominated in money, did not get added to the Bank of Spain's monetary reserves, the percentage of total reserves held in gold was even higher than it otherwise would have been.

Some bullion banks and associated analysts in London, seeing the Spanish and Swiss sales, tried to encourage private investors to sell gold positions. They used the argument that the European central banks tied in to the euro and European Central Bank system had a target of 15% of their total monetary reserves in gold. They suggested that given the sharp increase in the percentage of total reserves in gold, many European central banks would need to sell massive amounts of gold, in order to bring their gold holdings in line with this guideline. In fact, the ECB does not have any such guideline. The ECB and European central bankers have discussed the idea that holding around 15% of a country's monetary reserves in gold might be reasonable, but there is no policy requiring countries to move toward that level, and these countries' central banks do not operate under such a guideline. The attempt to scare investors appears to have failed and faded away.

2007 Sales Volumes

Through November of 2007 central banks sold a total of 15.64 million ounces and purchased a total of 1.86 million ounces. The selling was done by the central banks of eleven different countries and the European Central Bank. Purchasing of gold was done predominantly in small quantities by ten different countries. Net sales of gold by

central banks totaled 13.72 million ounces through November. This was up 15.7% from 11.86 million ounces of net sales in 2006, but 33.4% below the 20.6 million ounces of net sales recorded in 2005.

Including the European Central Bank, eight western European central banks accounted for 14.1 million ounces, or 90% of gross sales. The four non-Western European banks that sold gold in 2007 - Slovenia, Romania, Venezuela, and the Philippines - accounted for the remaining 550,000 ounces, or 3.5% of gross sales. Of western European countries, Spain and Switzerland each sold 4.4 million ounces of gold. France was

Central Bank Gold Reserve Levels

Annual, Projected Through 2008.

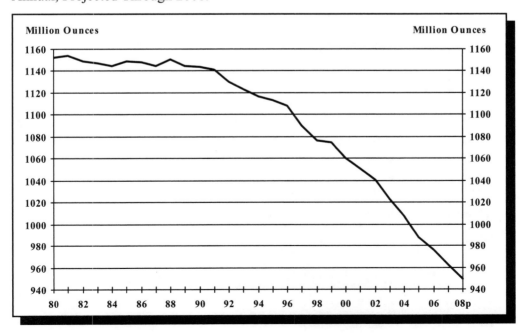

the next largest seller of gold in 2007 at 3.1 million ounces. No other central banks sold more than one million ounces of gold. The European Central Bank was close, at 960,000 ounces.

In 2006 a total of eighteen central banks sold gold. Nine were from Western Europe, and five sold more than one million ounces. The Bank for International Settlements also sold 1.0 million ounces of gold in 2007. One notable exception from the list of sellers in 2007 is the United States. The United States has 261.5 million ounces of gold reserves and no plans to sell gold in the immediate future.

Sales of central bank gold in 2008 should be expected to continue to be led by western European governments. Switzerland has been selling gold since May 2000. At that time the National Bank of Switzerland planned to reduce its gold reserves from 83.3 million ounces to 41.5 million ounces over five years. Switzerland reached this target in 2005 and did not sell any gold in 2006. It resumed sales in 2007, announcing plans to sell an additional 8.8 million ounces of gold prior to the end of the second Central Bank Gold Agreement in September 2009. Having sold 4.4 million ounces in 2007, the Swiss National Bank still had approximately 4.4 million ounces to be sold as of the end of November 2007.

ECB Member Weekly Gold Sales & Weekly Average Gold Price
Weekly, Through 18 January 2008.

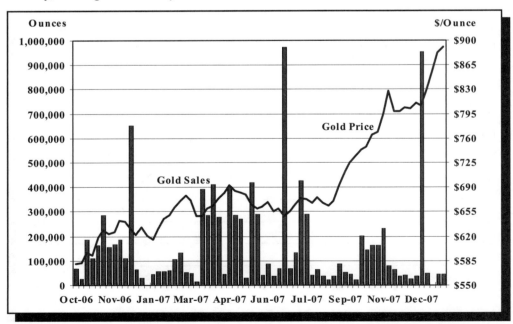

European Central Bank Member Gold Sales – Since January 2007

Week Ending	Gold Sales (Mil. Euros)	Average Price	Percent Change	Estimated Ounces Sold (at average)
2007				
5 January	-	$620.97	-1.90%	-
12 January	□28	$615.72	-0.84%	45,475
19 January	□37	$630.63	2.42%	58,672
26 January	□36	$644.20	2.15%	55,883
2 February	□39	$650.78	1.02%	59,928
9 February	□70	$661.44	1.64%	105,830
16 February	□90	$670.40	1.35%	134,248
23 February	□37	$678.68	1.23%	54,518
2 March	□34	$671.74	-1.02%	50,615
9 March	□9	$649.16	-3.36%	13,864
16 March	□256	$648.64	-0.08%	394,672
23 March	□189	$658.96	1.59%	286,816
30 March	□273	$663.54	0.70%	411,430
6 April	□189	$674.50	1.65%	280,208
13 April	□31	$681.94	1.10%	45,459
20 April	□281	$692.88	1.60%	405,554
27 April	□195	$685.22	-1.11%	284,580
4 May	□186	$682.00	-0.47%	272,727
11 May	□22	$679.92	-0.30%	32,357
18 May	□280	$665.06	-2.19%	421,015
25 May	□191	$658.98	-0.91%	289,842
1 June	□29	$662.05	0.47%	43,803
8 June	□59	$668.30	0.94%	88,284
15 June	□25	$655.88	-1.86%	38,117
22 June	□45	$659.16	0.50%	68,269
29 June	□631	$649.22	-1.51%	971,936
6 July	□44	$655.00	0.89%	67,176
13 July	□88	$664.92	1.51%	132,347
20 July	□288	$673.74	1.33%	427,465
27 July	□195	$672.60	-0.17%	289,920
3 August	□29	$667.46	-0.76%	43,448
10 August	□45	$674.94	1.12%	66,673
17 August	□26	$666.90	-1.19%	38,986
24 August	□16	$663.60	-0.49%	24,111
31 August	□25	$670.22	1.00%	37,301
7 September	□60	$692.70	3.35%	86,618
14 September	□38	$711.26	2.68%	53,426
21 September	□34	$724.48	1.86%	46,930
28 September	□17	$733.72	1.28%	23,170
5 October	□150	$743.42	1.32%	201,770
12 October	□108	$747.66	0.57%	144,451
19 October	□126	$764.72	2.28%	164,766
26 October	□126	$769.44	0.62%	163,755
2 November	□184	$795.58	3.40%	231,278
9 November	□66	$827.98	4.07%	79,712
16 November	□53	$799.14	-3.48%	66,321
23 November	□29	$798.18	-0.12%	36,333
30 November	□34	$803.66	0.69%	42,306
7 December	□22	$802.64	-0.13%	27,410
14 December	□32	$810.28	0.95%	39,493
21 December	□769	$806.14	-0.51%	953,929
28 December	□40	$830.13	2.98%	48,186
4 January	-	$858.20	3.38%	-
11 January	□40	$883.06	2.90%	45,297
18 January	□41	$890.04	0.79%	46,065
Total				10,754,055

Notes: Data released following Tuesday, prices average Comex settlement. Ounces estimated by dividing the level of gold sales in euroes by the average Comex price that week. Sales obviously are not actually at weekly average prices. ECB can sell up to 16.07 million ounces per year. It has sold 51.4% of this amount so far.
Fiscal year is from 1 October through end-September
Sources: ECB, CPM
28 January 2008

Changes in Central Bank Gold Reserves in 2007
Million Troy Ounces, Through November 2007

	Year-End 2006	YTD 2007	Net Change 2006-2007
Countries Increasing Reserves in 2007			
Russia	12.91	14.33	1.42
Qatar	0.02	0.40	0.38
Kazakhstan	2.16	2.22	0.06
South Korea	0.42	0.46	0.04
Mexico	0.09	0.12	0.03
Greece	3.59	3.62	0.03
Ukraine	0.81	0.84	0.03
Serbia	0.38	0.39	0.01
United Kingdom	9.97	9.98	0.01
South Africa	3.99	4.00	0.01
Subtotal Net Change			1.93

	Year-End 2006	YTD 2007	Net Change 2006-2007
Countries Decreasing Reserves in 2007			
Spain	13.40	9.05	-4.35
Switzerland	41.48	37.13	-4.35
France	87.44	84.37	-3.07
Bank for International Settlements	5.50	4.50	-1.00
European Central Bank	20.41	19.45	-0.96
Philippines	4.62	4.18	-0.44
Netherlands	20.61	20.00	-0.61
Austria	9.28	9.00	-0.28
Sweden	5.10	4.81	-0.29
Germany	110.04	109.87	-0.17
Slovenia	0.16	0.10	-0.06
Romania	3.37	3.33	-0.04
Venezuela	11.48	11.47	-0.01
Subtotal Net Change			-15.64
Total Net Changes, These Countries			-13.72

Notes: 2006 data through December. 2007 data through November.
Bank for International Settlements, Qatar, Philippines, Serbia, Ukraine, and South Korea through October.
Sources: International Monetary Fund, IFS; CPM Group.
January 20, 2008

Changes in Central Bank Gold Reserves in 2006

Million Troy Ounces, Through December 2006

	Year-End 2005	Year-End 2006	Net Change 2005-2006
Countries Increasing Reserves in 2006			
Russia	12.44	12.91	0.47
Kazakhstan	1.92	2.16	0.24
Mongolia	0.00	0.21	0.21
Greece	3.47	3.59	0.12
Lao People's Democratic Republic	0.15	0.21	0.06
Montenegro	0.00	0.04	0.04
Ukraine	0.78	0.81	0.03
Tajikistan	0.04	0.05	0.01
Malta	0.00	0.01	0.01
Venezuela	11.47	11.48	0.01
Suriname	0.03	0.04	0.01
Subtotal Net Change			1.20

	Year-End 2005	Year-End 2006	Net Change 2005-2006
Countries Decreasing Reserves in 2006			
France	90.85	87.44	-3.41
European Central Bank	22.98	20.41	-2.57
Netherlands	22.34	20.61	-1.73
Spain	14.72	13.40	-1.32
Portugal	13.42	12.30	-1.12
Indonesia	3.10	2.35	-0.75
Bank for International Settlements	6.00	5.50	-0.50
Austria	9.73	9.28	-0.44
Philippines	4.97	4.62	-0.35
Sweden	5.41	5.10	-0.31
Germany	110.21	110.04	-0.17
Colombia	0.33	0.22	-0.10
El Salvador	0.33	0.23	-0.09
United States	261.55	261.50	-0.05
South Korea	0.46	0.42	-0.04
Serbia	0.42	0.38	-0.04
Mexico	0.11	0.09	-0.02
United Kingdom	9.99	9.97	-0.02
Czech Republic	0.44	0.43	-0.01
Subtotal Net Change			-13.06
Total Net Changes, These Countries			-11.86

Sources: International Monetary Fund, IFS; CPM Group.
November 28, 2007

Reported Central Bank Gold Reserves By Country and Region

Million Troy Ounces

	1950	1960	1970	1980	1981	1982	1983	1984	1985	1986	1987	1988	1989	1990	1991	1992
Industrial																
United States	652.0	508.7	316.3	264.3	264.1	264.0	263.4	262.8	262.7	262.0	262.4	261.9	261.9	261.9	261.9	261.8
Canada	16.6	25.3	22.6	21.0	20.5	20.3	20.2	20.1	20.1	19.7	18.5	17.1	16.1	14.8	13.0	9.9
Australia	2.6	4.2	6.8	7.9	7.9	7.9	7.9	7.9	7.9	7.9	7.9	7.9	7.9	7.9	7.9	7.9
Japan	0.2	7.1	15.2	24.2	24.2	24.2	24.2	24.2	24.2	24.2	24.2	24.2	24.2	24.2	24.2	24.2
Austria	0.2	8.4	20.4	21.1	21.1	21.1	21.1	21.1	21.1	21.1	21.2	21.2	20.7	20.4	20.0	19.9
Belgium	16.8	33.4	42.0	34.2	34.2	34.2	34.2	34.2	34.2	34.2	33.6	33.7	30.2	30.2	30.2	25.0
Denmark	0.9	3.1	1.8	1.6	1.6	1.6	1.6	1.6	1.6	1.6	1.6	1.6	1.6	1.7	1.7	1.7
France	18.9	46.9	100.9	81.9	81.9	81.9	81.9	81.9	81.9	81.9	81.9	81.9	81.9	81.9	81.9	81.9
Germany	-	84.9	113.7	95.2	95.2	95.2	95.2	95.2	95.2	95.2	95.2	95.2	95.2	95.2	95.2	95.2
Greece	0.1	2.2	3.3	3.8	3.9	3.9	3.9	4.1	4.1	3.3	3.3	3.4	3.4	3.4	3.4	3.4
Italy	7.3	63.0	82.5	66.7	66.7	66.7	66.7	66.7	66.7	66.7	66.7	66.7	66.7	66.7	66.7	66.7
Netherlands	9.0	41.5	51.1	43.9	43.9	43.9	43.9	43.9	43.9	43.9	43.9	43.9	43.9	43.9	43.9	43.9
Norway	1.4	0.9	0.7	1.2	1.2	1.2	1.2	1.2	1.2	1.2	1.2	1.2	1.2	1.2	1.2	1.2
Portugal	5.5	15.7	25.8	22.2	22.1	22.1	20.4	20.3	20.2	20.2	20.1	16.1	16.1	15.8	15.9	16.1
Spain	3.2	5.1	14.2	14.6	14.6	14.6	14.6	14.6	14.7	14.8	11.9	14.0	15.7	15.6	15.6	15.6
Sweden	2.6	4.9	5.7	6.1	6.1	6.1	6.1	6.1	6.1	6.1	6.1	6.1	6.1	6.1	6.1	6.1
Switzerland	42.0	62.4	78.0	83.3	83.3	83.3	83.3	83.3	83.3	83.3	83.3	83.3	83.3	83.3	83.3	83.3
United Kingdom	81.8	80.0	38.5	18.8	19.0	19.0	19.0	19.0	19.0	19.0	19.0	19.0	19.0	18.9	18.9	18.6
Other	1.6	2.7	3.8	1.9	2.1	2.1	2.2	2.1	2.8	2.8	2.8	2.8	2.9	2.9	2.8	2.8
European Central Bank (ECB)	-	-	-	85.6	85.7	85.7	85.7	85.7	85.7	86.5	89.4	94.0	93.6	93.5	93.5	92.2
Subtotal	862.7	1,000.4	943.3	899.5	899.3	899.0	896.6	896.1	896.5	895.6	894.3	895.1	891.5	889.5	887.3	877.4
Developing-oil	20.8	20.3	33.5	40.6	43.4	43.6	43.8	42.1	43.8	42.0	42.0	42.1	42.1	41.5	42.0	42.0
Developing-Non-oil																
Africa	7.8	7.1	22.8	14.9	12.2	10.5	10.9	10.5	7.8	7.6	8.5	6.1	5.6	6.2	8.6	9.0
Asia	13.7	14.6	19.9	34.9	35.4	36.1	34.9	35.9	37.9	40.3	42.9	48.8	48.6	49.2	50.5	50.0
Europe	4.5	3.7	5.8	16.2	16.4	16.5	16.8	16.8	17.1	16.5	13.8	13.9	14.1	12.1	12.4	11.1
Middle East	3.5	8.9	13.7	14.9	14.9	14.9	14.8	14.8	14.7	15.0	15.0	14.7	14.3	14.3	14.0	13.5
Western Hemisphere	34.8	28.3	20.8	20.8	21.9	19.6	20.3	18.4	21.0	20.9	18.9	19.8	18.6	19.8	16.9	16.8
Subtotal	64.3	62.6	83.0	101.7	99.9	96.0	97.0	96.3	98.5	100.3	99.1	103.3	101.2	101.7	102.4	100.3
International Monetary Fund	42.7	69.6	124.0	103.4	103.4	103.4	103.4	103.4	103.4	103.4	103.4	103.4	103.4	103.4	103.4	103.4
Bank for International Settlements	1.5	-0.5	-8.1	7.5	7.6	7.3	6.6	6.6	6.7	6.4	6.1	6.6	6.6	7.8	6.6	6.8
Total	999.8	1,154.0	1,177.0	1,152.8	1,153.7	1,149.3	1,147.4	1,144.5	1,149.0	1,147.7	1,144.9	1,150.5	1,144.8	1,143.8	1,141.6	1,129.9

Notes: Totals do not equal sum of categories due to rounding. Asia, as of 1981, now includes non-members such as Taiwan. "Developing-oil" includes oil exporting countries; "Developing non-oil" consists of other developing countries. Data for 1980 and subsequent years excludes amounts transferred to the European Monetary Institute Accounts, formerly the European Monetary Cooperation Fund. Total for 1950, 1960, 1970 and 1980 includes reserves of non-members in the amounts of 7.8, 1.6, 0.3, and 0.1 million ounces, respectively. The European Central Bank replaced the European Monetary Institute on January 1, 1999. Year-end 1998 gold reserve figures for the European Union countries and the ECB reflect the return of 87 million ounces to the national central banks of Germany France, Italy, Netherlands, Portugal, Spain, Austria, Belgium, Finland, Ireland, Luxembourg, United Kingdom, Sweden, Denmark, and Greece. The 11 countries participating in the European Monetary Union transferred around 24 million ounces to the ECB at the beginning of 1999. Year-end-data. 2007 through November. Developing-oil, Developing-Non-oil, and BIS through October.
Sources: International Monetary Fund.
January 12, 2008

1993	1994	1995	1996	1997	1998	1999	2000	2001	2002	2003	2004	2005	2006	YTD 2007	
															Industrial
261.8	261.7	261.7	261.7	261.6	261.6	261.7	261.6	262.0	262.0	261.6	261.6	261.6	261.5	261.5	United States
6.1	3.9	3.4	3.1	3.1	2.5	1.8	1.2	1.1	0.6	0.1	0.1	0.1	0.1	0.1	Canada
7.9	7.9	7.9	7.9	2.6	2.6	2.6	2.6	2.6	2.6	2.6	2.6	2.6	2.6	2.6	Australia
24.2	24.2	24.2	24.2	24.2	24.2	24.2	24.6	24.6	24.6	24.6	24.6	24.6	24.6	24.6	Japan
18.6	18.3	12.0	10.8	7.9	9.6	13.1	12.1	11.2	10.2	10.2	9.9	9.7	9.3	9.0	Austria
25.0	25.0	20.5	15.3	15.3	9.5	8.3	8.3	8.3	8.3	8.3	8.3	7.3	7.3	7.3	Belgium
1.6	1.6	1.7	1.7	1.7	2.1	2.1	2.1	2.1	2.1	2.1	2.1	2.1	2.1	2.1	Denmark
81.9	81.9	81.9	81.9	81.9	102.4	97.2	97.3	97.3	97.3	97.3	96.0	90.9	87.4	84.4	France
95.2	95.2	95.2	95.2	95.2	119.0	111.5	111.5	111.1	110.8	110.6	110.4	110.2	110.0	109.9	Germany
3.4	3.5	3.5	3.5	3.6	3.6	4.2	4.3	3.9	3.9	3.5	3.5	3.5	3.6	3.6	Greece
66.7	66.7	66.7	66.7	66.7	83.4	78.8	78.8	78.8	78.8	78.8	78.8	78.8	78.8	78.8	Italy
35.1	34.8	34.8	34.8	27.1	33.8	31.6	29.3	28.4	27.4	25.0	25.0	22.3	20.6	20.0	Netherlands
1.2	1.2	1.2	1.2	1.2	1.2	1.2	1.2	1.2	1.2	1.2	0.0	0.0	0.0	0.0	Norway
16.1	15.0	16.1	16.1	16.1	20.1	19.5	19.5	19.5	19.0	16.6	14.9	13.4	12.3	12.3	Portugal
15.6	15.6	15.6	15.6	15.6	19.5	16.8	16.8	16.8	16.8	16.8	16.8	14.7	13.4	9.1	Spain
6.1	6.1	4.7	4.7	4.7	4.7	6.0	6.0	6.0	6.0	6.0	6.0	5.4	5.1	4.8	Sweden
83.3	83.3	83.3	83.3	83.3	83.3	83.3	77.8	70.7	61.6	52.5	43.5	41.5	41.5	37.1	Switzerland
18.5	18.4	18.4	18.4	18.4	23.0	20.6	15.7	11.4	10.1	10.1	10.0	10.0	10.0	10.0	United Kingdom
2.7	2.7	2.3	2.3	2.3	2.8	1.9	1.9	1.9	1.9	1.9	1.9	1.9	1.9	1.9	Other
89.6	89.9	93.7	92.0	89.5	0.0	24.0	24.0	24.6	24.6	24.6	24.7	23.0	20.4	19.4	European Central Bank (ECB)
860.4	856.9	848.7	840.1	821.9	809.0	810.4	796.5	783.5	769.8	754.3	740.6	723.6	712.6	698.5	Subtotal
42.4	42.4	41.9	42.5	42.3	41.6	41.2	41.8	42.3	41.7	38.3	38.3	38.2	37.5	37.9	Developing-oil
															Developing-Non-oil
7.3	6.5	7.2	6.1	6.4	6.7	7.0	8.7	8.4	8.8	6.9	7.0	7.0	7.0	7.0	Africa
50.5	50.5	52.2	53.4	53.7	52.9	52.6	54.1	58.5	62.3	61.8	60.9	58.8	58.7	58.2	Asia
21.9	20.8	22.0	26.8	30.2	30.6	30.1	29.5	30.9	29.6	29.6	30.2	30.6	31.5	32.2	Europe
12.6	12.5	13.1	13.1	13.5	12.8	12.0	11.9	12.1	13.1	17.0	13.1	13.4	13.4	13.6	Middle East
15.8	16.4	17.4	16.3	12.0	12.7	11.3	8.3	5.7	5.3	5.2	6.9	6.7	6.5	6.6	Western Hemisphere
108.1	106.6	111.9	115.5	115.8	115.7	113.0	112.4	115.6	119.1	120.5	118.1	116.5	117.1	117.6	Subtotal
103.4	103.4	103.4	103.4	103.4	103.4	103.4	103.4	103.4	103.4	103.4	103.4	103.4	103.4	103.4	International Monetary Fund
8.6	7.0	7.3	6.6	6.2	6.4	6.4	6.4	6.3	6.3	6.2	6.7	6.0	5.5	4.5	Bank for International Settlements
1,123.0	1,116.2	1,113.2	1,108.2	1,089.7	1,076.1	1,074.4	1,060.5	1,051.2	1,040.3	1,022.7	1,007.1	987.8	976.1	961.8	Total

Central Bank Reserves Since 1920

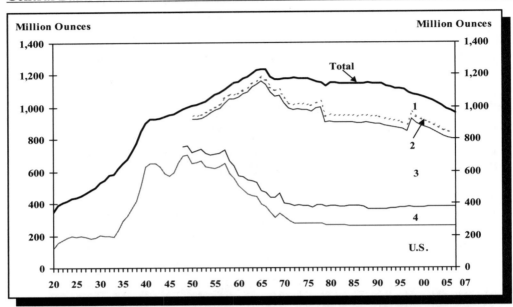

Notes: 1) Intergovernmental agencies: International Monetary Fund, Bank for International Settlements, and the European Monetary Cooperation Fund, European Central Bank after 1998. 2) Oil Exporting developing countries. 3) Industrialized nations, excluding the United States. 4) Non-oil exporting developing nations.

U.S. as a Percent of Total Gold Reserves

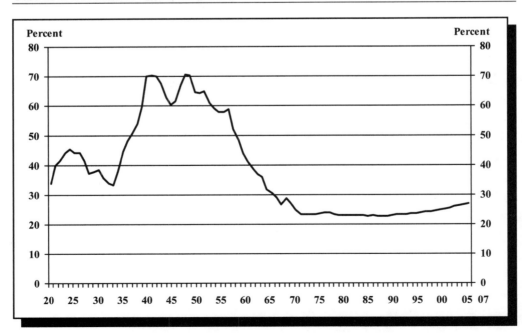

A number of countries that were sellers of gold in 2006 became buyers of small volumes of gold in 2007. The United Kingdom purchased 10,000 ounces of gold in 2007, half of the 20,000 ounces it sold in 2006. Mexico also purchased gold in 2007, 30,000 ounces, after selling 40,000 ounces of gold in 2006. These two central banks' gold activities reflect gold commemorative and bullion coin programs. Serbia meanwhile purchased 10,000 ounces of gold in 2007, after selling 40,000 ounces in 2006. This represented the role of the central bank in Serbia as a financial market maker in that country. It buys and sells gold to industrial users, jewelers, refiners, and others. The final country that purchased gold in 2007 after selling gold in 2006

was South Korea, which purchased the same amount, 40,000 ounces, that it sold. Venezuela was the only country to move in the opposite direction, becoming a net seller of gold in 2007 after purchasing gold in 2006. In both cases, the central banks were acting as national gold market makers for domestic entities seeking to buy or sell gold.

Overall, 2007 saw a smaller number of central banks involved in gold transactions than did 2006. In terms of both total gold sales and purchases there was more activity in 2007 than 2006, however. Some countries that were active in 2006 were no longer active in 2007, while others were added to the activity list after not being present in 2006.

Gold Held at the New York Federal Reserve Bank

Quarterly, Through Third Quarter 2007.

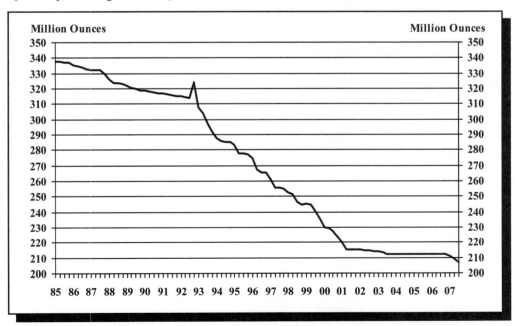

Gold Held at the Federal Reserve Bank in New York

Year	Quarter	Kilograms	Thou. Troy Ounces	Change
1994	1st	8,947,239	287,660	-4,310
	2nd	8,888,298	285,765	-1,895
	3rd	8,872,828	285,268	-497
	4th	8,864,725	285,007	-261
1995	1st	8,813,892	283,373	-1,634
	2nd	8,637,821	277,712	-5,661
	3rd	8,640,031	277,783	71
	4th	8,620,877	277,167	-616
1996	1st	8,538,366	274,514	-2,653
	2nd	8,321,776	267,551	-6,964
	3rd	8,258,420	265,514	-2,037
	4th	8,248,843	265,206	-308
1997	1st	8,128,760	261,345	-3,861
	2nd	7,951,952	255,661	-5,685
	3rd	7,951,215	255,637	-24
	4th	7,929,114	254,927	-711
1998	1st	7,856,181	252,582	-2,345
	2nd	7,821,556	251,468	-1,113
	3rd	7,663,902	246,400	-5,069
	4th	7,619,700	244,979	-1,421
1999	1st	7,622,647	245,073	95
	2nd	7,609,386	244,647	-426
	3rd	7,481,200	240,526	-4,121
	4th	7,317,652	235,268	-5,258
2000	1st	7,154,105	230,009	-5,258
	2nd	7,137,161	229,465	-545
	3rd	7,087,065	227,854	-1,611
	4th	6,962,562	223,851	-4,003
2001	1st	6,843,217	220,014	-3,837
	2nd	6,703,980	215,538	-4,477
	3rd	6,703,980	215,538	0
	4th	6,703,244	215,514	-24
2002	1st	6,702,507	215,490	-24
	2nd	6,687,036	214,993	-497
	3rd	6,672,302	214,519	-474
	4th	6,663,462	214,235	-284
2003	1st	6,663,462	214,235	0
	2nd	6,633,257	213,264	-971
	3rd	6,608,946	212,482	-782
	4th	6,608,946	212,482	0
2004	1st	6,608,946	212,482	0
	2nd	6,608,946	212,482	0
	3rd	6,605,999	212,387	-95
	4th	6,605,999	212,387	0
2005	1st	6,605,999	212,387	0
	2nd	6,605,999	212,387	0
	3rd	6,605,999	212,387	0
	4th	6,605,999	212,387	0
2006	1st	6,605,999	212,387	0
	2nd	6,605,999	212,387	0
	3rd	6,605,999	212,387	0
	4th	6,605,999	212,387	0
2007	1st	6,566,217	211,108	-1,279
	2nd	6,501,388	209,024	-2,084
	3rd	6,436,558	206,940	-2,084

Note: Gold held on foreign and international account.
Source: CPM Group.
January 8, 2008

Many of these countries bought or sold small quantities of gold. Of those countries that were not active in 2007, Mongolia was the largest purchaser in 2006, at 210,000 ounces and Indonesia was the largest seller in 2006 at 750,000 ounces. The largest additions to the list in 2007 were Qatar, on the purchasing side at 380,000 ounces, and Switzerland on the selling side at 4.4 million ounces. Russia was the largest purchaser of gold for the second consecutive year in 2007. In 2007 Russia purchased 1.42 million ounces of gold, 76.4% of the total 1.93 million ounces purchased. The Russian central bank has begun buying relatively small amounts of gold from domestic miners and refiners. Two countries, Russia and Qatar totaled 1.8 million

ounces of purchases. Eight other countries comprised the 210,000 ounces of purchases. The third largest purchase was by Kazakhstan, which purchased 60,000 ounces of gold. Geographically, the purchasers of gold are not as uniform as the sellers. Eastern Europe is the most prevalent purchaser, with the Ukraine and Serbia joining Russia. The United Kingdom, as previously mentioned, and Greece were the only western European countries that purchased gold, 10,000 ounces and 30,000 ounces in 2007, respectively. South Korea, Mexico, and South Africa were also net purchasers of gold.

Gold Prices and Shifts in Central Bank Gold Reserves

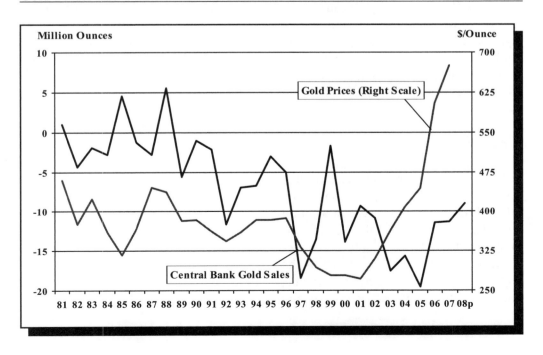

Gold's Role as a Reserve Asset

As a reserve asset, gold is not seen as being particularly useful or interesting by most central bank managers. Gold is not an interest-bearing asset, in contrast to government bonds and other common reserve holdings. Another reason that central banks do not view gold as being particularly useful as a reserve asset is that if they needed to mobilize their reserves, perhaps to defend their national currency from a sharp sudden round of selling and declining values, it is much harder, costly, and difficult to first sell one's gold, to earn dollars, and then use the dollars to defend one's currency. The gold market is much less liquid and much more transparent than currency markets. If a central bank has to sell its gold first, and then use the resulting dollars to buy its own currencies, the entire market will see it coming, spreads on the gold sales will move quickly and sharply against the central bank, and the bank will incur two sets of transaction costs, from gold to dollars and then from dollars to its currency. Because of this, gold is not seen as a useful reserve asset.

On top of this, most central bankers do not see gold as ever playing a central role in a future international currency regime. The gold market is too small and illiquid to play a useful role in a future monetary system, unless the world economy utterly and irrevocably collapsed. That tends not to happen. Even in the event of the most cataclysmic events, the international monetary system and global economy probably would dust itself off and move forward from where it was, rather than dissolving into small national economies reminiscent of the medieval ages.

Another reason that is commonly cited for not holding gold as a reserve asset is that the gold price is less predictable than that of the U.S. dollar. That may not be a completely accurate opinion, since the track records of governments and private sector economists in projecting the dollar as well as gold suggest that both markets are hard to predict on an on-going basis. Looking at the period from the end of 1999 to the end of 2007, the trade weighted U.S. dollar index lost 14.0% percent of its value, falling to 98.82 on 31 December 2007 from 114.85 on 31 December 1999. Over this period the trade weighted U.S. dollar index reached a high of 130.08 on 27 February 2002 and a low of 97.38 on 13 November 2007. Gold meanwhile gained 189.4% to $838 from $289.60 with settlement low of $256.60 and high of $842.70.

Composition of Global Monetary Reserves

Through October 2007.

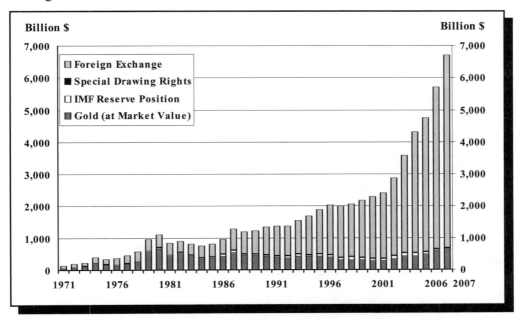

Gold as a Percent of Total Reserves

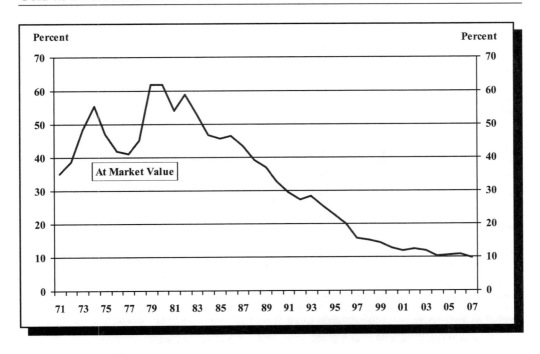

Official Gold Transactions
Thousand Troy Ounces

Year	IMF	United States	South Africa	Portugal	Canada	Germany	United Kingdom
1960	1,900	-48,700	-150	140	-2,100	9,541	8,197
1961	-10,300	-24,500	3,400	-3,100	1,700	19,779	-15,264
1962	3,300	-25,400	5,700	800	-7,000	445	8,975
1963	3,400	-13,200	3,800	700	3,100	4,701	-2,750
1964	-3,800	-3,600	-1,600	700	6,000	11,550	-9,937
1965	-8,900	-40,200	-4,300	1,500	3,600	4,627	3,650
1966	22,400	-23,700	6,100	1,900	-3,000	-3,376	-9,236
1967	400	-33,400	-1,600	1,600	-900	-1,834	-18,608
1968	-11,200	-33,500	18,900	4,500	-4,300	8,904	5,233
1969	600	27,600	-3,700	500	300	-13,131	-36
1970	58,000	-22,500	-12,800	800	-2,300	-2,854	-3,534
1971	11,200	-24,700	-7,300	500	100	2,763	-16,339
1972	18,200	-15,600	6,200	600	-1,000	888	-1,102
1973	-	-	1,100	700	-	255	-75
1974	-	-	-700	300	-	4	21
1975	-	-1,260	-500	-100	-	-1	-
1976	-3,900	-30	-5,100	-100	-300	-	1
1977	-17,900	2,870	-3,000	-3,600	-	682	1,198
1978	-13,400	-1,140	100	-2,000	-	343	601
1979	-5,500	-11,810	240	-	-50	-23,386	-4,578
1980	-3,400	-280	2,120	40	-1,200	-70	590
1981	-	-210	-2,860	-30	-520	-	190
1982	-	-80	1,720	-50	-200	-	-20
1983	-	-640	220	-1,660	-90	-	-
1984	-	-600	-430	-130	-30	-	20
1985	-	-140	-2,520	-200	-30	-	-
1986	-	-610	-20	-70	-390	-	-20
1987	-	340	1,010	-100	-1,200	-	-
1988	-	-510	-2,360	-3,990	-1,380	-	-10
1989	-	60	-390	-20	-1,040	-	-10
1990	-	-20	1,010	-220	-1,340	-	-50
1991	-	-	2,380	40	-1,800	-	-50
1992	-	-70	180	190	-3,020	-	-280
1993	-	-50	-1,890	-	-3,890	-	-160
1994	-	-60	-560	10	-2,160	-	-10
1995	-	-30	50	-	-480	-	-10
1996	-	-40	-460	-	-320	-	-
1997	-	-20	200	-	-	-	-10
1998	-	-30	10	4,020	-600	23,800	4,580
1999	-	60	-60	-580	-680	-7,460	-2,450
2000	-	-60	1,960	-	-630	-	-4,880
2001	-	390	-180	-	-130	-390	-4,250
2002	-	-	-140	-480	-370	-340	-1,330
2003	-	-	-1,600	-2,400	-491	-210	-20
2004	11	36	4	-1,770	-	-202	-31
2005	-	-35	-3	-1,421	-	-18	-46
2006	-	-52	-2	-1,142	-	-17	-23
2007YTD	-	-	13	-	-	-17	10

Notes: Sales from official reserves indicated with negative numbers. Reported transactions include only transactions reported reported to the IMF member countries. Unreported transactions reflect estimates of additional purchases and sales. The large transactions shown for Western European countries in 1979, as well as the large "other reported" figures for 1979 represent the 85 million ounces transferred to the European Monetary Cooperation Fund by member countries in that year. Further shifts to the EMCF were made by Spain in 1987, Portugal in 1988 and Austria in 1995. The large transactions shown for Western European countries and the "other reported" figures for 1998 reflect the return of 87 million ounces from the European Monetary Institute to the 15 European Union member countries' national central banks at the end of 1998. On January 1, 1999, the European Central Bank replaced the EMI, and the 11 countries participation in the European Monetary Union transferred 24 million ounces to the ECB. Year-end data. 2007 through November. South Africa through October 2006. Sources: International Monetary Fund; Bank for International Settlements; Consolidated Gold Fields; CPM Group. January 18, 2008

134

France	Brazil	Colombia	Mexico	Reported		Unreported	Total	Year
				Other	Total			
10,030	-1,134	200	-171	29,347	7,100	-600	6,500	1960
13,710	-57	285	-686	32,519	17,486	-286	17,200	1961
13,310	-271	-885	-514	11,769	10,229	271	10,500	1962
16,800	284	142	1,285	8,509	26,771	-3,371	23,400	1963
15,830	-5,549	-114	858	6,605	16,943	3,257	20,200	1964
27,920	-804	-657	-315	21,365	7,486	-1,186	6,300	1965
15,200	-503	-286	-1,400	-6,128	-2,029	829	-1,200	1966
-120	-	172	1,629	8,204	-44,457	-643	-45,100	1967
-38,770	-7	-	-29	27,469	-22,800	0	-22,800	1968
-9,430	-	-143	115	382	3,057	-157	2,900	1969
-430	-	-257	200	-5,896	8,429	-829	7,600	1970
-250	31	-86	228	32,824	-1,029	-2,071	-3,100	1971
30	4	29	-314	-1,964	5,971	-1,071	4,900	1972
220	1	-	-314	-687	1,200	-1,400	-200	1973
20	-	-	-966	2,521	1,200	-1,800	-600	1974
-	-	697	-3	-4,004	-5,171	4,871	-300	1975
90	-	287	-2,058	339	-10,771	8,871	-1,900	1976
650	188	318	153	23,412	4,971	-13,671	-8,700	1977
320	94	230	138	7,457	-7,257	-4,443	-11,700	1978
-20,070	90	360	90	46,157	-18,457	945	-17,512	1979
-70	180	470	80	5,430	3,890	3,510	7,400	1980
-	320	580	200	1,500	-830	5,330	4,500	1981
-	-2,050	450	-190	-4,464	-4,884	5,894	1,010	1982
-	390	400	240	-1,000	-2,140	-271	-2,411	1983
-	930	-2,850	110	2,009	-971	-499	-1,529	1984
-	1,630	470	-60	3,450	2,600	-1,100	1,500	1985
-	-670	170	210	1,657	257	658	915	1986
-	-	-1,330	-30	-1,620	-2,930	30	-2,900	1987
-	-30	420	10	13,450	5,600	-343	5,257	1988
-	250	-490	-1,520	-2,411	-5,571	-610	-6,181	1989
-	1,590	20	-110	-2,023	-1,143	-857	-2,000	1990
-	-2,550	230	-	-417	-2,167	-633	-2,800	1991
-	210	-380	-230	-8,286	-11,686	-414	-12,100	1992
-	700	-180	-210	-1,280	-6,960	-15,040	-22,000	1993
-	780	-10	-50	-4,703	-6,763	-237	-7,000	1994
-	870	-20	80	-3,464	-3,004	-4,996	-8,000	1995
-	-890	-20	-250	-3,060	-5,040	-4,960	-10,000	1996
40	-660	110	-70	-18,067	-18,477	-1,523	-20,000	1997
20,480	1,570	-	30	-67,436	-13,576	-	-14,596	1998
-5,130	-1,430	-30	-60	16,090	-1,730	-12,180	-13,910	1999
10	-1,280	-	90	-9,120	-13,910	-	-13,910	2000
-	-1,430	-	-20	-3,257	-9,267	-	-9,267	2001
-	-20	-	10	-8,200	-10,870	-	-10,870	2002
-	-	-	-50	-12,813	-17,584	-	-17,584	2003
-1,270	-1	-	-31	-12,385	-15,650	-	-15,650	2004
-5,128	-6	-	-31	-12,607	-19,295	-1,100	-20,395	2005
-3,412	-	-105	-18	-6,927	-11,697	-	-11,697	2006
-2,480	-	-	40	-11,833	-14,267	-	-14,267	2007 YTD

Top 15 Central Banks by Gold Holdings

Country	Gold Reserves Million Troy Ounces	Percent of Total Central Bank Gold Reserves
United States	261.50	31%
Germany	109.87	13%
France	84.37	10%
Italy	78.83	9%
Switzerland	37.13	4%
Japan	24.60	3%
Netherlands	20.00	2%
European Central Bank	19.44	2%
China,P.R.: Mainland	19.29	2%
Russia	14.33	2%
Portugal	12.30	1%
India	11.50	1%
Venezuela, Rep. Bol.	11.47	1%
United Kingdom	9.98	1%
Spain	9.05	1%
Total for all countries	853.94	84%

Note: Gold reserves as of November 2007. China, Venezuela and total for all countries as of October 2007.
Sources: International Monetary Fund; CPM Group.
January 12, 2007

Top 15 Central Banks by Foreign Exchange Holdings

Country	Foreign Exchange Reserves Billion US $	Percent of Total Central Bank Foreign Exchange Reserves
China	1,462.4	24%
Japan	943.8	15%
Russia	450.5	7%
Taiwan	261.8	4%
India	264.0	4%
Korea	261.0	4%
Brazil	176.2	3%
Singapore	158.5	3%
Hong Kong	142.9	2%
Malaysia	99.4	2%
Mexico	84.4	1%
Algeria	106.7	2%
Thailand	74.8	1%
Turkey	82.2	1%
Libya	72.3	1%
Total for all countries	6,168.5	
China and Hong Kong	1,605.4	26%
China, Hong Kong, and Taiwan	1,867.2	30%
China, Hong Kong, Taiwan, and Korea	2,128.2	35%
China, Hong Kong, Taiwan, Korea, and Japan	3,072.0	50%
China, Hong Kong, Taiwan, Japan, and Singapore	2,969.5	48%
China, Hong Kong, Taiwan, Japan, Korea, and Singapore	3,230.5	52%

Note: Total reserves excluding gold as of November.
Total for all countries, China, Hong Kong, Singapore, Korea, Malaysia, Lybia, and Norway through October 2007.
Tiawan through October 2006. Sources: International Monetary Fund; The Economist; CPM Group.
January 12, 2008

IMF Gold Transactions, 1976 - 1980
Thousand Troy Ounces

	Auctions	Non-Competitive Sales	Restitutions
1976	3,900	-	-
1977	6,030	-	11,914
1978	5,915	1,384	6,086
1979	5,458	96	5,800
1980	2,220	-	1,200
TOTAL	23,523	1,480	25,000

Notes: Totals do not equal due to rounding.
Sources: International Monetary Fund, CPM Group.
October 23, 1996

IMF Gold Sales
Thousand Troy Ounces

Competitive Sales

1976	June-December	3,900	5 auctions of 780,000 ounces each
1977	January	780	
	March-December	5,250	10 auctions of 525,000 ounces each
		6,030	
1978	January-May	2,625	5 auctions of 525,000 ounces each
	June-December	3,290	7 auctions of 470,000 ounces each
		5,915	
1979	January-May	2,350	5 auctions of 470,000 ounces each
	June-December	3,108	7 auctions of 444,000 ounces each
		5,458	
1980	January-May	2,220	5 auctions of 444,000 ounces each
	Subtotal	23,523	

Noncompetitive Sales

1978-1979	1,480	
	TOTAL SALES	25,003

Notes: Totals do not equal due to rounding.
Sources: International Monetary Fund, CPM Group.
October 23, 1996

IMF Gold Sales, Non-Competitive Bids, 1978-1979
Thousand Troy Ounces

Country	Entitlement	Awarded
Colombia	134.4	134.4
Cyprus	22.4	4.0
India	804.8	804.8
Kenya	41.0	41.0
Korea	68.8	68.8
Malaysia	159.2	159.2
Mauritius	18.8	18.8
Mexico	316.8	60.0
Nepal	10.8	10.8
Paraguay	16.4	16.4
Philippines	132.8	132.8
Tanzania	36.0	9.2
Uraguay	59.0	20.0
Subtotal	1,821.2	1,480.2

Other countries entitled to submit non-competitive bids	1,844.6	
TOTAL	3,665.8	

Source: **Annual Report 1979**, IMF.
October 23, 1996

IMF Gold Restitution, 1977-1980

Industrial Countries	Quotas as Percent of Total	Gold Restitution (Thousand Troy Oz.)
United States	22.94	5,734.0
Canada	3.77	941.4
Japan	4.11	1,027.0
Belgium	2.23	556.3
France	5.13	1,283.7
Germany	5.48	1,369.3
Italy	3.42	855.8
Netherlands	2.40	599.1
United Kingdom	9.59	2,396.3
Other Industrial Countries	3.81	952.5
Subtotal	62.88	15,715.4
Other Europe	5.29	1,323.0
Australia, New Zealand, South Africa	4.07	1,018.0
Less Developed Areas - Oil Exporting Countries	5.22	1,305.0
Less Developed Areas - Non-Oil Exporting		
Other Western Hemisphere	7.47	1,868.0
Other Middle East	1.59	398.0
Other Asia	9.54	2,385.0
Other Africa	3.98	995.0
Subtotal	22.58	5,646.0
TOTAL	100.00	25,007.4

Notes: Totals do not equal due to rounding.
Sources: International Monetary Fund, CPM Group.
October 23, 1996

Fabrication Demand

Fabrication Demand

Fabrication demand for gold rose sharply in 2007, in spite of the dramatic increase in gold prices. Part of this increase reflected increased demand for gold jewelry in India and other countries where jewelry and gold decorative objects are used as a form of savings and investment. This quasi-investment demand for gold jewelry accounted for three-quarters of the increased use of gold in the manufacture of fabricated products last year. Demand also rose sharply in electronics and in various other industrial applications in which there is low price elasticity, due to the critical need for gold in those applications.

Gold use fell in the manufacture of jew-

elry in industrialized nations, where gold jewelry is more of a luxury and discretionary purchase than it is an investment decision. Also, these countries continue to lose manufacturing jobs, including in gold jewelry manufacturing, to countries from Thailand to Turkey.

Fabrication demand rose 8.3% in total in 2007, to 82.95 million ounces from 76.6 million ounces the year before. Jewelry demand in developing countries accounted for 4.7 million ounces of the 6.3 million ounce increase in total gold use in fabricated products last year.

While it may seem extraordinary that fabrication demand would rise in an

Annual Total Demand

Projected Through 2008.

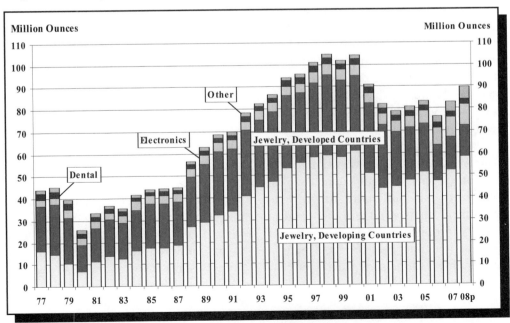

environment of rapidly increasing prices, the fact that most of the increase came in the sector that represents investment demand helps explain much of the seemingly incongruous development.

Furthermore, the increase in 2007 fabrication demand, both in the developing country jewelry market and in total, represented the mirror image of a sharp decline the year before. Total fabrication demand fell 7.9% in 2006, to 76.6 million ounces. The big declines were in jewelry. While total fabrication use of gold dropped 6.5 million ounces, a large portion of the decrease, 3.9 million ounces, occurred in jewelry demand in developing countries. To some extent the increase in gold use in 2007 was a recovery from a loss in volume the year before. Even with the sharp increase in 2007, total gold use, at 82.9 million ounces, was slightly less than the 83.1 million ounces estimated to have been used in 2005. (In reality, the margin of error in estimating the vast amounts of gold used in jewelry manufacturing by small jewelers around the world is such that one should say that total gold use in 2007 was virtually the same as it had been in 2005.)

Thus, much of the sharp variation in fabrication demand for gold over the past two years has had more to do with investment demand patterns for gold in jewelry form than it have with the use of gold in manufactured products bought by customers for reasons other than their gold content.

Gold demand is projected to rise another 8.2% this year, to 89.8 million ounces. Another sharp increase is projected for jewelry demand in developing countries, while demand in electronics and other industrial products is projected to continue to expand at a robust pace. Demand for gold for use in jewelry manufacturing in industrialized economies meanwhile is projected to continue to decline, affected by a combination of rising prices for gold and jewelry, and reductions in consumer spending on luxury discretionary purchases such as jewelry during a time of fiscal stringency and uncertainty.

Meanwhile, all of these variations are occurring in the context of a market that remains 20% smaller in volume of gold ounces used than it was at its peak of 104.6 million ounces in 1998, and 104.3 million ounces in 2000. This longer term decline partly represents the negative effects on gold use of the rise in prices over the past seven years. It also partly has been due to a shift away from using gold jewelry as a form of savings and investment in parts of India, other Asian nations, and the Middle East. In these countries gold jewelry continues to play a vital role as an investment and alternative savings mechanism, but there have been two secular shifts that have reduced this role somewhat. The first has been a shift away from gold jewelry toward gold bars, coins, and medallions as the preferred method of investing in gold by some investors in these regions. The second has been a shift toward a more diversified portfolio by some investors in these regions: Whereas until recently most of these investors' savings went in to gold and silver, today a portion of their assets have been transferred into stocks, bonds, certificates of deposit, savings accounts at banks, and other financial assets, which are seen as less risky and more worthy than they used to be seen in these regions.

Jewelry

Gold use in jewelry consists of two distinct markets. As described above, the majority of gold jewelry purchased in the world today actually represents a form of gold investment and savings. A distinct gold jewelry market exists in which gold jewelry is a luxury good and discretionary consumer purchase.

To a large extent, the quasi-investment gold jewelry market exists in India, Pakistan, other parts of Asia, and the Middle East. The market for gold jewelry as a luxury item exists more in industrialized nations, in North America, Europe, Japan, and elsewhere. As with all such simplistic divisions, there is some overlap in the geographic divisions between these two markets. In the investment-oriented markets most of the gold jewelry is sold at a relatively small mark-up over the gold content of the jewelry. A gold necklace may be sold in Dubai, Mumbai, Turkey, or Hong Kong for around 3% more than the value of the gold content. In the latter market, where gold jewelry is more a luxury item, gold jewelry has an enormous premium, often two to four times the value

of the gold content, at the retail sales level. A $200 necklace bought in the United States might have $50 worth of gold in it, while a similarly priced necklace in Europe might have even less gold content and value.

In total, around 67.0 million ounces of gold was used in the manufacture of jewelry last year. Gold jewelry absorbed roughly 53% of the 126.7 million ounces of gold that entered the physical gold market from all sources last year.

This share of the physical gold market is off sharply from what it was even just a few years ago. As recently as 2000 jewelry absorbed 94.9 million ounces, or 80% of the 118.8 million ounces of total available new gold supply. In 2000 investment demand for gold was very low, as most investors seemed convinced that they would never want to buy gold again, and low gold prices were combining with strong real economic growth worldwide to stimulate heavy demand for gold jewelry. By 2007 investment demand had been at unprecedented historical highs for six years, while jewelry demand had been pounded down by a combination of high gold prices and weaker economic conditions in parts of the world.

As prices rose after 2001, while economic conditions became decidedly less stable, investors began buying more gold, and the use of gold in jewelry, at least luxury gold jewelry, declined. Gold use in jewelry is negatively correlated to the gold price, especially in the noninvestment jewelry markets. As prices rise, gold use in jewelry falls for two reasons. On the wholesale level, jewelers use less gold per piece of jewelry, in order to maintain a price point for retail sales and keep their products affordable. On a retail level, consumers buy less gold jewelry in industrialized markets when the prices raise, both for gold and jewelry. Even if jewelry prices do not rise proportionately to gold bullion prices, history has shown that consumers pull back from jewelry purchases.

The gold jewelry market is divided roughly into two sub-markets. One is gold jewelry in developing countries,

much of which is purchased as a form of investment or savings. This market is the largest market. Last year, 52.1 million ounces of gold were used in the manufacture of gold jewelry in developing economies. This was 77.7% of the 67.0 million ounces of total gold use in jewelry. It also was 9.9% more than the 47.4 million ounces used in these regions in jewelry manufacturing in 2006. As mentioned above, this growth was something of a recovery, in that gold use in jewelry in developing countries had declined from 51.3 million ounces in 2005 to 47.4 million ounces in 2006.

Demand was strong in numerous national markets. Indian gold use in jewelry

Gold Jewelry Demand and Gold Prices

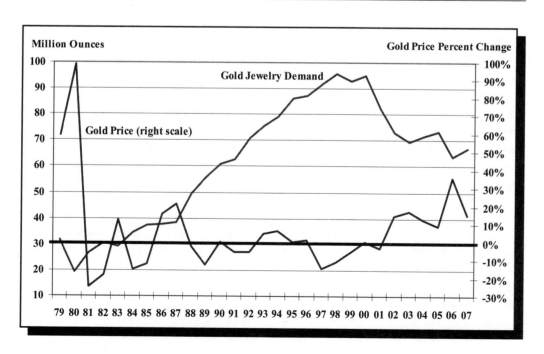

and decorative objects rose from 5.4 million ounces to 9.1 million ounces last year. Demand rose from 19.0 to 20.7 million ounces in Middle Eastern markets. The growth was not universal. The increase in gold jewelry purchases was strongest in India, with Pakistan and Iran continuing to be strong markets for such gold purchases. Countries in the Middle East saw modest increases in demand for gold jewelry. Some southeast Asian markets saw a decline in gold jewelry demand last year.

Demand is projected to continue to be strong this year. Gold use in jewelry in developing countries is projected to rise another 11.9%, or 6.2 million ounces, to 58.3 million ounces in 2008. Demand is projected to continue to be strong in India, Pakistan, and Iran. Demand is expected to pick up more forcefully in the Middle East, while southeast Asian demand also is expected to rise sharply.

Gold use in jewelry in developing countries meanwhile continued to contract last year. Demand fell an estimated 8.0% to 14.9 million ounces in 2007. This followed a 26.4% drop from 22.0 million ounces in 2005 to 16.2 million ounces in 2006.

Demand for gold for use in jewelry manufacturing in developed economies is projected to continue to decline in 2008, as the combination of higher gold prices and weaker economic sentiments continue to constrict these markets. Gold use may fall another 4.7%, to around 14.2 million ounces.

Demand in these countries has been hit hard by higher gold prices, lower consumer interest in solid gold jewelry, and increased concerns about economic conditions. While the higher gold price may not stimulate sharp declines in consumer demand for gold jewelry, given the high price mark-up on jewelry in such countries, it has limited the amount of gold being used in jewelry through the efforts of jewelry manufacturers.

Jewelers need to keep their products affordable, both at the highly competitive wholesale level and at the retail level. In order to do this, they reduce the amount of gold per piece of jewelry as gold prices rise. The average piece of gold jewelry sold in the United States is sold for a price around $70 or less these days. The average price for gold jewelry is lower in Europe and higher in Japan. Jewelry manufacturers will make lighter pieces as the gold price rises, so that their jewelry still can be marketed at such a price level. As prices have risen sharply over the past two years, jewelry retailers have had to increase their prices at the consumer level. This has offered some relief to manufacturers, but not complete protection from rising prices. Jewelers also face extremely tough competition from other jewelry manufacturers, so they strive to offer the most attractive, heavier, and more likely to sell gold jewelry designs to their distributions and retail customers. This limits the reductions in per-unit gold use to some extent, although a shift toward using colored precious and semi-precious gemstones in increasing volumes of jewelry allows jewelry manufacturers to reduce their gold content while still increasing the perceived value of their products.

Electronics

Electronics applications used an estimated 8.9 million ounces of gold in 2007. This was up 19.4% from 7.5 million ounces in 2006, which in turn was up 36.5% from 5.5 million ounces the year before that. Gold use in electronic products has been rising sharply for several years. This trend is projected to continue in the long run, but there could be slowing down temporarily in 2008 reflecting the weaker world economy. Electronics use of gold still is projected to increase this year on a worldwide basis, but the increase may be a relatively modest 5.4% to 9.4 million ounces.

Gold is used in many electronic components that are now contained ubiquitously in products ranging from the obvious electronic consumer products that seem indispensible to life around the world, to processers and process control devices in everything from electronic manufacturing equipment to automobiles, household appliances, thermostats, and so many other products. The demand for these goods is among the strongest segments of consumer preferences, showing strong resilience during times of economic weakness. Consumer demand for electronic goods, most of which have some small amount of gold in them, seems insatiable.

The data here represents gold use where it is fabricated into the first manufactured products. These products range from plating salts to sputtering targets and various wires and pastes used in manufacturing electronic switches, gears, controllers, connectors, and other components that go into consumer and industrial products.

Most of the increases are occurring in Japan and a wide range of Asian countries that are emerging as important manufacturers of electronic components. India is a leader in this area, but demand also is rising in Taiwan, Thailand, Malaysia, and other countries. China also is growing in importance as a site for the manufacture of gold-bearing electronic microchips, connectors, contacts, and other products. Chinese demand for gold for use in conversion into plating salts, sputtering targets, wire, tubes, and other forms of gold semi-fabricated products that are used in electronics components is not included in these figures, however, as good data are not available yet.

Dental and Medical

Gold use in dental alloys, dental constructions, and a wide range of medical devices is estimated to have declined a modest 0.3% to 2.4 million ounces in 2007. This would mark the sixth year of the past seven years in which gold use in these applications has fallen slightly. In 2008 gold use in these products is projected to rise 1.1% to around 2.43 million ounces. The manufacturing of these products is spread around the world. In recent years there has been a shift away from Europe and to a lesser extent the United States and Japan, to having alloys and medical devices manufactured in various Asian nations.

Most of the gold used in dental and medical applications is used in dental fillings and crowns. In these uses, gold competes with palladium, ceramics, epoxies, and other materials. In the late 1990s gold and palladium were losing market share in fillings to more natural looking ceramics and epoxies. Tighter health insurance regulations have limited the amount of payments for fillings in many countries over the past few years, in ways which have encouraged patients to choose metal fillings instead of ceramics and epoxies. Generally speaking, insurance companies and national health insurance programs will pay a maximum amount per filling that covers the less expensive metal fillings, offering to allow the patients to choose the more expensive epoxies and ceramics if they will pay the difference. As a result of this, a larger number of patients have shifted back toward using metals fillings at the lower cost. Due to this, gold-palladium alloys have re-gained market share in dental fillings.

Meanwhile, the relative values of gold and palladium, used in alloy together, have shifted dramatically. While gold used to be relatively low priced, its price has risen sharply. Palladium prices earli-

er had shot up to $1,080, in early 2001, in a period of extremely tight palladium supplies. As a result of the tight supplies and high prices for palladium, many dental alloys had shifted to lower palladium content and a higher gold content. As the prices of the two metals reversed, with palladium falling and gold soaring, dental alloys have shifted back toward using more palladium and less gold.

The shift back to metals from ceramics and epoxies and the shift back toward palladium from gold as the dominant metal in alloys have largely negated each other in terms of their effects on gold usage in dental alloys. As a result, the volume of gold used in these products has been relatively flat since 2002.

Not all gold use in dental and medical applications goes into dental alloys. There also are a wide range of dental constructions, such as caps, that use gold. Medical implants often use gold because of the low level of interaction gold has with chemicals inside the human body. In India there has been aurvedic medicine using gold for many centuries. Last year around 64,000 ounces of gold were used in aurvedic medicines in India. There is a growing interest in some of these medicines outside of India, although the volumes of gold used outside of India are low at present.

Other Industrial

Another 4.6 million ounces of gold is estimated to have been used in other manufactured products in 2007. This marked a big increase in usage. It followed a 62.4% increase in gold use from 1.9 million ounces in 2005 to 3.1 million ounces in 2006. Much of the growth was in India, although demand also is estimated to have risen sharply in other Asian nations that are developing various industries using gold. This growth rate may continue this year, with the potential for at least an 18.7% increase to 5.5 million ounces in gold use in these various applications.

In many of these applications the amount of gold used is small per unit of manufactured product, the value of the gold contained in the products is low compared to the value of the product, the use of gold is indispensible due to gold's physical or chemical properties, and thus the use of gold in these applications is highly price inelastic.

The uses of gold are enormous. Gold is used in optical equipment, as a highly effective reflector. It is used in high-quality mirrors, used in a variety of industrial and scientific applications. Gold plated mirrors are used to bake paints and finishes on metal for high-corrosion resistance, for example. Gold also is being used increasing in some solar power units. While the volumes are low at present, these applications could represent a large growth area for future gold use in the next few years.

In India around 225,000 ounces of gold were used last year in the manufacture of jari, a cloth containing gold and silver threads that is popular for use in saris and other traditional clothes.

Gold is used in plating and decorative applications, ranging from gold leaf put on architectural features and office signs. It is used to plate a wide range of other things, from watch bands and pens to buttons on electronic stereo components.

Gold also is used in architectural plate glass. A thin coating, deposited using sputter targets and vapor deposition, can reflect heat while allowing sunshine into a building, reducing heating and cooling costs.

World Gold Use Per Capita

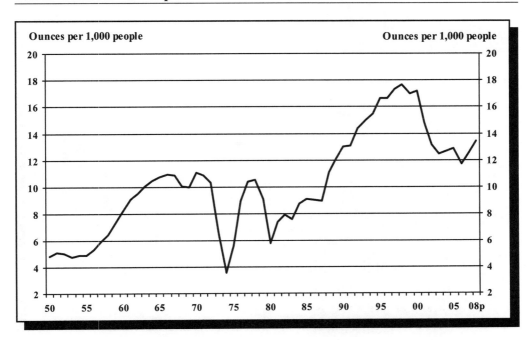

World Gold Use Per Unit of GDP

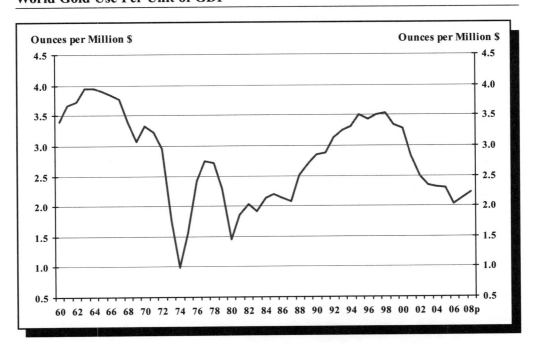

Annual Indian Gold Demand

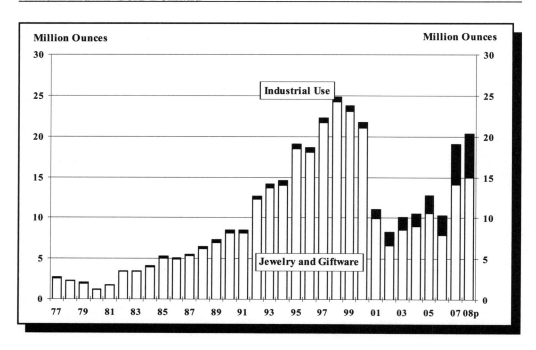

Annual Thai Demand

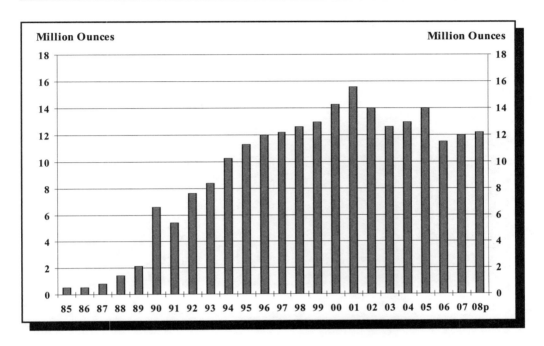

Annual U.S. Gold Demand

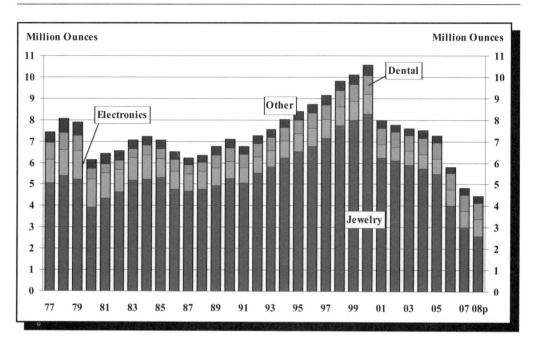

Annual Japanese Gold Demand

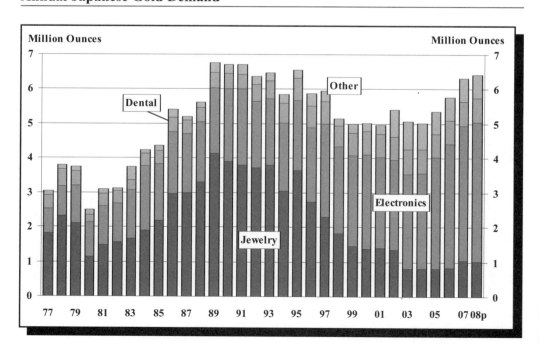

Annual European Gold Demand

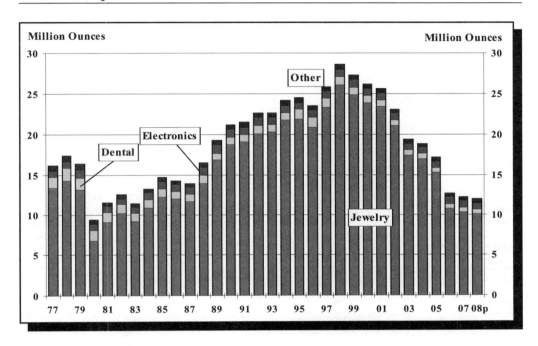

Annual Italian Fabrication Demand

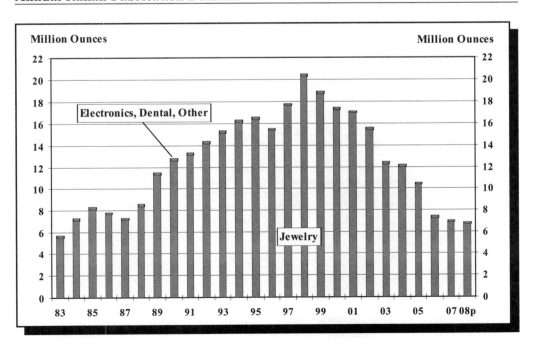

Annual Gold Use
Thousand Troy Ounces

	1985	1986	1987	1988	1989	1990	1991	1992	1993	1994	1995	1996
Electronics												
United States	900	830	800	820	835	825	750	750	760	798	835	867
Japan	1,641	1,788	1,721	1,752	1,900	2,124	2,200	1,914	1,923	2,000	2,019	2,160
Europe	923	910	920	1,039	1,096	1,000	957	902	870	872	863	869
Other	106	157	220	241	248	264	240	235	230	240	300	365
Subtotal	3,570	3,685	3,661	3,852	4,079	4,213	4,147	3,801	3,783	3,910	4,017	4,261
% of Total	8.1%	8.3%	8.1%	6.8%	6.5%	6.1%	5.9%	4.9%	4.6%	4.5%	4.3%	4.4%
% Change Year Ago	-9.7%	3.2%	-0.7%	5.2%	5.9%	3.3%	-1.6%	-8.3%	-0.5%	3.4%	2.7%	6.1%
Dental/Medical												
United States	444	525	400	425	600	625	620	620	620	625	654	678
Japan	390	428	383	418	434	418	430	510	530	570	638	605
Europe	936	862	785	961	781	849	910	1,064	871	918	1149	1153
Other	80	77	111	113	113	125	110	110	110	120	145	170
Subtotal	1,850	1,892	1,679	1,917	1,928	2,017	2,070	2,304	2,131	2,233	2,586	2,606
% of Total	4.2%	4.3%	3.7%	3.4%	3.1%	2.9%	2.9%	2.9%	2.6%	2.6%	2.7%	2.7%
% Change Year Ago	0.4%	2.3%	-11.3%	14.2%	0.6%	4.6%	2.6%	11.3%	-7.5%	4.8%	15.8%	0.8%
Other Industrial												
United States	410	400	350	360	425	400	380	375	380	400	418	434
Japan	150	218	103	161	289	270	268	215	216	250	246	367
Europe	492	463	476	526	569	612	638	628	620	645	639	628
Other	135	183	220	174	206	250	185	180	180	200	240	280
Subtotal	1,187	1,264	1,149	1,221	1,489	1,532	1,471	1,398	1,396	1,495	1,543	1,709
% of Total	2.7%	2.8%	2.6%	2.2%	2.4%	2.2%	2.1%	1.8%	1.7%	1.7%	1.6%	1.8%
% Change Year Ago	3.0%	6.5%	-9.1%	6.2%	22.0%	2.9%	-4.0%	-4.9%	-0.1%	7.1%	3.2%	10.8%
Jewelry												
United States	5,295	4,773	4,693	4,773	4,923	5,250	5,040	5,520	5,821	6,228	6,514	6,762
Japan	2,184	2,967	2,999	3,295	4,145	3,900	3,810	3,724	3,798	3,035	3,655	2,745
Europe	12,323	12,057	11,764	13,947	16,834	18,751	19,029	20,066	20,285	21,760	21,897	20,908
Other developed	437	447	459	490	566	604	608	616	624	640	670	800
Developing	17,281	17,410	18,568	27,065	29,113	32,362	33,987	40,830	44,835	47,274	53,527	55,995
Subtotal	37,520	37,654	38,483	49,570	55,581	60,867	62,474	70,756	75,363	78,937	86,263	87,210
% of Total	85.0%	84.6%	85.6%	87.6%	88.1%	88.7%	89.0%	90.4%	91.2%	91.2%	91.4%	91.0%
% Change Year Ago	8.2%	0.4%	2.2%	28.8%	12.1%	9.5%	2.6%	13.3%	6.5%	4.7%	9.3%	1.1%
Total	44,127	44,495	44,973	56,560	63,077	68,628	70,161	78,259	82,674	86,575	94,409	95,788
% Change Year Ago	6.0%	0.8%	1.1%	25.8%	11.5%	8.8%	2.2%	11.5%	5.6%	4.7%	9.0%	1.5%

Notes: These statistics represent total fabrication demand, including metal recovered from old scrap but excluding gold use
in investment-related medals, medallions, and coins. Gold use in transitional economies also is excluded. There may be
discrepancies in sums and percentage changes due to rounding. e -- estimates. p--projections.
Longer term projections are available in CPM Group's Gold Supply, Demand, and Price: 10-Year Projections report.
Source: CPM Group.
January 19, 2008

1997	1998	1999	2000	2001	2002	2003	2004	2005	2006	2007e	2008p	
												Electronics
878	882	890	900	630	625	650	670	715	750	765	775	United States
2,722	2,533	2,650	2,725	2,625	2,585	2,735	2,775	3,238	3,575	3,900	4,019	Japan
873	912	916	933	894	811	773	783	813	838	843	841	Europe
383	458	460	475	550	533	575	650	700	2,300	3,400	3,750	Other
4,856	4,785	4,916	5,033	4,699	4,554	4,733	4,878	5,466	7,463	8,908	9,385	Subtotal
4.8%	4.6%	4.8%	4.8%	5.2%	5.6%	6.0%	6.0%	6.6%	9.7%	10.7%	10.5%	% of Total
14.0%	-1.5%	2.7%	2.4%	-6.6%	-3.1%	3.9%	3.1%	12.1%	36.5%	19.4%	5.4%	% Change Year Ago
												Dental/Medical
697	731	775	900	765	720	730	740	750	755	760	762	United States
642	602	640	682	669	700	720	687	671	691	694	707	Japan
1160	1024	938	842	780	724	680	679	612	574	569	580	Europe
180	251	260	300	345	335	345	375	400	390	380	380	Other
2,679	2,608	2,613	2,724	2,559	2,479	2,475	2,481	2,433	2,410	2,403	2,429	Subtotal
2.6%	2.5%	2.6%	2.6%	2.8%	3.0%	3.1%	3.1%	2.9%	3.1%	2.9%	2.7%	% of Total
2.8%	-2.7%	0.2%	4.2%	-6.1%	-3.1%	-0.2%	0.2%	-1.9%	-0.9%	-0.3%	1.1%	% Change Year Ago
												Other Industrial
445	449	460	470	353	340	350	360	365	320	325	328	United States
306	195	246	240	255	763	794	760	647	675	670	670	Japan
628	640	595	625	609	545	513	511	501	491	488	481	Europe
287	283	275	285	360	350	358	380	400	1,620	3,133	4,000	Other
1,666	1,567	1,576	1,620	1,577	1,998	2,015	2,011	1,913	3,106	4,616	5,479	Subtotal
1.6%	1.5%	1.5%	1.6%	1.7%	2.4%	2.6%	2.5%	2.3%	4.1%	5.6%	6.1%	% of Total
-2.5%	-5.9%	0.6%	2.8%	-2.7%	26.7%	0.9%	-0.2%	-4.9%	62.4%	48.6%	18.7%	% Change Year Ago
												Jewelry
7,145	7,752	7,985	8,300	6,225	6,100	5,900	5,750	5,465	4,000	3,000	2,600	United States
2,280	1,817	1,448	1,375	1,415	1,358	815	800	806	840	1,053	1,026	Japan
23,261	26,086	24,871	23,862	23,375	21,060	17,395	16,920	15,235	10,841	10,404	10,107	Europe
867	860	325	400	415	400	385	460	525	475	485	470	Other developed
58,400	59,085	58,274	61,000	50,926	44,058	45,027	47,690	51,282	47,430	52,081	58,272	Developing
91,953	95,600	92,903	94,937	82,356	72,976	69,522	71,620	73,313	63,586	67,023	72,475	Subtotal
90.9%	91.4%	91.1%	91.0%	90.3%	89.0%	88.3%	88.4%	88.2%	83.0%	80.8%	80.7%	% of Total
5.4%	4.0%	-2.8%	2.2%	-13.3%	-11.4%	-4.7%	3.0%	2.4%	-13.3%	5.4%	8.1%	% Change Year Ago
101,155	104,559	102,008	104,314	91,190	82,007	78,745	80,990	83,125	76,565	82,950	89,767	Total
5.6%	3.4%	-2.4%	2.3%	-12.6%	-10.1%	-4.0%	2.9%	2.6%	-7.9%	8.3%	8.2%	% Change Year Ago

Notes: These statistics represent total fabrication demand, including metal recovered
from old scrap but excluding gold use in investment-related medals, medallions, and
coins. Gold use in transitional economies also is excluded. There may be discrepancies
in sums and percentage changes due to rounding. e -- estimate, p -- projections.
Source: CPM Group.

Fabrication Demand by Country and Region

Thousand Troy Ounces

	1983	1984	1985	1986	1987	1988	1989	1990	1991	1992	1993	1994	1995
Japan	3,742	4,253	4,365	5,401	5,206	5,626	6,768	6,712	6,708	6,278	6,467	5,855	6,558
United States	7,085	7,237	7,049	6,528	6,243	6,378	6,792	7,100	6,790	7,265	7,581	8,051	8,421
Western Europe	11,484	13,256	14,674	14,291	13,995	16,473	19,326	21,211	21,534	22,660	22,647	24,195	24,547
Canada	383	373	370	363	347	360	421	355	327	289	334	350	360
Australia	93	56	64	87	83	79	87	95	81	81	81	81	83
South Africa	87	71	58	58	80	87	93	105	88	84	84	80	81
Latin America	743	653	784	1,193	849	981	1,151	850	893	937	1,000	930	850
Middle East	4,964	5,305	5,466	6,395	5,961	6,884	8,253	10,700	10,900	11,000	11,200	11,200	11,372
Indian Subcontinent	3,925	4,533	5,835	5,684	6,138	7,183	8,073	9,400	9,420	14,000	15,650	16,050	21,065
Far East (excluding Japan)	2,643	5,446	4,970	3,945	5,427	11,459	10,996	10,650	12,000	14,200	16,250	18,453	19,747
Africa (excluding South Africa)	450	457	492	550	643	1,051	1,116	1,450	1,420	1,380	1,380	1,330	1,325
Total	35,599	41,640	44,127	44,495	44,972	56,560	63,077	68,628	70,161	78,174	82,674	86,575	94,409

Notes: Fabrication statistics in this table are estimates of net offtake of gold including
secondary metal recovered from industrial scrap and dishoarded materials. This table
excludes gold consumed in the fabrication of official coins and medallions. It also
excludes fabrication demand in the transitional economies.
Sources: U.S. Bureau of Mines; Consolidated Gold Fields; industry sources; CPM Group.
January 19, 2008

1996	1997	1998	1999	2000	2001	2002	2003	2004	2005	2006	2007e	2008p	
5,877	5,950	5,147	4,984	5,022	4,964	5,406	5,064	5,022	5,362	5,781	6,317	6,422	Japan
8,741	9,165	9,814	10,110	10,570	7,973	7,785	7,630	7,520	7,295	5,825	4,850	4,465	United States
23,559	25,922	28,661	27,320	26,262	25,658	23,140	19,361	18,893	17,161	12,744	12,304	12,008	Western Europe
382	390	400	408	416	425	404	395	400	406	350	360	390	Canada
87	89	91	93	94	96	92	85	90	88	80	82	90	Australia
82	83	84	84	83	84	81	80	85	83	75	75	80	South Africa
980	1,000	1,010	1,025	1,056	1,072	965	1,000	1,030	1,050	945	970	960	Latin America
12,600	12,935	12,642	12,300	12,788	13,399	11,541	13,940	15,600	17,000	19,000	20,700	22,962	Middle East
21,157	23,220	25,700	24,500	22,000	10,866	7,343	9,540	10,000	11,600	7,900	14,082	14,900	Indian Subcontinent
													Far East
20,975	21,050	19,700	19,900	24,726	25,344	24,100	20,600	21,300	22,000	22,875	22,200	26,500	(excluding Japan)
													Africa (excluding
1,348	1,351	1,310	1,284	1,297	1,310	1,150	1,050	1,050	1,080	990	1,010	990	South Africa)
95,788	101,155	104,559	102,008	104,314	91,190	82,007	78,745	80,990	83,125	76,565	82,950	89,767	Total

Indian Fabrication Demand

Thousand Ounces

	1977	1978	1979	1980	1981	1982	1983
Jewelry	2,571.0	2,215.7	1,945.1	1,159.3	1,698.7	3,371.6	3,393.2
Industrial Use	135.3	116.6	102.4	61.0	89.4	177.5	178.6
Total	2,706.3	2,332.3	2,047.5	1,220.3	1,788.1	3,549.1	3,571.8
% Change Year Ago	--	-13.8%	-12.2%	-40.4%	46.5%	98.5%	0.6%

	1984	1985	1986	1987	1988	1989	1990
Jewelry	3,918.8	5,044.4	4,913.8	5,306.0	6,209.3	6,979.1	8,126.3
Industrial Use	206.3	265.5	258.6	279.2	326.8	367.3	427.7
Total	4,125.1	5,309.9	5,172.4	5,585.2	6,536.1	7,346.4	8,554.0
% Change Year Ago	15.5%	28.7%	-2.6%	8.0%	17.0%	12.4%	16.4%

	1991	1992	1993	1994	1995	1996	1997
Jewelry	8,143.6	12,230.4	13,632.0	13,957.0	18,486.7	18,004.4	21,700.0
Industrial Use	428.6	509.6	568.0	643.0	578.7	643.0	643.0
Total	8,572.2	12,740.0	14,200.0	14,600.0	19,065.4	18,647.4	22,343.0
% Change Year Ago	0.2%	48.6%	11.5%	2.8%	30.6%	-2.2%	19.8%

	1998	1999	2000	2001	2002	2003	2004
Jewelry and Giftware	24,209.5	23,065.0	21,000.0	8,841.4	4,951.2	6,912.3	7,394.7
Industrial Use	707.3	735.0	770.0	1,125.3	1,671.8	1,607.5	1,607.5
Total	24,916.8	23,800.0	21,770.0	9,966.7	6,623.0	8,519.8	9,002.2
% Change Year Ago	11.5%	-4.5%	-8.5%	-54.2%	-33.5%	28.6%	5.7%
Investment				11,574.3	9,838.1	12,860.3	16,075.4

	2005	2006	2007e	2008p
Jewelry and Giftware	8,359.2	5,400.0	9,098.6	9,400.0
Industrial Use	2,250.5	2,500.0	4,983.4	5,500.0
Total	10,609.7	7,900.0	14,082.0	14,900.0
% Change Year Ago	17.9%	-25.5%	78.3%	5.8%
Investment	19,290.4	20,500.0	15,432.3	16,000.0

Notes: Totals may not equal the sums of individual categories due to rounding. Jewelry
includes decorative and investment items through 2000.
Sources: Indian market sources; CPM Group.
January 18, 2008

Thai Gold Market

Thousand Troy Ounces

	1985	1986	1987	1988	1989	1990	1991
Supply							
Official Imports	140.2	130.6	213.8	360.3	526.4	1,655.4	1,359.2
Smuggling	420.5	391.9	641.3	1,081.0	1,579.3	4,966.3	4,077.7
Total	560.6	522.6	855.0	1,441.4	2,105.7	6,621.7	5,436.9
% Change Year Ago	-	-6.8%	63.6%	68.6%	46.1%	214.5%	-17.9%
Fabrication Demand	560.6	522.6	855.0	1,441.4	2,105.7	6,621.7	5,436.9
% Change Year Ago	-	-6.8%	63.6%	68.6%	46.1%	214.5%	-17.9%

	1992	1993	1994	1995	1996	1997	1998
Supply							
Official Imports	1,911.4	2,102.5	3,858.1	4,822.6	5,112.0	5,215.0	-
Smuggling	5,734.1	6,307.5	6,400.0	6,477.0	6,866.0	7,010.0	-
Total	7,645.5	8,410.0	10,258.1	11,299.6	11,978.0	12,225.0	-
% Change Year Ago	40.6%	10.0%	22.0%	10.2%	6.0%	2.1%	-
Fabrication Demand	7,645.5	8,410.0	10,258.1	11,299.6	11,978.0	12,225.0	12,653.0
% Change Year Ago	40.6%	10.0%	22.0%	10.2%	6.0%	2.1%	3.5%

	1999	2000	2001	2002	2003	2004	2005
Fabrication Demand	13,000.0	14,300.0	15,600.0	14,000.0	12,600.0	13,000.0	14,000.0
% Change Year Ago	2.7%	10.0%	9.1%	-10.3%	-10.0%	3.2%	7.7%

	2006	2007e	2008p
Fabrication Demand	11,500.0	12,000.0	12,200.0
% Change Year Ago	-17.9%	4.3%	1.7%

Sources: Trade sources, CPM Group.
January 22, 2008

Total European Fabrication Demand
Thousand Ounces

	1983	1984	1985	1986	1987	1988	1989	1990	1991
Jewelry	9,262.6	10,944.1	12,323.4	12,056.5	11,764.2	13,947.4	16,834.1	18,751.2	19,029.2
Electronics	778.0	884.1	922.7	909.9	919.6	1,038.5	1,096.4	999.5	957.4
Dental/Medical	961.3	951.7	935.6	861.6	784.5	961.3	826.4	849.1	909.5
Other	482.3	475.8	491.9	463.0	476.2	526.2	569.1	611.5	637.5
Total	11,484.3	13,255.8	14,673.6	14,291.0	13,944.5	16,473.4	19,326.0	21,211.3	21,533.6
% Change Year Ago	--	15.4%	10.7%	-2.6%	-2.4%	18.1%	17.3%	9.8%	1.5%
Medals	67.5	77.1	67.5	86.8	167.1	215.4	218.5	254.2	241.2
Total Including Medals	11,551.7	13,332.9	14,741.1	14,377.8	14,111.6	16,688.8	19,544.4	21,465.4	21,774.7
% Change Year Ago	--	15.4%	10.6%	-2.5%	-1.9%	18.3%	17.1%	9.8%	1.4%

	1992	1993	1994	1995	1996	1997	1998	1999	2000
Jewelry	20,066.0	20,285.0	21,760.0	21,897.0	20,908.1	23,261.0	26,085.7	24,871.0	23,862.0
Electronics	902.1	870.2	872.0	862.7	869.0	872.7	911.8	916.0	933.0
Dental/Medical	1,064.3	871.4	918.0	1,148.7	1,153.1	1,160.0	1,023.6	938.0	842.0
Other	627.9	619.9	645.0	638.8	628.4	628.0	640.3	595.0	625.0
Subtotal	22,660.3	22,646.5	24,195.0	24,547.2	23,558.6	25,921.7	28,661.4	27,320.0	26,262.0
% Change Year Ago	5.2%	-0.1%	6.8%	1.5%	-4.0%	10.0%	10.6%	-4.7%	-3.9%
Medals	235.3	134.3	93.0	70.4	51.4	47.2	47.2	29.0	
Total Including Medals	22,895.5	22,780.8	24,288.0	24,617.6	23,610.0	25,968.9	28,708.6	27,349.0	
% Change Year Ago	5.1%	-0.5%	6.6%	1.4%	-4.1%	10.0%	10.5%	-4.7%	

	2001	2002	2003	2004	2005	2006	2007e	2008p	
Jewelry	23,375.0	21,060.0	17,395.0	16,920.0	15,235.0	10,841.0	10,404.0	10,107.0	
Electronics	894.0	811.0	773.0	783.0	813.0	838.0	843.0	841.0	
Dental/Medical	780.0	724.0	680.0	679.0	612.0	574.0	569.0	579.5	
Other	609.0	545.0	513.0	511.0	501.0	491.0	488.0	480.5	
Subtotal	25,658.0	23,140.0	19,361.0	18,893.0	17,161.0	12,744.0	12,304.0	12,008.0	
% Change Year Ago	-2.3%	-9.8%	-16.3%	-2.4%	-9.2%	-25.7%	-3.5%	-2.4%	

Notes: Totals may not equal the sums of individual categories due to rounding. Gold use in coinage is excluded.
Sources: Consolidated Gold Fields; CPM Group.
January 26, 2008

Italian Fabrication Demand

Thousand Ounces

	1983	1984	1985	1986	1987	1988	1989	1990
Jewelry	5,529.9	7,073.2	8,134.1	7,651.9	7,137.5	8,423.6	11,252.7	12,600.0
Electronics	35.4	41.8	41.8	41.8	22.5	32.2	35.4	35.1
Dental/Medical	147.9	147.9	141.5	141.5	141.5	144.7	144.7	148.0
Other	61.1	61.1	61.1	64.3	48.2	54.7	57.9	58.0
Total	5,774.2	7,324.0	8,378.4	7,899.5	7,349.7	8,655.0	11,490.7	12,841.1
% Change Year Ago	-	26.8%	14.4%	-5.7%	-7.0%	17.8%	32.8%	11.8%
Medals	19.3	22.5	25.7	32.2	128.6	141.5	128.6	192.9
Total Including Medals	5,793.5	7,346.5	8,404.2	7,931.6	7,478.3	8,796.5	11,619.3	13,034.0
% Change Year Ago	-	26.8%	14.4%	-5.6%	-5.7%	17.6%	32.1%	12.2%

	1991	1992	1993	1994	1995	1996	1997	1998
Jewelry	13,104.6	14,150.0	15,141.0	16,100.0	16,325.0	15,330.0	17,600.0	20,240.0
Electronics	35.1	28.9	29.0	26.0	27.0	27.3	27.7	28.0
Dental/Medical	157.5	154.3	155.0	146.0	150.0	141.0	141.0	148.0
Other	61.1	64.3	65.0	66.0	66.0	62.0	60.0	62.0
Total	13,358.3	14,397.5	15,389.8	16,337.8	16,567.8	15,560.3	17,828.7	20,478.0
% Change Year Ago	4.0%	7.8%	6.9%	6.2%	1.4%	-6.1%	14.6%	14.9%
Medals	192.9	192.9	96.5	50.0	29.0	16.0	15.0	15.0
Total Including Medals	13,551.2	14,590.4	15,486.3	16,387.8	16,596.8	15,576.3	17,843.7	20,493.0
% Change Year Ago	4.0%	7.7%	6.1%	5.8%	1.3%	-6.1%	14.6%	14.8%

	1999	2000	2001	2002	2003	2004	2005	2006
Jewelry	18,722.0	17,225.0	16,900.0	15,375.0	12,250.0	12,000.0	10,380.0	7,266.0
Electronics	28.0	30.0	29.0	30.0	30.0	30.0	28.0	30.0
Dental/Medical	150.0	160.0	153.0	145.0	135.0	132.0	130.0	130.0
Other	62.0	65.0	63.0	50.0	48.0	48.0	42.0	40.0
Total	18,962.0	17,480.0	17,145.0	15,600.0	12,463.0	12,210.0	10,580.0	7,466.0
% Change Year Ago	-7.4%	-7.8%	-1.9%	-9.0%	-20.1%	-2.0%	-13.3%	-29.4%

	2007e	2008p
Jewelry	6,900.0	6,700.0
Electronics	31.0	30.0
Dental/Medical	131.0	130.0
Other	40.0	39.0
Total	7,102.0	6,899.0
% Change Year Ago	-4.9%	-2.9%

Notes: Totals may not equal the sums of individual categories due to rounding. Gold use in coinage is excluded.
Sources: Consolidated Gold Fields; CPM Group.
January 26, 2008

U.S. Gold Fabrication Demand
Thousand Troy Ounces

	1976	1977	1978	1979	1980	1981	1982	1983
Jewelry	4,575	5,070	5,382	5,220	3,952	4,335	4,641	5,170
Electronics	935	1,060	1,229	1,340	1,293	1,205	1,043	1,070
Dental/Medical	729	797	811	716	466	415	428	420
Other	624	527	632	611	452	470	449	425
Total	6,863	7,454	8,054	7,887	6,163	6,425	6,561	7,085
% Change Year Ago	--	8.6%	8.0%	-2.1%	-21.9%	4.3%	2.1%	8.0%

	1984	1985	1986	1987	1988	1989	1990	1991
Jewelry	5,242	5,295	4,773	4,693	4,773	4,932	5,250	5,040
Electronics	1,120	900	830	800	820	835	825	750
Dental/Medical	435	444	525	400	425	600	625	620
Other	440	410	400	350	360	425	400	380
Total	7,237	7,049	6,528	6,243	6,378	6,792	7,100	6,790
% Change Year Ago	2.1%	-2.6%	-7.4%	-4.4%	2.2%	6.5%	4.5%	-4.4%

	1992	1993	1994	1995	1996	1997	1998	1999
Jewelry	5,520	5,821	6,228	6,514	6,762	7,145	7,752	7,985
Electronics	750	760	798	835	867	878	882	890
Dental/Medical	620	620	625	654	678	697	731	775
Other	375	380	400	418	434	445	449	460
Total	7,265	7,581	8,051	8,421	8,741	9,165	9,814	10,110
% Change Year Ago	7.0%	4.3%	6.2%	4.6%	3.8%	4.9%	7.1%	3.0%

	2000	2001	2002	2003	2004	2005	2006	2007e
Jewelry	8,300	6,225	6,100	5,900	5,750	5,465	4,000	3,000
Electronics	900	630	625	650	670	715	750	765
Dental/Medical	900	765	720	730	740	750	755	760
Other	470	353	340	350	360	365	320	325
Total	10,570	7,973	7,785	7,630	7,520	7,295	5,825	4,850
% Change Year Ago	4.5%	-24.6%	-2.4%	-2.0%	-1.4%	-3.0%	-20.2%	-16.7%

	2008p
Jewelry	2,600
Electronics	775
Dental/Medical	762
Other	328
Total	4,465
% Change Year Ago	-7.9%

Notes: Investment-related articles have been excluded from these figures.
Sources: U.S. Bureau of Mines; CPM Group.
January 18, 2008

Japanese Gold Fabrication Demand

Thousand Troy Ounces

	1976	1977	1978	1979	1980	1981	1982	1983
Jewelry	1,886	1,817	2,304	2,117	1,156	1,492	1,559	1,654
Electronics	768	703	883	1,081	976	1,109	1,113	1,428
Dental/Medical	469	402	472	429	206	374	363	275
Other	171	134	138	128	164	132	86	385
Total	3,294	3,056	3,797	3,755	2,502	3,107	3,121	3,742
% Change Year Ago	--	-7.2%	24.2%	-1.1%	-33.4%	24.2%	0.5%	19.9%

	1984	1985	1986	1987	1988	1989	1990	1991
Jewelry	1,911	2,184	2,967	2,999	3,295	4,145	3,900	3,810
Electronics	1,868	1,641	1,788	1,721	1,752	1,900	2,124	2,200
Dental/Medical	369	390	428	383	418	434	418	430
Other	105	150	218	103	161	289	270	268
Total	4,253	4,365	5,401	5,206	5,626	6,768	6,712	6,708
% Change Year Ago	13.7%	2.6%	23.7%	-3.6%	8.1%	20.3%	-0.8%	-0.1%

	1992	1993	1994	1995	1996	1997	1998	1999
Jewelry	3,724	3,798	3,035	3,655	2,745	2,280	1,817	1,448
Electronics	1,914	1,923	2,000	2,019	2,160	2,722	2,533	2,650
Dental/Medical	510	530	570	638	605	642	602	640
Other	215	216	250	246	367	306	195	246
Total	6,363	6,467	5,855	6,558	5,877	5,950	5,147	4,984
% Change Year Ago	-5.1%	1.6%	-9.5%	12.0%	-10.4%	1.2%	-13.5%	-3.2%

	2000	2001	2002	2003	2004	2005	2006	2007e
Jewelry	1,375	1,415	1,358	815	800	806	840	1,053
Electronics	2,725	2,625	2,585	2,735	2,775	3,238	3,575	3,900
Dental/Medical	682	669	700	720	687	671	691	694
Other	240	255	763	794	760	647	675	670
Total	5,022	4,964	5,406	5,064	5,022	5,362	5,781	6,317
% Change Year Ago	0.8%	-1.2%	8.9%	-6.3%	-0.8%	6.8%	7.8%	9.3%

	2008p
Jewelry	1,026
Electronics	4,019
Dental/Medical	707
Other	670
Total	6,422
% Change Year Ago	1.7%

Notes: Investment-related articles have been excluded from these figures. Categories were revised based on Japanese trade sources for the years starting 2003
Sources: Japanese trade sources; CPM Group.
January 26, 2008

German Fabrication Demand
Thousand Ounces

	1983	1984	1985	1986	1987	1988	1989
Jewelry	1,061.0	1,115.6	1,157.4	1,221.7	1,366.4	1,607.6	1,190.0
Electronics	215.4	263.6	286.1	270.1	295.8	344.0	385.8
Dental/Medical	553.0	549.8	536.9	353.7	379.4	562.6	373.0
Other	183.3	189.7	192.9	160.8	167.2	183.3	215.4
Total	2,012.6	2,118.7	2,173.4	2,102.7	2,208.8	2,697.4	2,164.2
% Change Year Ago	-	5.3%	2.6%	-3.3%	5.0%	22.1%	-19.8%

	1990	1991	1992	1993	1994	1995	1996
Jewelry	1,286.0	1,446.8	1,286.0	1,221.7	1,344.0	1,151.0	1,093.1
Electronics	321.5	305.4	257.2	225.1	226.0	234.7	234.7
Dental/Medical	385.8	450.1	463.0	446.9	475.0	443.7	450.1
Other	241.1	257.2	244.3	234.7	240.0	221.8	215.4
Total	2,234.4	2,459.5	2,250.5	2,128.3	2,284.9	2,051.2	1,993.3
% Change Year Ago	3.2%	10.1%	-8.5%	-5.4%	7.4%	-10.2%	-2.8%
Medals	12.9	12.9	13.0	10.0	13.0	10.0	10.0
Total Including Medals	2,247.3	2,472.4	2,263.5	2,138.3	2,297.9	2,061.2	2,003.3
% Change Year Ago	3.1%	10.0%	-8.4%	-5.5%	7.5%	-10.3%	-2.8%

	1997	1998	1999	2000	2001	2002	2003
Jewelry	1,093.0	1,040.0	1,180.0	1,300.0	1,245.0	800.0	800.0
Electronics	235.0	245.0	250.0	255.0	245.0	215.0	190.0
Dental/Medical	451.0	293.0	265.0	325.0	300.0	275.0	240.0
Other	215.0	220.0	200.0	212.0	205.0	185.0	165.0
Total	1,994.0	1,798.0	1,895.0	2,092.0	1,995.0	1,475.0	1,395.0
% Change Year Ago	0.0%	-9.8%	5.4%	10.4%	-4.6%	-26.1%	-5.4%
Medals	10.0	10.0	10.0				
Total Including Medals	2,004.0	1,808.0	1,905.0				
% Change Year Ago	0.0%	-9.8%	5.4%				

	2004	2005	2006	2007e	2008p
Jewelry	750.0	750.0	565.0	555.0	540.0
Electronics	195.0	205.0	210.0	213.0	210.0
Dental/Medical	245.0	210.0	175.0	172.0	170.0
Other	165.0	165.0	160.0	160.0	158.0
Total	1,355.0	1,330.0	1,110.0	1,100.0	1,078.0
% Change Year Ago	-2.9%	-1.8%	-16.5%	-0.9%	-2.0%

Notes: Totals may not equal the sums of individual categories due to rounding. Gold use in coinage is excluded.
Sources: Consolidated Gold Fields; CPM Group.
January 26, 2008

United Kingdom Fabrication Demand

Thousand Ounces

	1983	1984	1985	1986	1987	1988	1989
Jewelry	366.5	411.5	463.0	482.3	514.4	617.3	707.3
Electronics	228.3	270.1	279.7	282.9	289.4	331.2	350.4
Dental/Medical	16.1	12.9	12.9	12.9	12.9	12.9	12.9
Other	64.3	70.7	73.9	64.3	64.3	67.5	64.3
Total	675.2	765.2	829.5	842.3	880.9	1,028.9	1,134.9
% Change Year Ago	-	13.3%	8.4%	1.6%	4.6%	16.8%	10.3%
Medals	3.2	3.2	3.2	6.4	6.4	6.4	6.4
Total Including Medals	678.4	768.4	832.7	848.8	887.4	1,035.3	1,141.3
% Change Year Ago	-	13.3%	8.4%	1.9%	4.5%	16.7%	10.2%

	1990	1991	1992	1993	1994	1995	1996
Jewelry	735.0	645.0	655.0	668.0	735.0	800.0	850.0
Electronics	330.0	320.1	315.0	303.0	280.0	265.0	268.0
Dental/Medical	13.0	13.0	12.0	13.0	15.0	17.0	17.0
Other	67.0	63.6	62.0	62.3	64.0	66.0	66.0
Total	1,145.0	1,041.7	1,044.0	1,046.3	1,094.0	1,148.0	1,201.0
% Change Year Ago	0.9%	-9.0%	0.2%	0.2%	4.6%	4.9%	4.6%
Medals	6.4	6.4	6.4	6.4	6.4	3.0	3.0
Total Including Medals	1,151.4	1,048.1	1,050.4	1,052.7	1,100.4	1,151.0	1,204.0
% Change Year Ago	0.9%	-9.0%	0.2%	0.2%	4.5%	4.6%	4.6%

	1997	1998	1999	2000	2001	2002	2003
Jewelry	905.0	977.0	995.0	1,150.0	1,185.0	1,070.0	1,040.0
Electronics	271.0	282.0	280.0	285.0	265.0	240.0	245.0
Dental/Medical	18.0	19.0	18.0	25.0	20.0	18.0	20.0
Other	67.0	68.3	68.0	70.0	68.0	65.0	65.0
Total	1,261.0	1,346.3	1,361.0	1,530.0	1,538.0	1,393.0	1,370.0
% Change Year Ago	5.0%	6.8%	1.1%	12.4%	0.5%	-9.4%	-1.7%
Medals	3.0	3.0	3.0				
Total Including Medals	1,264.0	1,349.3	1,364.0				
% Change Year Ago	5.0%	6.7%	1.1%				

	2004	2005	2006	2007e	2008p
Jewelry	1,000.0	970.0	575.0	558.0	540.0
Electronics	255.0	265.0	280.0	278.0	280.0
Dental/Medical	20.0	20.0	20.0	18.0	18.0
Other	65.0	65.0	65.0	64.0	64.0
Total	1,340.0	1,320.0	940.0	918.0	902.0
% Change Year Ago	-2.2%	-1.5%	-28.8%	-2.3%	-1.7%

Notes: Totals may not equal the sums of individual categories due to rounding. Gold use in coinage is excluded.
Sources: Consolidated Gold Fields; CPM Group.
January 26, 2008

French Fabrication Demand
Thousand Ounces

	1983	1984	1985	1986	1987	1988	1989
Jewelry	559.4	536.9	562.6	639.8	655.9	717.0	787.7
Electronics	96.5	86.8	83.6	73.9	77.2	83.6	86.8
Dental/Medical	35.4	32.2	32.2	25.7	25.7	22.5	22.5
Other	73.9	57.9	61.1	73.9	77.2	86.8	93.2
Total	765.2	713.7	739.5	813.4	835.9	909.9	990.2
% Change Year Ago	-	-6.7%	3.6%	10.0%	2.8%	8.9%	8.8%
Medals	6.4	3.2	6.4	3.2	6.4	3.2	6.4
Total Including Medals	771.6	717.0	745.9	816.6	842.3	913.1	996.6
% Change Year Ago	-	-7.1%	4.0%	9.5%	3.1%	8.4%	9.1%

	1990	1991	1992	1993	1994	1995	1996
Jewelry	945.2	913.0	925.0	934.2	1,020.0	1,061.0	1,070.0
Electronics	86.8	86.8	85.0	95.0	105.0	100.0	100.0
Dental/Medical	22.5	22.2	20.0	21.0	24.0	26.0	27.0
Other	100.0	100.0	96.0	97.0	110.0	110.0	110.0
Total	1,154.5	1,122.0	1,126.0	1,147.2	1,259.0	1,297.0	1,307.0
% Change Year Ago	16.6%	-2.8%	0.4%	1.9%	9.7%	3.0%	0.8%
Medals	6.4	6.4	6.4	4.8	4.0	3.0	3.0
Total Including Medals	1,160.9	1,128.4	1,132.4	1,152.0	1,263.0	1,300.0	1,310.0
% Change Year Ago	16.5%	-2.8%	0.4%	1.7%	9.6%	2.9%	0.8%

	1997	1998	1999	2000	2001	2002	2003
Jewelry	1,085.0	1,110.0	1,120.0	1,200.0	1,160.0	1,090.0	930.0
Electronics	100.0	110.0	110.0	112.0	112.0	102.0	95.0
Dental/Medical	27.0	27.0	24.0	35.0	30.0	25.0	25.0
Other	110.0	110.0	100.0	105.0	103.0	90.0	85.0
Total	1,322.0	1,357.0	1,354.0	1,452.0	1,405.0	1,307.0	1,135.0
% Change Year Ago	1.1%	2.6%	-0.2%	7.2%	-3.2%	-7.0%	-13.2%
Medals	3.0	3.0	3.0				
Total Including Medals	1,325.0	1,360.0	1,357.0				
% Change Year Ago	1.1%	2.6%	-0.2%				

	2004	2005	2006	2007e	2008p
Jewelry	895.0	885.0	675.0	670.0	657.0
Electronics	93.0	96.0	97.0	98.0	98.0
Dental/Medical	22.0	24.0	23.0	23.0	22.5
Other	80.0	80.0	80.0	80.0	77.5
Total	1,090.0	1,085.0	875.0	871.0	855.0
% Change Year Ago	-4.0%	-0.5%	-19.4%	-0.5%	-1.8%

Notes: Totals may not equal the sums of individual categories due to rounding. Gold use in coinage is excluded.
Sources: Consolidated Gold Fields; CPM Group.
January 26, 2008

Swiss Fabrication Demand

Thousand Ounces

	1983	1984	1985	1986	1987	1988	1989
Jewelry	479.0	572.3	652.7	652.7	598.0	813.4	835.9
Electronics	99.7	99.7	99.7	93.2	106.1	115.7	122.2
Dental/Medical	115.7	115.7	115.7	109.3	109.3	102.9	102.9
Other	57.9	57.9	61.1	64.3	80.4	90.0	93.2
Total	752.3	845.6	929.2	919.5	893.8	1,122.0	1,154.2
% Change Year Ago	-	12.4%	9.9%	-1.0%	-2.8%	25.5%	2.9%
Medals	12.9	25.7	3.2	28.9	12.9	45.0	51.4
Total Including Medals	765.2	871.3	932.4	948.4	906.7	1,167.0	1,205.7
% Change Year Ago	-	13.9%	7.0%	1.7%	-4.4%	28.7%	3.3%

	1990	1991	1992	1993	1994	1995	1996
Jewelry	1,000.0	850.0	875.0	893.0	965.0	900.0	885.0
Electronics	120.0	126.0	136.0	137.4	150.0	150.0	151.0
Dental/Medical	103.0	105.9	106.0	106.5	118.0	125.0	128.0
Other	102.0	112.2	112.0	112.3	120.0	126.0	126.0
Total	1,325.0	1,194.1	1,229.0	1,249.2	1,353.0	1,301.0	1,290.0
% Change Year Ago	14.8%	-9.9%	2.9%	1.6%	8.3%	-3.8%	-0.8%
Medals	26.0	13.0	7.0	7.0	10.0	19.0	13.0
Total Including Medals	1,351.1	1,207.2	1,236.0	1,256.2	1,363.0	1,320.0	1,303.0
% Change Year Ago	12.1%	-10.7%	2.4%	1.6%	8.5%	-3.2%	-1.3%

	1997	1998	1999	2000	2001	2002	2003
Jewelry	867.0	936.0	1,050.0	1,100.0	1,060.0	945.0	815.0
Electronics	151.0	154.0	155.0	157.0	150.0	135.0	130.0
Dental/Medical	128.0	134.0	122.0	130.0	125.0	115.0	110.0
Other	126.0	127.0	115.0	120.0	118.0	105.0	100.0
Total	1,272.0	1,351.0	1,442.0	1,507.0	1,453.0	1,300.0	1,155.0
% Change Year Ago	-1.4%	6.2%	6.7%	4.5%	-3.6%	-10.5%	-11.2%
Medals	10.0	10.0	10.0				
Total Including Medals	1,282.0	1,361.0	1,452.0				
% Change Year Ago	-1.6%	6.2%	6.7%				

	2004	2005	2006	2007e	2008p
Jewelry	780.0	785.0	555.0	545.0	530.0
Electronics	130.0	138.0	139.0	140.0	140.0
Dental/Medical	112.0	110.0	110.0	110.0	109.0
Other	103.0	102.0	100.0	100.0	99.0
Total	1,125.0	1,135.0	904.0	895.0	878.0
% Change Year Ago	-2.6%	0.9%	-20.4%	-1.0%	-1.9%

Notes: Totals may not equal the sums of individual categories due to rounding. Gold use in coinage is excluded.
Sources: Consolidated Gold Fields; CPM Group.
January 26, 2008

Spanish Fabrication Demand

Thousand Ounces

	1983	1984	1985	1986	1987	1988	1989	1990
Jewelry	430.8	405.1	466.2	501.6	572.3	771.6	964.5	1,093.0
Electronics	9.6	9.6	9.6	9.6	9.6	9.6	12.9	12.9
Dental/Medical	9.6	9.6	9.6	9.6	9.6	6.4	6.4	6.4
Other	16.1	16.1	16.1	16.1	16.1	19.3	25.7	25.7
Total	466.2	440.5	501.6	537.0	607.7	806.7	1,009.5	1,138.0
% Change Year Ago	-	-5.5%	13.9%	7.1%	13.2%	32.8%	25.1%	12.7%
Medals	3.2	-	3.2	3.2	-	3.2	6.4	6.4
Total Including Medals	469.4	440.5	504.8	540.2	607.7	806.7	1,009.5	1,144.4
% Change Year Ago	-	-6.2%	14.6%	7.0%	12.5%	32.8%	25.1%	13.4%

	1991	1992	1993	1994	1995	1996	1997	1998
Jewelry	983.0	985.8	677.7	746.0	760.0	768.0	784.0	840.0
Electronics	9.0	8.6	9.0	11.0	12.0	13.0	13.0	14.0
Dental/Medical	6.4	6.5	6.5	7.0	8.0	8.0	8.0	8.0
Other	23.2	22.1	24.3	27.0	29.0	29.0	30.0	31.0
Total	1,021.6	1,023.0	717.3	790.8	808.8	818.0	835.0	893.0
% Change Year Ago	-10.2%	0.1%	-29.9%	10.2%	2.3%	1.1%	2.1%	6.9%
Medals	6.4	6.4	6.4	6.4	3.2	3.2	3.2	3.2
Total Including Medals	1,028.0	1,029.4	723.7	797.2	812.0	821.2	838.2	896.2
% Change Year Ago	-10.2%	0.1%	-29.7%	10.2%	1.9%	1.1%	2.1%	6.9%

	1999	2000	2001	2002	2003	2004	2005	2006
Jewelry	850.0	900.0	860.0	835.0	750.0	720.0	700.0	570.0
Electronics	14.0	14.0	13.0	12.0	13.0	10.0	10.0	10.0
Dental/Medical	7.0	12.0	10.0	8.0	10.0	8.0	8.0	8.0
Other	30.0	32.0	31.0	30.0	30.0	30.0	28.0	28.0
Total	901.0	958.0	914.0	885.0	803.0	768.0	746.0	616.0
% Change Year Ago	0.9%	6.3%	-4.6%	-3.2%	-9.3%	-4.4%	-2.9%	-17.4%

	2007e	2008p
Jewelry	555.0	540.0
Electronics	10.0	10.0
Dental/Medical	8.0	8.0
Other	27.0	27.0
Total	600.0	585.0
% Change Year Ago	-2.6%	-2.5%

Notes: Totals may not equal the sums of individual categories due to rounding. Gold use in coinage is excluded.
Sources: Consolidated Gold Fields; CPM Group.
January 26, 2008

Greek Fabrication Demand

Thousand Ounces

	1983	1984	1985	1986	1987
Jewelry	254.0	257.2	289.4	289.4	273.3
Dental/Medical	3.2	3.2	3.2	16.1	16.1
Total	257.2	260.4	292.6	305.5	289.4
% Change Year Ago	--	1.3%	12.3%	4.4%	-5.3%

	1988	1989	1990	1991	1992
Jewelry	311.9	321.5	310.0	297.0	296.5
Dental/Medical	19.3	19.3	19.3	19.3	19.4
Total	331.0	340.8	329.3	316.3	315.9
% Change Year Ago	14.4%	3.0%	-3.4%	-3.9%	-0.1%

	1993	1994	1995	1996	1997
Jewelry	204.0	250.0	270.0	277.0	282.0
Dental/Medical	19.4	19.8	20.0	21.0	21.0
Total	223.4	269.8	290.0	298.0	303.0
% Change Year Ago	-29.3%	20.8%	7.5%	2.8%	1.7%

	1998	1999	2000	2001	2002
Jewelry	288.0	292.0	305.0	295.0	285.0
Dental/Medical	22.5	22.0	25.0	22.0	20.0
Total	310.5	314.0	330.0	317.0	305.0
% Change Year Ago	2.5%	1.1%	5.1%	-3.9%	-3.8%

	2003	2004	2005	2006	2007e
Jewelry	250.0	240.0	240.0	215.0	208.0
Dental/Medical	20.0	20.0	20.0	18.0	17.0
Total	270.0	260.0	260.0	233.0	225.0
% Change Year Ago	-11.5%	-3.7%	0.0%	-10.4%	-3.4%

	2008p
Jewelry	200.0
Dental/Medical	16.0
Total	216.0
% Change Year Ago	-4.0%

Notes: Totals may not equal the sums of individual categories due
to rounding. Gold use in coinage is excluded.
Sources: Consolidated Gold Fields; CPM Group.
January 26, 2008

Other European Fabrication Demand

Thousand Ounces

	1983	1984	1985	1986	1987	1988	1989
Jewelry	581.9	572.3	598.0	617.3	646.4	685.0	774.9
Electronics	93.2	112.5	122.2	138.2	119.0	122.2	102.9
Dental/Medical	80.4	80.4	83.6	96.5	90.0	90.0	99.7
Other	25.7	22.5	25.7	19.3	22.8	24.6	19.4
Total	781.2	787.7	829.5	871.4	878.2	921.6	996.9
% Change Year Ago	-	0.8%	5.3%	5.1%	0.8%	4.9%	8.2%
Medals	6.4	6.4	6.4	3.2	3.2	3.2	3.2
Total Including Medals	787.6	794.1	835.9	874.6	881.4	924.8	1,000.1
% Change Year Ago	-	0.8%	5.3%	4.6%	0.8%	4.9%	8.1%

	1990	1991	1992	1993	1994	1995	1996
Jewelry	782.0	789.8	793.0	545.1	600.0	630.0	635.0
Electronics	93.2	75.0	71.4	71.7	73.0	74.0	75.0
Dental/Medical	102.9	103.0	103.1	103.1	114.0	119.0	121.0
Other	17.7	15.1	14.3	14.3	18.0	20.0	20.0
Total	995.8	982.9	981.8	734.2	805.0	843.0	851.0
% Change Year Ago	-0.1%	-1.3%	-0.1%	-25.2%	9.6%	4.7%	0.9%
Medals	3.2	3.2	3.2	3.2	3.2	3.2	3.2
Total Including Medals	999.0	986.1	985.0	737.4	808.2	846.2	854.2
% Change Year Ago	-0.1%	-1.3%	-0.1%	-25.1%	9.6%	4.7%	0.9%

	1997	1998	1999	2000	2001	2002	2003
Jewelry	645.0	654.7	662.0	682.0	670.0	660.0	560.0
Electronics	75.0	78.8	79.0	80.0	80.0	77.0	70.0
Dental/Medical	121.0	127.1	120.0	130.0	120.0	118.0	120.0
Other	20.0	22.0	20.0	21.0	21.0	20.0	20.0
Total	861.0	882.6	881.0	913.0	891.0	875.0	770.0
% Change Year Ago	1.2%	2.5%	-0.2%	3.6%	-2.4%	-1.8%	-12.0%
Medals	3.0	3.0	3.0				
Total Including Medals	864.0	885.6	884.0				
% Change Year Ago	1.1%	2.5%	-0.2%				

	2004	2005	2006	2007e	2008p
Jewelry	535.0	525.0	420.0	413.0	400.0
Electronics	70.0	71.0	72.0	73.0	73.0
Dental/Medical	120.0	110.0	108.0	107.0	106.0
Other	20.0	19.0	18.0	17.0	16.0
Total	745.0	725.0	618.0	610.0	595.0
% Change Year Ago	-3.2%	-2.7%	-14.8%	-1.3%	-2.5%

Notes: Totals may not equal the sums of individual categories due to rounding. Gold use in coinage is excluded.
Sources: Consolidated Gold Fields; CPM Group.
January 26, 2008

Markets

Markets

Market interest in gold continued to increase last year, although clearing volume in the London interbank, or dealer, market declined slightly. New York's Commodities Exchange (Comex) remained the dominant futures and options exchange, compared to the Chicago Board of Trade (CBOT), the Tokyo Commodity Exchange (Tocom), and the Multi Commodity Exchange (MCX) in India.

Futures and Options

In 2007, the combined trading volume for gold contracts traded on the Comex, CBOT, Tocom, and MCX rose to 4.5 billion ounces. This was up 15.7% from the 3.9 billion ounce trading volume of 2006. Total trading volume increased due to a large increase in trading volume on the Comex. There were decreases in CBOT, Tocom, and MCX volumes.

Combined open interest on the three major futures and options exchanges rose 28.9% in 2007 to a record 61.9 million ounces from 48.0 million ounces in 2006. Comex accounted for all of this increase, as it did with the rise in combined trading volume. Tocom and CBOT each saw a decline in open interest at the end of 2007 compared to the end of 2006. Tocom open interest fell 2.1 million ounces from 7.8 million ounces to 5.6 million ounces, the lowest level since a reported 4.2 million ounces at the end of 1988.

The Gold Market 1997 - 2007

2007 through December.

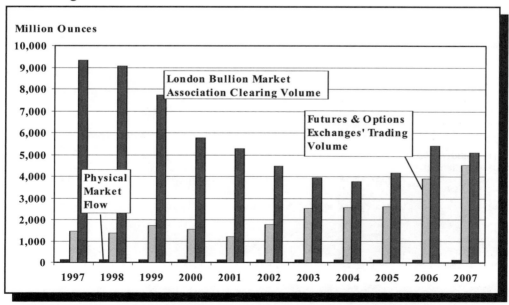

The Comex, based in New York, is the largest futures market for gold trading. In 2007 Comex futures trading volume was 2.5 billion ounces, or approximately 55.2% of the total 4.5 billion ounce trading volume. The 2007 Comex trading volume established a new record by surpassing the previous high of 1.6 billion ounces in 2006. Comex open interest increased 19.8 million ounces to 54.3 million ounces at the end of 2007 from 34.5 million ounces at the end of 2006.

Comex gold options trading volume declined 5.6% in 2007 to 355.5 million ounces from 376.5 million ounces. Gold options trading volume remained high by historical standards, however. Since 1985 options trading volume has only been higher than this level on three occasions: 2003, 2004, and 2006. Trading volumes in 2007 were down from 2006 levels for both call options

and put options. Call option trading volume was down 3.5% to 220.7 million ounces from 228.6 million ounces and put option trading volume was down 8.8% to 134.8 million ounces from 147.9 million ounces. Open interest meanwhile rose in both call and put options. Total option open interest at the end of 2007 stood at 38.5 million ounces, up 7.7 million ounces from the 30.8 million ounces recorded at the end of 2006. A majority, 65.5% of this total was made up by a 5.0 million ounce increase in put option open interest while the remainder was accounted for by a 2.7 million ounce increase in call option open interest.

Trading volume on the CBOT fell 8.1% to 838.0 million ounces in 2007 from 911.5 million ounces in 2006. The CBOT comprises of two types of gold futures contracts: a regular 100 ounce

The Gold Market in 1997-2007

Million Ounces

	1997	1998	1999	2000	2001	2002	2003	2004	2005	2006	2007
Physical Market Flow	112.6	119.6	119.7	118.8	113.3	119.0	128.9	122.1	129.1	116.7	126.0
Futures and Options Exchanges' Trading Volume	1,446.4	1,395.4	1,754.3	1,547.5	1,203.1	1,755.7	2,515.9	2,565.0	2,615.9	3,915.1	4,531.7
London Bullion Market Association Clearing Volume	9,313.8	9,052.9	7,744.0	5,799.7	5,288.8	4,481.0	3,962.4	3,773.4	4,161.7	5,413.9	5,130.3
Total	10,872.8	10,567.8	9,618.0	7,466.0	6,605.1	6,355.7	6,607.2	6,460.4	6,906.7	9,445.8	9,788.0

Note: 2007 through December.
Source: CPM Group
January 18, 2008

contract like those traded on the Comex and a mini contract. The mini-sized gold contract has caught the attention of many market participants over the past years. In 2007, however, trading volumes decreased on both CBOT gold contracts. CBOT gold trading volume rose at a rapid rate from 2002 through 2006. In 2001 CBOT gold trading volume totaled just 194,730 ounces and combined exchange trading volume totaled 1.0 billion ounces. CBOT's share of total exchange trading volume rose from 0.02% that year to a high of 23.3% in 2006 and 18.5% in 2007. CBOT open interest declined 3.8 million ounces to 1.9 million ounces at the end of 2007 from 5.7 million ounces at the end of 2006. Despite the large fall, CBOT gold

open interest at the end of 2007 was the second largest total on record, behind 2006.

In 2007 gold trading volume on the Tocom fell to 586.7 million ounces in 2007 from 714.7 million ounces in 2006. This was a 17.9% decrease. The only year Tocom gold trading volume was higher than the 2006 total was during 2003, when it stood at 856.4 million ounces. In 2004 trading volume fell 34.7% to 559 million ounces before increasing through 2006. Open interest declined to 5.7 million ounces at the end of 2007 from 7.8 million ounces at the end of 2006, the lowest level since 4.2 million ounces were reported at the end of 1988.

Trading Volume in the Futures Markets

Annual Total. 2007 Through December.

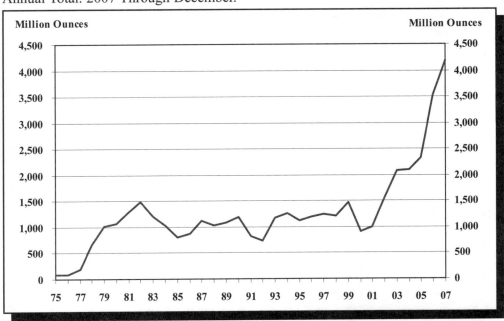

The Multi Commodity Exchange of India began trading gold futures in November 2003. Trading volumes increased each year from inception through 2006. In 2007, however, trading volume on the MCX fell 30.7% to 245.4 million ounces from 320.7 million ounces in 2006. Open interest on the MCX rose 92,089 ounces to 467,687 ounces at the end of 2007 from 375,598 ounces at the end of 2006.

London Bullion Market Association

Each month the London Bullion Market Association (LBMA) reports the amount of gold cleared by members. As of January 2008 there are six clearing members. Reported statistics track the volume of gold in millions of ounces that is transferred on average each day, the value in dollars of that gold using the London PM fixing price, and the average number of transfers recorded each day.

The average number of ounces transferred per month declined 5.7% to 20.3 million ounces in 2007 from 21.5 million ounces in 2006. In 2007 the average number of ounces transferred was highest at the end of the year. Average transfers were above 20 million ounces from September through December and above 25 million ounces in November and December. This compares to 2006, when the average number of ounces transferred was highest during the period from March through July.

Open Interest in the Futures Markets
Year-end, Through 2007.

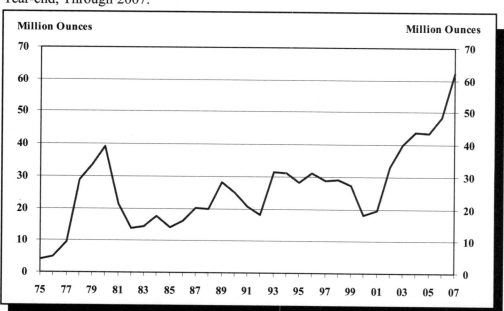

The average size of trades executed by LBMA members declined substantially in 2007. This decline started in January when the average trade size stood at 12,491 ounces, 18.5% below the December 2006 average trade size of 15,319 ounces and the lowest average trade size since the LBMA began publicly reporting such data in the fourth quarter of 1996. Average trade size fell further, to 11,291 ounces, in February. From March through September average trade volume fluctuated between a low of 11,327 ounces recorded in July and a high of 13,369 ounces recorded in April. In October average trade size reached a new all time low at 10,812 ounces. Average trade size then rose in November and December to finish the year at a high of 13,974 ounces.

Offsetting some of the decline in average trade size was an increase in the average number of transfers. The average number of transfers increased on a monthly basis in eight months of 2007. A record high for average monthly transfers was first established in June at 1,649 transfers. This was surpassed in September, October, and November with a record high of 2,165 transfers reported for November.

London Bullion Market Association - Average Trade Size

Ounces of Gold Transferred Divided by Number of Transfers.

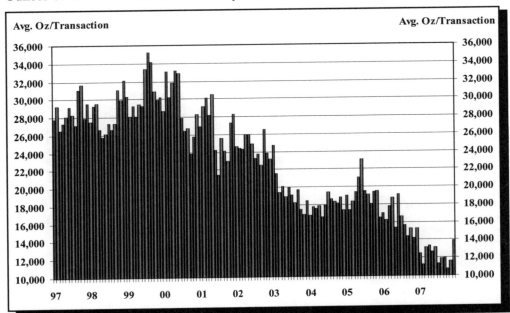

London Bullion Market Clearing Turnover for Gold

Daily Averages

Ounces Transferred (Million Ounces)

	1996	1997	1998	1999	2000	2001	2002	2003	2004	2005	2006	2007
January	-	37.2	37.5	28.9	22.2	19.7	16.3	18.7	14.1	14.8	17.6	17.1
February	-	40.3	37.0	26.7	30.0	24.2	20.1	19.0	15.4	13.9	19.7	16.0
March	-	36.3	38.5	28.5	24.2	28.7	17.4	16.8	15.6	16.0	20.6	20.6
April	-	32.1	34.5	25.2	25.2	25.1	19.2	15.4	17.0	14.3	26.1	20.2
May	-	32.4	32.5	32.6	25.5	28.7	19.3	15.9	14.5	16.8	24.5	19.5
June	-	32.2	35.0	30.5	28.2	20.5	21.0	15.8	13.8	19.1	25.8	21.8
July	-	37.0	30.0	34.8	20.5	16.1	17.3	13.6	15.1	14.6	23.2	17.5
August	-	33.2	28.6	36.4	19.8	19.9	17.1	14.3	13.8	15.2	19.5	18.2
September	-	34.3	34.0	37.1	21.1	19.5	16.4	16.5	12.4	17.5	20.5	21.5
October	27.5	42.0	35.8	37.2	18.9	16.7	17.5	14.1	14.7	18.4	21.6	20.9
November	31.0	40.8	27.5	25.3	18.6	18.0	14.7	13.7	16.6	17.4	19.3	25.2
December	29.8	43.7	30.4	28.5	23.6	20.4	17.7	14.3	15.4	20.0	19.9	25.0

Value in Billions of Dollars

	1996	1997	1998	1999	2000	2001	2002	2003	2004	2005	2006	2007
January	-	13.2	10.8	8.3	6.3	5.2	4.5	6.7	5.8	6.3	9.7	10.8
February	-	14.0	11.0	7.7	9.0	6.3	5.9	6.8	6.2	5.9	10.9	10.6
March	-	12.8	11.4	8.1	6.9	7.5	5.1	5.7	6.4	6.9	11.5	13.5
April	-	11.1	10.6	7.1	7.1	6.5	5.8	5.1	6.9	6.1	15.9	13.7
May	-	11.1	9.7	9.0	7.0	7.8	6.1	5.7	5.6	7.1	16.5	13.0
June	-	11.0	10.2	8.0	8.0	5.5	6.7	5.6	5.4	8.2	15.4	14.3
July	-	12.0	8.8	8.9	5.8	4.3	5.4	4.8	6.0	6.2	14.7	11.7
August	-	10.7	8.1	9.3	5.4	5.4	5.3	5.1	5.5	6.7	12.3	12.1
September	-	11.1	9.8	9.8	5.8	5.5	5.2	6.3	5.0	8.0	12.3	15.3
October	* 10.5	13.6	10.6	11.5	5.1	4.7	5.5	5.3	6.2	8.7	12.7	15.8
November	11.7	12.5	8.1	7.4	4.9	4.9	4.7	5.3	7.3	8.3	12.1	20.3
December	11.0	12.6	8.9	8.1	6.4	5.6	5.9	5.8	6.8	10.2	12.6	20.1

Number of Transfers

	1996	1997	1998	1999	2000	2001	2002	2003	2004	2005	2006	2007
January	-	1,336	1,362	952	774	730	662	755	839	775	1,036	1,369
February	-	1,378	1,265	950	907	830	822	883	863	800	1,210	1,417
March	-	1,365	1,304	975	800	954	714	866	884	869	1,156	1,562
April	-	1,174	1,292	898	791	890	739	764	950	736	1,388	1,511
May	-	1,154	1,262	1,107	768	940	744	837	872	799	1,588	1,538
June	-	1,105	1,339	1,044	857	844	842	788	768	828	1,345	1,649
July	-	1,309	1,098	1,043	734	751	744	711	775	748	1,391	1,545
August	-	1,223	1,073	1,034	747	776	718	783	740	795	1,246	1,520
September	-	1,104	1,245	1,087	789	807	728	838	674	965	1,424	1,789
October	* 1,086	1,326	1,153	1,205	792	725	659	804	808	947	1,415	1,933
November	1,124	1,460	919	845	721	659	617	809	881	889	1,358	2,165
December	1,172	1,480	947	942	833	721	762	776	886	1,206	1,299	1,789

Note: * partly estimated.

Value is calculated using the monthly average London PM fixing price.

Allocations between Clearing Members where the sole purpose is for overnight credit and physical movements arranged by Clearing Members in locations other than London are excluded.

Source: London Bullion Market Association, CPM Group.

January 22, 2008

London Bullion Market Association - Daily Activity
Ounces of Gold Transferred

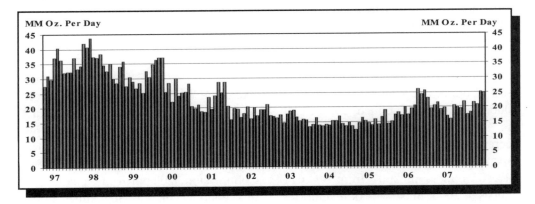

Value of Gold Transferred

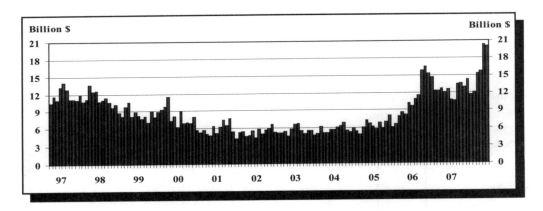

Number of Transfers

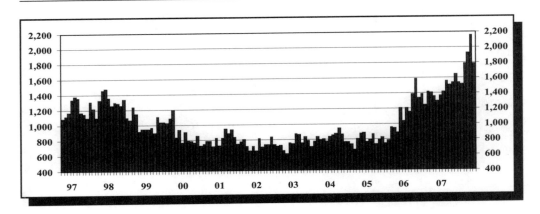

Inventories

Combined inventories held in Nymex, CBOT, and Tocom approved warehouses declined during 2007. Combined inventories stood at 7.6 million ounces at the end of 2007, down 4.0% from 7.9 million ounces recorded at the end of 2006. Inventories declined on each of the three exchanges. The largest decrease in percentage terms occurred in Japan, where inventories fell 38.9% to 247,303 ounces in 2007 from 404,617 ounces in 2006. In New York inventories fell 2.1% to 7.4 million ounces from 7.5 million ounces and in Chicago inventories fell 5.5% to 3,844 ounces from 4,069 ounces. At the end of 2007 Comex inventories accounted for approximately 96.7% of combined warehouse inventories, the highest total since 2004.

The Continued Rise of New Exchanges

On 9 January the Shanghai Futures Exchange (SHFE) began trading gold futures contracts, joining a gold contract already trading on the Shanghai Gold Exchange for a couple of years. The China Securities Regulatory Commission had approved the launch of this contract on 11 September 2007. Each SHFE gold futures contract is one kilogram in size and the market participant is not allowed to take physical delivery. The SHFE trading is not

Comex Gold Stocks in 2000-2007

Daily, Through 31 December 2007.

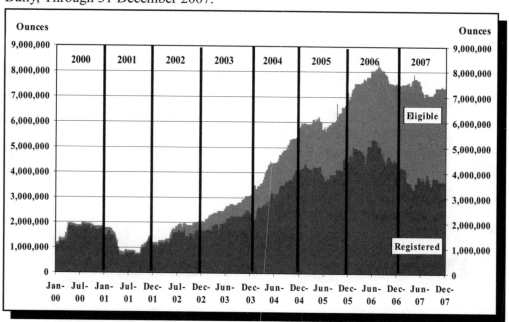

expected to have a large effect on prices, but it represents the amount of interest in the gold market in China and elsewhere. Investors and institutions around the world want to be able to participate in the gold market.

Large Speculative Comex Gold Positions

Weekly, Through 22 January 2008.

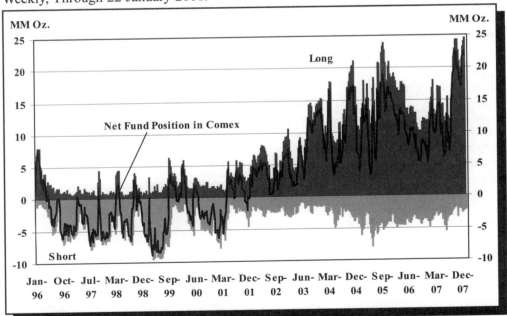

Multi Commodity Exchange Gold Open Interest
Troy Ounces

	2003	2004	2005	2006	2007
January	-	13,544	136,315	347,263	329,669
February	-	27,930	108,321	403,964	350,860
March	-	13,988	119,001	288,520	272,004
April	-	38,579	117,231	278,568	351,740
May	-	17,561	196,393	232,291	386,708
June	-	41,607	184,602	212,204	431,254
July	-	33,543	154,472	237,493	297,053
August	-	83,210	152,984	413,653	325,694
September	-	130,990	471,329	512,761	404,916
October	-	131,562	429,551	508,478	417,922
November	2,131	101,006	441,631	367,885	320,698
December	5,418	162,066	323,401	375,598	467,687

Notes: Month-end data.
Source: Multi Commodity Exchange of India.
January 9, 2008

Multi Commodity Exchange Gold Trading Volume
Troy Ounces

	2003	2004	2005	2006	2007
January	-	205,768	2,833,938	26,115,173	19,375,476
February	-	278,122	2,800,766	22,699,759	20,298,390
March	-	464,217	3,383,390	29,494,873	22,840,263
April	-	507,199	2,644,997	26,266,521	14,535,670
May	-	634,247	3,674,330	32,027,711	18,775,329
June	-	896,241	4,445,628	27,180,861	16,634,831
July	-	1,675,898	5,223,569	32,907,979	17,158,818
August	-	1,927,496	5,323,279	26,260,458	14,898,296
September	-	2,838,913	11,525,203	30,036,560	19,452,679
October	-	3,067,888	10,030,374	27,611,048	26,715,735
November	9,897	4,319,933	11,620,664	23,825,655	31,489,776
December	55,398	3,555,953	21,756,275	16,311,557	23,207,582
Total	65,295	20,371,877	85,262,413	320,738,155	245,382,845

Notes: Monthly total volume.
Source: Multi Commodity Exchange of India.
January 9, 2008

Exchange Activity

Troy Ounces

Trading Volume	Comex	IMM	CBT	Tocom	Total
1975	39,351,700	40,696,800	5,334,237	-	85,382,737
1976	47,396,300	34,092,100	1,055,196	-	82,543,596
1977	98,155,100	90,818,000	1,327,000	-	190,300,100
1978	374,237,800	281,287,000	5,446,701	-	660,971,501
1979	654,189,300	355,896,000	10,989,742	-	1,021,075,042
1980	800,141,000	254,341,900	7,147,624	-	1,061,630,524
1981	1,037,370,600	254,341,900	1,474,800	-	1,293,187,300
1982	1,228,944,800	251,843,500	1,951,500	2,692,075	1,485,431,875
1983	1,038,280,500	153,346,600	10,403,885	2,627,677	1,204,658,662
1984	911,550,400	99,413,200	9,732,442	8,861,408	1,029,557,450
1985	775,770,400	-	5,399,625	17,613,665	798,783,690
1986	835,603,000	-	3,957,569	33,129,303	872,689,872
1987	1,026,538,600	26,160,000	6,211,144	69,405,163	1,128,314,907
1988	953,240,300	13,500	11,818,793	65,535,987	1,030,608,580
1989	998,857,700	-	8,303,679	86,378,771	1,093,540,150
1990	973,004,100	-	1,959,691	220,981,535	1,195,945,326
1991	679,991,700	-	596,396	146,852,502	827,440,598
1992	600,200,900	-	321,120	134,800,651	735,322,671
1993	891,619,500	-	699,323	281,782,913	1,174,101,736
1994	850,336,600	-	796,834	401,275,941	1,252,409,375
1995	776,000,300	-	715,591	351,893,720	1,128,609,611
1996	890,217,900	-	602,149	305,783,411	1,196,603,460
1997	954,190,400	-	448,452	285,239,885	1,239,878,737
1998	899,004,800	-	450,030	301,377,736	1,200,832,566
1999	957,578,600	-	329,848	514,795,787	1,472,704,235
2000	664,346,400	-	230,917	252,083,736	916,661,053
2001	690,544,000	-	194,730	314,810,363	1,005,549,093
2002	901,818,300	-	301,537	659,303,216	1,561,423,053
2003	1,223,568,900	-	4,819,744	856,427,035	2,084,815,679
2004	1,495,959,700	-	22,917,953	558,964,547	2,077,842,200
2005	1,589,061,700	-	75,629,368	577,369,987	2,242,061,055
2006	1,591,758,400	-	911,479,744	714,652,125	3,217,890,269
2007	2,506,044,000	-	838,019,525	586,708,968	3,930,772,493

Exchange Activity

Troy Ounces

Open Interest	Comex	IMM	CBT	Tocom	Total
1975	2,971,200	881,000	282,607	-	4,134,807
1976	3,491,200	1,317,000	37,810	-	4,846,010
1977	5,427,600	3,749,000	280,678	-	9,457,278
1978	18,621,200	10,118,700	201,490	-	28,941,390
1979	24,810,500	8,109,600	628,287	-	33,548,387
1980	29,929,100	8,940,900	305,600	-	39,175,600
1981	17,933,900	3,272,600	8,700	-	21,215,200
1982	13,042,900	746,300	8,900	165,865	13,963,965
1983	13,806,900	137,300	90,816	256,112	14,291,128
1984	16,740,700	300	79,572	762,486	17,583,058
1985	13,224,300	-	45,460	871,991	14,141,751
1986	14,074,400	-	48,643	2,096,258	16,219,301
1987	15,010,600	27,200	73,497	5,013,355	20,124,652
1988	15,273,100	-	299,080	4,175,444	19,747,624
1989	15,093,100	-	51,733	13,176,418	28,321,251
1990	10,761,000	-	68,144	14,280,312	25,109,456
1991	11,414,400	-	10,385	9,195,019	20,619,804
1992	10,769,700	-	8,141	7,471,308	18,249,149
1993	16,312,100	-	23,105	15,077,553	31,412,758
1994	17,607,200	-	25,475	13,362,731	30,995,406
1995	14,217,900	-	12,089	13,951,957	28,181,946
1996	18,980,500	-	13,006	12,017,867	31,011,373
1997	17,777,000	-	16,429	11,014,219	28,807,648
1998	16,291,200	-	7,748	12,729,491	29,028,439
1999	15,591,400	-	11,831	11,875,150	27,478,382
2000	11,130,700	-	12,700	7,010,557	18,153,956
2001	11,496,300	-	4,854	8,055,294	19,556,448
2002	20,691,400	-	11,985	12,491,094	33,194,479
2003	27,938,100	-	76,028	12,148,785	40,162,913
2004	31,873,500	-	660,400	11,062,606	43,596,506
2005	32,324,700	-	1,103,636	9,644,342	43,072,678
2006	34,532,800	-	5,677,010	7,804,357	48,014,167
2007	54,349,300	-	1,852,356	5,693,535	61,895,191

Note: Trading volumes are annual totals, open interest is year-end levels. Tocom open interest prior to 1984 is highest recorded for month of December. Warehouse inventories are year-end levels. Only inventories in Chicago vaults are listed in the International Money Market to avoid double counting of stocks in New York vaults that are also registered with Comex.

Sources: New York Commodity Exchange, Tokyo Commodity Exchange, Chicago Mercantile Exchange's International Money Market, Chicago Board of Trade, CPM Group.
January 10, 2008

Exchange Activity

Troy Ounces

Warehouse Stocks	New York	Chicago	Japan	Total
1975	493,237	81,198	-	574,435
1976	292,099	28,260	-	320,359
1977	1,831,631	20,870	-	1,852,501
1978	2,604,394	200,232	-	2,804,626
1979	2,253,352	186,042	-	2,439,394
1980	4,814,587	183,677	-	4,998,264
1981	2,383,355	71,042	-	2,454,397
1982	2,243,146	56,093	-	2,299,239
1983	2,485,201	50,385	-	2,535,586
1984	2,307,069	49,699	-	2,356,768
1985	2,110,000	32,717	120,501	2,263,218
1986	2,787,206	29,470	214,542	3,031,218
1987	2,630,000	58,604	373,045	3,061,648
1988	1,434,967	60,542	520,456	2,015,965
1989	2,241,913	50,560	585,914	2,878,387
1990	1,636,038	21,672	952,175	2,609,885
1991	1,604,105	14,548	859,356	2,478,009
1992	1,497,132	11,868	875,239	2,384,238
1993	2,524,266	11,482	491,166	3,026,914
1994	1,577,427	15,442	660,793	2,253,662
1995	1,458,371	15,381	571,865	2,045,617
1996	666,165	9,374	355,844	1,031,383
1997	489,158	7,802	322,439	819,399
1998	809,467	6,812	242,673	1,058,953
1999	1,219,446	6,166	288,006	1,513,618
2000	1,701,224	6,098	285,723	1,993,045
2001	1,220,253	7,952	233,768	1,461,973
2002	2,041,791	8,261	230,006	2,280,058
2003	3,122,237	8,178	246,017	3,376,432
2004	5,795,566	6,279	182,745	5,984,590
2005	6,657,742	4,069	249,361	6,911,172
2006	7,534,516	4,069	404,617	7,943,201
2007	7,375,310	3,844	247,303	7,626,457

Note: Trading volumes are annual totals, open interest is year-end levels. Tocom open interest prior to 1984 is highest recorded for month of December. Warehouse inventories are year-end levels. Only inventories in Chicago vaults are listed in the International Money Market to avoid double counting of stocks in New York vaults that are also registered with Comex. 2003 through December.
Sources: New York Commodity Exchange, Tokyo Commodity Exchange, Chicago Mercantile Exchange's International Money Market, Chicago Board of Trade, CPM Group.
January 10, 2008

Comex Trading Activity - Trading Volume

Monthly, Through December 2007.

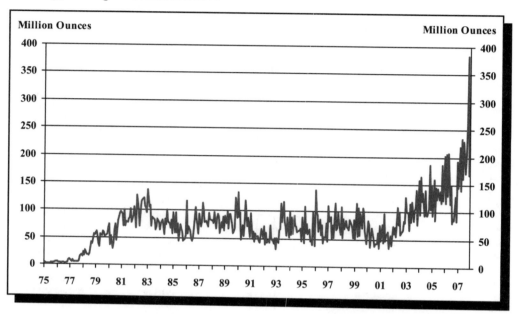

Comex Trading Activity - Open Interest

Monthly, End-December 2007.

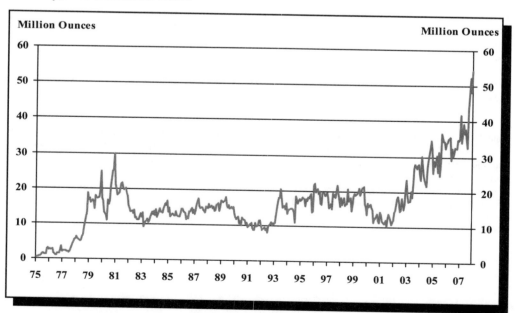

Tocom - Trading Volume

Monthly, Through December 2007.

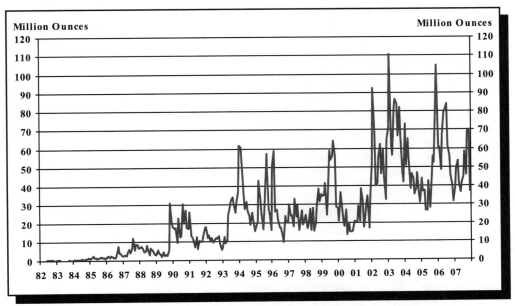

Tocom - Open Interest

Monthly, End-December 2007.

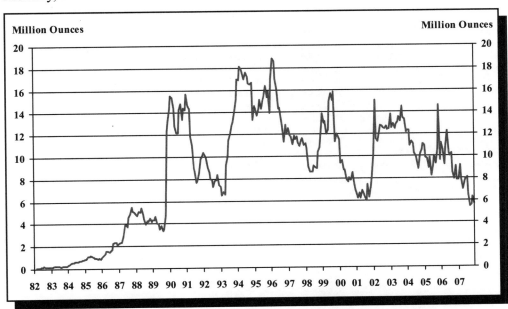

Comex Trading Volume

Troy Ounces

	1975	1976	1977	1978	1979	1980
January	2,924,200	4,466,300	7,075,200	23,515,400	60,785,000	73,401,100
February	2,181,100	2,697,900	4,210,000	17,001,200	51,568,900	35,668,700
March	2,295,100	3,130,600	8,844,900	26,770,700	38,443,100	53,186,200
April	2,186,600	1,818,800	5,691,200	17,655,500	33,497,500	29,736,400
May	2,114,400	3,838,600	4,931,200	17,659,600	55,792,500	39,195,100
June	2,067,700	3,243,200	5,131,200	16,249,800	52,047,600	64,907,000
July	3,777,500	2,583,500	4,889,400	20,268,000	60,169,300	73,272,400
August	1,921,100	2,231,100	4,553,000	41,140,600	59,037,500	44,953,300
September	4,022,100	3,745,300	6,190,800	37,440,000	51,849,000	80,599,000
October	2,711,100	2,916,000	14,215,200	46,542,200	52,855,200	86,599,700
November	4,767,800	8,510,300	18,485,300	55,195,700	55,803,000	94,252,100
December	4,706,600	10,038,500	14,523,600	55,134,800	67,302,100	97,231,900
Total	35,675,300	49,220,100	98,741,000	374,573,500	639,150,700	773,002,900

	1981	1982	1983	1984	1985	1986
January	92,992,800	92,236,900	136,899,900	74,950,800	95,030,200	116,237,400
February	70,866,600	66,895,900	104,743,800	78,641,200	58,985,400	57,415,000
March	99,901,600	126,469,700	108,764,600	82,919,500	96,276,600	70,389,200
April	70,213,300	98,556,600	71,267,800	56,122,200	59,808,300	61,790,800
May	78,226,900	71,140,600	87,232,700	83,355,500	75,257,400	49,597,900
June	77,627,100	94,258,800	84,056,000	73,781,300	44,859,200	44,957,800
July	83,764,200	115,349,600	81,860,700	100,689,800	73,808,900	49,315,600
August	86,206,600	118,272,100	64,782,400	79,127,700	65,766,300	65,989,000
September	102,237,800	122,465,200	69,413,200	75,316,800	61,608,600	104,885,200
October	76,877,700	107,411,900	83,268,500	67,131,300	43,864,600	84,688,400
November	88,682,500	104,418,000	78,053,200	81,488,500	47,912,200	72,431,400
December	105,051,800	95,115,100	64,384,200	57,768,100	54,544,500	57,905,300
Total	1,032,648,900	1,212,590,400	1,034,727,000	911,292,700	777,722,200	835,603,000

	1987	1988	1989	1990	1991	1992
January	93,642,600	81,501,400	90,039,100	132,713,100	95,734,500	72,978,900
February	70,679,700	77,867,400	77,999,900	88,509,000	49,780,100	38,836,100
March	79,479,500	96,499,400	99,380,600	97,564,700	61,766,400	60,733,700
April	113,480,000	67,370,400	68,237,700	47,241,400	44,613,000	42,544,700
May	100,260,000	86,622,800	93,198,700	74,515,900	58,440,000	48,539,000
June	79,780,000	94,628,300	93,664,900	54,102,600	51,996,700	42,723,700
July	80,540,000	88,423,800	75,609,600	74,743,200	55,141,900	73,464,300
August	75,970,000	58,745,500	59,114,400	119,146,700	45,717,000	50,022,700
September	70,170,000	79,089,600	63,003,400	72,936,100	42,910,300	46,527,300
October	95,126,600	69,448,300	68,124,800	87,990,900	55,103,700	41,411,900
November	84,710,200	89,549,900	122,843,700	70,531,200	67,727,500	50,412,800
December	82,700,000	63,493,500	87,640,900	53,009,300	51,060,600	32,005,800
Total	1,026,538,600	953,240,300	998,857,700	973,004,100	679,991,700	600,200,900

Comex Trading Volume

Troy Ounces

	1993	1994	1995	1996	1997	1998
January	50,600,600	98,183,100	88,185,800	138,473,200	110,279,100	107,821,400
February	42,579,700	58,400,000	43,507,600	98,749,600	83,020,600	53,417,300
March	66,142,000	88,954,200	108,747,900	94,357,100	89,943,900	87,723,300
April	67,242,100	58,923,600	61,297,200	64,712,100	50,854,600	69,814,000
May	114,066,500	92,261,900	77,703,500	85,845,500	76,213,000	84,527,100
June	80,965,500	74,024,100	58,805,000	58,208,000	52,272,700	71,866,200
July	117,165,900	72,378,700	66,990,100	74,975,700	114,753,700	71,244,000
August	80,883,300	62,598,000	46,335,500	42,457,200	66,782,500	67,988,300
September	72,893,800	64,562,000	49,553,900	54,189,900	71,575,500	85,173,700
October	56,524,500	65,120,500	38,770,800	52,848,000	98,798,900	76,961,300
November	89,233,500	68,779,800	98,294,000	79,519,700	80,882,400	70,564,700
December	53,322,100	46,150,700	37,809,000	45,881,900	58,813,500	51,903,500
Total	891,619,500	850,336,600	776,000,300	890,217,900	954,190,400	899,004,800

	1999	2000	2001	2002	2003	2004
January	86,076,100	61,638,500	75,523,600	73,356,600	126,028,800	158,132,000
February	51,744,600	83,345,700	48,333,300	61,317,300	100,746,500	96,259,600
March	114,755,200	76,770,600	76,656,900	71,769,200	98,762,300	164,952,100
April	56,110,600	36,223,800	43,806,600	55,977,900	66,781,100	120,287,700
May	106,956,000	70,152,200	97,159,700	108,963,200	116,030,100	134,478,500
June	57,356,000	62,546,200	48,143,500	77,553,900	82,425,800	93,058,700
July	96,431,100	53,247,600	57,825,400	99,891,700	119,166,600	140,500,700
August	70,964,600	37,442,600	64,742,000	58,579,300	83,746,200	95,295,700
September	106,728,200	43,016,400	34,103,400	62,182,600	103,397,800	94,485,800
October	99,375,600	42,488,000	48,144,600	66,902,100	109,126,300	106,719,100
November	67,466,200	62,573,700	57,367,000	84,477,900	139,729,600	186,465,300
December	43,614,400	34,901,100	38,738,000	80,846,600	77,627,800	105,324,500
Total	957,578,600	664,346,400	690,544,000	901,818,300	1,223,568,900	1,495,959,700

	2005	2006	2007
January	150,234,300	201,884,700	192,980,400
February	94,440,100	116,272,900	145,585,100
March	159,903,500	205,265,100	219,589,500
April	85,808,000	130,290,500	140,517,200
May	145,167,400	207,097,300	233,664,800
June	123,995,300	114,855,500	161,078,600
July	143,241,200	148,722,900	229,224,400
August	123,437,600	80,448,600	171,068,500
September	138,021,000	88,465,400	202,461,800
October	117,396,300	85,714,900	258,442,200
November	185,265,000	128,466,000	383,709,900
December	122,152,000	84,274,600	167,721,600
Total	1,589,061,700	1,591,758,400	2,506,044,000

Notes: Monthly total volume.

Source: New York Commodities Exchange.

January 9, 2008

Comex Open Interest

Troy Ounces

	1975	1976	1977	1978	1979	1980
January	367,000	2,557,300	1,877,400	5,599,300	16,797,200	17,116,800
February	537,100	2,785,200	2,331,900	6,321,500	17,281,300	16,388,000
March	523,600	2,605,700	2,359,800	5,748,500	15,980,400	13,118,300
April	677,000	2,621,300	2,226,600	5,164,400	16,581,900	12,491,000
May	693,500	1,617,800	1,928,700	4,994,700	16,251,900	10,887,000
June	920,800	1,212,300	1,938,700	5,292,400	14,152,500	16,759,200
July	1,509,800	1,009,000	1,845,900	6,146,900	17,816,800	15,314,200
August	1,467,400	1,107,800	2,036,200	6,661,100	17,436,400	16,414,700
September	1,169,600	1,408,200	2,744,400	8,673,400	17,220,800	20,499,900
October	1,143,100	1,603,400	4,154,200	11,639,700	17,456,700	25,020,400
November	2,845,400	2,323,500	4,700,800	12,836,300	19,516,400	25,357,300
December	2,971,200	3,491,200	5,427,600	18,621,200	24,810,500	29,929,100

	1981	1982	1983	1984	1985	1986
January	21,102,200	15,281,300	11,878,400	12,334,900	13,543,400	14,414,900
February	20,006,700	14,498,800	13,094,200	14,269,300	14,613,900	14,375,200
March	18,180,300	13,523,900	9,286,500	11,920,400	12,139,400	13,656,800
April	18,608,500	13,623,300	10,619,700	13,394,500	12,904,900	13,208,800
May	20,001,200	12,963,100	10,956,900	14,515,700	12,822,400	11,503,800
June	21,359,800	13,906,300	11,385,500	13,421,500	12,456,200	12,095,400
July	21,586,100	11,805,000	10,542,400	13,444,100	12,404,900	11,698,600
August	20,287,900	11,967,600	10,889,000	13,220,300	13,713,200	13,695,900
September	19,770,400	11,115,500	11,869,400	14,316,200	12,472,200	13,657,400
October	20,285,100	11,275,300	13,399,700	16,039,700	12,285,100	14,677,800
November	18,639,600	12,187,700	12,588,200	15,550,200	12,274,700	13,167,900
December	17,933,900	13,042,900	13,806,900	16,740,700	13,224,300	14,074,400

	1987	1988	1989	1990	1991	1992
January	13,007,800	14,619,200	17,022,100	13,199,400	9,349,600	10,294,000
February	14,001,600	15,822,300	16,577,400	12,192,000	9,802,500	8,760,700
March	15,683,200	14,831,000	16,364,900	11,681,200	10,254,100	9,024,500
April	17,543,700	15,418,400	16,848,800	12,360,100	10,821,700	9,456,500
May	15,096,400	14,646,100	17,951,300	10,462,500	9,148,500	8,602,900
June	14,696,000	15,164,500	15,785,800	11,214,200	8,734,900	9,116,200
July	15,052,300	13,938,200	14,827,900	9,892,300	8,749,000	8,076,700
August	14,881,500	14,263,000	15,659,500	12,314,700	10,799,300	9,934,900
September	14,263,400	15,654,600	14,746,800	11,662,000	9,790,400	9,919,100
October	13,342,200	16,089,500	14,114,200	14,775,900	10,194,600	10,880,300
November	15,220,600	14,028,600	14,775,900	10,194,600	11,549,600	9,967,200
December	15,010,600	15,273,100	15,093,100	10,761,000	11,414,400	10,769,700

Comex Open Interest

Troy Ounces

	1993	1994	1995	1996	1997	1998
January	10,576,800	13,406,100	17,177,700	21,634,800	19,584,400	15,794,600
February	10,675,500	14,496,400	17,428,500	22,161,000	18,052,000	18,086,900
March	12,822,500	14,606,000	18,252,900	19,545,500	15,156,900	16,106,500
April	16,599,900	15,038,700	17,706,200	20,665,800	16,554,300	18,180,800
May	17,889,100	14,814,300	15,680,300	19,087,000	15,032,600	16,044,500
June	17,906,800	14,724,900	17,592,800	19,920,400	19,434,100	16,471,600
July	20,358,400	13,807,500	17,079,200	16,523,700	18,471,300	16,527,100
August	17,591,300	11,064,400	18,053,600	16,247,100	19,196,600	20,600,400
September	15,251,300	18,512,400	17,804,400	19,546,500	18,228,400	17,220,800
October	15,564,300	16,435,500	19,294,200	19,369,900	21,630,500	18,228,800
November	14,717,500	17,216,900	13,919,300	18,591,100	19,442,200	14,395,600
December	16,312,100	17,607,200	14,217,900	18,980,500	17,777,000	16,291,200

	1999	2000	2001	2002	2003	2004
January	18,749,000	13,499,000	14,169,300	11,838,600	23,414,800	25,254,000
February	19,354,300	16,650,900	13,509,300	14,174,000	19,082,700	23,432,500
March	18,818,200	15,760,400	11,810,800	14,698,000	17,126,700	30,204,000
April	19,328,500	16,498,000	11,041,200	18,082,900	17,452,800	24,587,200
May	19,874,100	15,519,200	10,985,800	18,553,800	20,057,000	23,457,600
June	20,851,900	14,856,700	11,967,200	17,116,300	18,417,100	22,425,100
July	18,918,900	11,107,400	10,094,300	14,372,500	21,903,200	21,566,400
August	19,869,200	12,406,700	12,350,200	14,924,700	26,911,400	26,957,500
September	20,924,100	12,404,400	13,606,300	18,050,700	27,792,200	29,033,600
October	21,400,800	13,781,800	11,941,100	15,001,900	26,751,900	32,365,400
November	16,357,400	11,594,000	10,703,200	16,369,500	27,719,700	34,564,600
December	15,591,400	11,130,700	11,496,300	20,691,400	27,938,100	31,873,500

	2005	2006	2007
January	25,361,000	33,964,500	35,138,100
February	28,780,100	33,985,900	41,731,600
March	27,281,300	34,995,100	34,195,100
April	30,261,400	35,570,000	39,370,900
May	25,599,500	29,229,500	36,492,200
June	31,292,200	32,378,900	37,736,100
July	24,751,400	30,240,600	35,118,500
August	28,734,600	31,076,200	32,625,500
September	36,535,700	32,682,800	43,692,700
October	34,334,100	32,348,100	52,228,400
November	34,251,000	34,949,000	48,227,800
December	32,324,700	34,532,800	54,349,300

Notes: Month-end data.
Source: New York Commodities Exchange.
January 9, 2008

Tocom Trading Volume

Troy Ounces

	1982	1983	1984	1985	1986	1987	1988	1989	1990
January		249,554	336,907	1,149,548	1,769,735	2,677,382	7,147,068	2,916,390	17,564,410
February		328,387	651,212	1,361,196	2,423,070	3,151,605	7,294,158	5,339,878	16,724,633
March	83,013	294,372	623,145	2,234,441	1,569,533	2,454,384	6,123,390	4,161,233	17,485,737
April	167,505	172,006	478,692	1,657,240	2,516,403	4,342,595	4,439,980	2,968,731	9,159,413
May	149,404	127,863	566,463	1,728,357	1,989,389	5,857,536	4,876,747	2,038,869	22,936,309
June	247,785	196,055	694,841	1,030,848	1,709,163	3,841,141	7,766,548	4,570,351	12,534,208
July	321,539	220,586	1,193,016	1,431,253	1,645,859	6,635,519	5,721,764	2,607,647	12,822,664
August	579,452	161,622	668,092	1,562,653	2,904,301	11,843,225	2,908,449	2,984,421	30,580,363
September	555,886	172,746	571,993	1,824,199	7,263,454	5,198,318	6,601,246	2,302,826	20,147,976
October	255,341	252,801	776,086	1,256,803	3,841,848	8,567,744	5,215,937	5,356,500	27,080,213
November	206,568	225,184	861,703	1,291,301	3,252,526	8,449,590	4,608,449	31,354,970	17,187,089
December	125,581	226,502	1,439,258	1,085,826	2,244,022	6,386,126	2,832,252	19,776,957	16,758,520
Total	2,692,075	2,627,677	8,861,408	17,613,665	33,129,303	69,405,163	65,535,987	86,378,771	220,981,535

	1991	1992	1993	1994	1995	1996	1997	1998	1999
January	26,211,887	17,596,175	6,323,560	61,910,127	17,324,533	50,889,092	30,115,818	24,143,568	34,634,695
February	12,964,416	11,974,882	12,379,756	60,710,874	20,701,739	58,625,387	23,485,508	16,858,348	35,294,138
March	12,239,997	13,364,242	8,967,120	52,320,152	43,013,425	26,162,504	23,981,529	18,853,203	41,456,270
April	9,463,848	10,075,258	10,493,474	35,037,479	32,668,101	26,965,339	18,020,789	27,544,083	24,242,785
May	6,767,401	11,629,358	24,039,786	27,491,388	25,142,490	21,620,992	33,154,316	15,889,744	33,838,965
June	12,461,258	9,575,186	29,117,442	31,677,538	16,194,790	17,488,888	23,178,468	28,104,245	58,712,419
July	6,133,293	10,472,930	31,919,954	26,872,005	25,329,382	17,322,894	29,854,819	15,427,513	53,596,085
August	10,406,378	11,882,320	33,940,755	23,641,278	45,597,955	13,015,632	15,759,341	19,888,069	55,746,356
September	10,022,081	11,422,629	30,470,022	18,724,471	57,404,528	9,276,120	19,995,228	29,251,414	64,398,881
October	9,752,143	12,628,891	25,812,961	25,786,790	27,021,409	23,919,156	26,746,039	38,382,663	55,975,751
November	13,064,469	8,778,106	31,035,649	21,866,945	25,815,276	20,097,403	18,980,166	31,408,212	28,819,502
December	17,365,333	5,400,675	37,282,434	15,236,892	15,680,089	20,400,005	21,967,866	35,626,673	28,079,939
Total	146,852,502	134,800,651	281,782,913	401,275,941	351,893,720	305,783,411	285,239,885	301,377,736	514,795,787

	2000	2001	2002	2003	2004	2005	2006	2007
January	20,696,981	20,405,117	51,399,163	71,163,002	73,204,572	44,152,171	59,576,501	39,176,882
February	36,311,547	20,050,752	92,334,785	110,800,861	51,017,535	37,152,931	60,725,117	48,737,439
March	30,899,588	29,246,881	68,667,240	61,839,106	65,238,400	37,629,147	48,632,628	53,505,098
April	20,100,200	20,650,202	39,963,320	56,474,794	53,372,252	26,849,178	67,074,623	41,519,639
May	18,022,750	38,752,878	41,480,930	81,401,103	38,296,210	26,647,947	80,021,388	36,710,569
June	27,390,660	31,328,285	55,020,039	86,538,882	46,522,288	42,326,589	80,665,656	41,348,469
July	13,198,152	17,417,513	62,073,292	84,081,186	43,755,142	28,344,121	83,957,213	45,083,892
August	19,979,088	21,327,617	46,514,411	66,634,126	35,729,073	36,916,205	61,187,444	58,457,258
September	14,786,686	31,352,784	59,634,533	81,883,107	38,757,122	55,632,575	55,609,748	46,170,257
October	14,705,923	34,807,634	44,766,281	66,715,339	47,108,042	52,240,193	45,283,650	69,204,031
November	15,417,386	16,835,650	32,632,414	47,008,021	34,778,570	84,665,075	40,135,680	69,880,312
December	20,574,776	32,635,050	64,816,808	41,887,507	31,185,343	104,813,854	31,782,478	36,915,122
Total	252,083,736	314,810,363	659,303,216	856,427,035	558,964,547	577,369,987	714,652,125	586,708,968

Notes: Monthly total volume and annual totals.

Source: Tokyo Commodity Exchange.

January 18, 2008

Tocom Open Interest
Troy Ounces

	1982	1983	1984	1985	1986	1987	1988	1989	1990
January		170,688	347,935	827,848	997,668	2,228,944	4,773,157	4,345,746	14,317,253
February		193,194	377,096	843,313	1,143,793	2,290,127	4,739,495	4,304,818	15,488,600
March	46,426	264,761	489,687	1,082,707	1,291,365	2,299,418	5,109,132	4,618,319	15,345,143
April	66,166	238,655	563,730	1,089,426	1,535,710	2,840,161	5,014,834	4,031,633	14,440,390
May	78,319	216,310	570,578	1,157,618	1,517,674	3,846,413	5,393,569	3,978,842	12,793,181
June	120,533	225,730	612,792	1,082,546	1,472,824	3,972,380	4,880,541	3,452,085	12,137,211
July	154,645	209,687	609,867	1,011,718	1,576,831	3,694,951	4,421,814	3,823,361	12,179,007
August	193,804	193,001	638,031	942,498	1,682,414	4,539,164	3,988,101	3,340,201	14,244,946
September	183,838	202,357	668,863	927,934	2,230,262	4,849,001	4,244,953	3,509,152	14,769,067
October	157,024	244,988	694,937	883,662	2,340,410	5,524,165	4,201,518	4,723,420	13,400,251
November	179,208	259,231	758,049	941,598	2,292,956	5,126,268	4,461,360	12,351,624	14,436,565
December	165,865	256,112	762,486	871,991	2,096,258	5,013,355	4,175,444	13,176,418	14,280,312

	1991	1992	1993	1994	1995	1996	1997	1998	1999
January	15,691,696	10,354,615	7,253,359	16,966,278	14,553,690	16,976,952	12,536,940	11,184,778	13,887,431
February	14,634,581	10,075,451	6,545,883	16,896,768	14,326,127	18,852,463	11,872,836	10,740,970	13,020,037
March	14,323,169	9,906,595	6,816,688	18,145,405	13,729,378	18,587,992	11,777,991	9,082,316	13,191,368
April	11,881,677	9,070,613	6,559,965	17,934,046	14,328,088	16,983,832	11,099,933	8,625,422	12,037,415
May	11,025,118	8,594,622	9,193,428	17,285,502	15,142,883	16,023,073	11,876,018	8,591,214	12,413,578
June	9,012,516	7,969,901	10,029,347	16,996,886	14,360,239	14,336,286	11,546,892	8,578,289	14,956,088
July	8,669,886	7,902,610	11,477,414	17,565,503	15,105,299	14,455,791	11,815,607	9,146,199	15,649,353
August	7,659,165	7,321,454	12,034,843	17,216,346	15,464,069	13,351,993	11,268,788	8,993,065	15,051,832
September	7,818,568	7,840,398	12,895,356	16,625,641	16,380,428	12,820,574	10,933,231	8,927,896	15,784,450
October	8,548,196	7,928,652	13,085,496	16,515,204	15,381,859	11,342,060	11,477,285	10,406,635	11,353,955
November	9,855,572	8,390,690	14,027,929	16,638,630	15,885,114	12,850,153	11,631,062	10,749,876	12,000,956
December	9,915,019	7,471,308	15,077,553	13,362,731	13,951,957	12,017,867	11,014,219	12,729,491	11,875,150

	2000	2001	2002	2003	2004	2005	2006	2007	
January	11,498,923	6,728,081	10,057,993	13,792,522	12,361,333	10,917,992	11,169,475	7,823,069	
February	9,369,550	6,190,649	15,056,526	12,580,312	12,354,357	9,869,204	10,565,009	9,166,615	
March	9,647,461	6,635,519	11,565,539	12,967,856	10,927,509	9,758,380	9,261,684	7,889,878	
April	8,735,056	6,229,809	11,338,137	12,513,824	11,327,978	8,911,499	10,698,885	6,961,913	
May	8,752,417	6,861,860	12,222,989	12,879,056	11,055,565	9,828,855	12,209,518	7,654,599	
June	7,929,199	6,481,292	12,755,758	13,080,577	10,256,170	8,237,363	10,234,468	7,944,084	
July	7,690,126	6,306,713	12,738,975	13,537,181	10,028,382	9,153,015	9,964,595	8,057,190	
August	8,029,091	5,932,769	12,573,239	13,173,492	9,209,986	10,033,333	10,234,725	6,481,356	
September	7,836,219	7,432,567	12,487,043	14,486,495	8,828,357	9,329,587	8,538,808	5,408,166	
October	8,524,437	6,307,678	12,744,730	13,497,989	10,152,580	10,600,182	7,893,511	5,575,028	
November	7,914,602	7,324,605	12,433,994	13,318,363	10,541,154	14,564,524	9,056,402	6,274,209	
December	7,010,557	8,055,294	12,491,094	12,148,785	11,062,606	9,644,342	7,804,357	5,693,535	

Notes: Open interest for the period March 1982 through October 1984 are the largest open interest
for the month. Data for the months November 1984 to the present are month-end figures.
Source: Tokyo Commodity Exchange.
January 18, 2008

Comex Options Trading Volume - Puts and Calls
Monthly, Through December 2007.

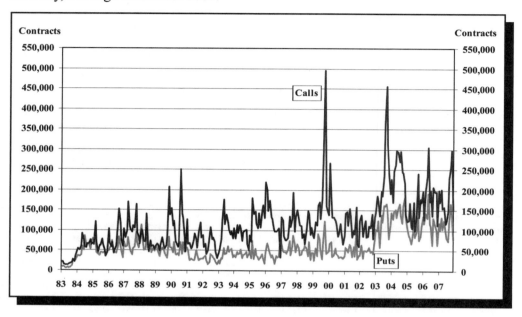

Comex Options Open Interest - Puts and Calls
Monthly, End-December 2007.

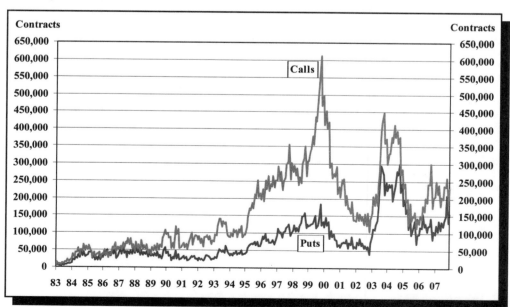

Put/Call Ratio

Monthly Open Interest, Through December 2007.

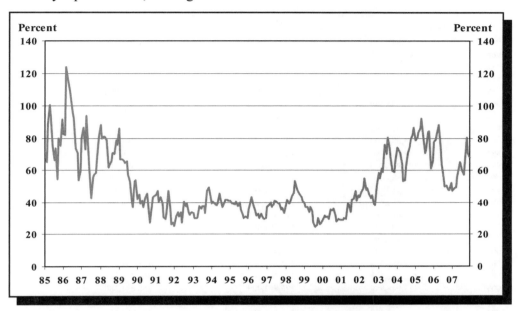

Annual Comex Gold Options Activity
Troy Ounces

	Trading Volume		
	Puts	Calls	Total
1985	62,847,100	76,742,500	139,589,600
1986	66,367,200	98,311,900	164,679,100
1987	75,486,400	132,520,300	208,006,700
1988	78,375,600	91,494,000	169,869,600
1989	60,769,500	99,610,400	160,379,900
1990	62,095,600	131,084,800	193,180,400
1991	41,959,600	97,885,500	139,845,100
1992	33,997,800	81,287,600	115,285,400
1993	49,051,100	122,650,400	171,701,500
1994	49,026,900	109,879,600	158,906,500
1995	45,965,500	154,704,000	200,669,500
1996	53,503,000	154,463,300	207,966,300
1997	68,410,500	138,077,800	206,488,300
1998	61,482,000	133,054,600	194,536,600
1999	69,613,400	211,969,700	281,583,100
2000	53,800,300	169,791,200	223,591,500
2001	62,432,900	135,069,000	197,501,900
2002	61,787,900	132,468,500	194,256,400
2003	148,481,500	282,550,300	431,031,800
2004	175,990,600	290,761,700	466,752,300
2005	113,048,900	175,572,400	288,621,300
2006	147,857,400	228,641,500	376,498,900
2007	134,772,100	220,731,700	355,503,800

	Open Interest		
	Puts	Calls	Total
1985	3,365,200	3,671,400	7,036,600
1986	3,399,900	5,686,300	9,086,200
1987	5,217,200	6,463,500	11,680,700
1988	3,913,700	5,151,800	9,065,500
1989	5,830,100	10,821,900	16,652,000
1990	2,615,400	5,829,700	8,445,100
1991	2,485,600	9,083,200	11,568,800
1992	2,601,800	7,705,200	10,307,000
1993	4,249,200	9,173,900	13,423,100
1994	3,917,200	9,540,600	13,457,800
1995	6,370,300	21,303,400	27,673,700
1996	7,652,500	25,184,200	32,836,700
1997	10,198,500	30,241,800	40,440,300
1998	12,594,300	30,631,300	43,225,600
1999	13,267,200	49,662,400	62,929,600
2000	6,789,400	23,462,300	30,251,700
2001	6,251,100	13,946,500	20,197,600
2002	7,207,100	14,077,600	21,284,700
2003	24,664,900	37,387,200	62,052,100
2004	24,485,000	28,352,900	52,837,900
2005	9,564,400	14,483,200	24,047,600
2006	10,553,900	20,206,700	30,760,600
2007	15,606,600	22,863,900	38,470,500

Notes: Trading volume is monthly total. Open interest is month-end.
Sources: New York Commodity Exchange.
January 9, 2008

Prices

Prices

In 2007 the price of gold averaged a record $700.11. This was up 14.4% from the previous record average of $611.98 from 1980 and 15.4% from the 2006 average price of $606.67. Gold prices settled for 2007 at $838.00 on 31 December, up 31.4% from a settlement of $638.00 on 29 December 2006. (Unless otherwise specified, all prices in this report are Comex nearby active futures settlement prices.) On a settlement basis the high for the year was $842.70 on 28 December and the low for the year was $606.90 on 5 January. Intraday prices reached a high of $848 on 7 November and a low of $603 on 5 January.

Annual price volatility meanwhile moved slightly lower to 17% in 2007, compared to 24.3% in 2006. Annual price volatility averaged 16.3% from 2000 through 2006 after averaging 11.4% from 1991 through 1999. Annual price volatility was at its highest level between 1975 and 1987, when price volatility averaged 24.1% and reached a peak of 46.1% in 1980. In 2006 market activity was lowest in the final quarter, at 18.7%. Market activity continued to decrease on a quarterly basis through the first three quarters of 2007, reaching 14.6% during the third quarter. In the fourth quarter price volatility picked up, reaching 20.2%.

Weekly London Gold Prices

Through 18 January 2008.

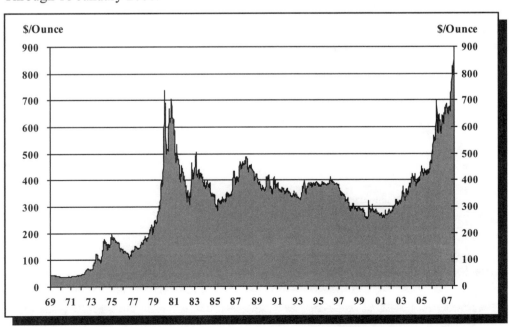

Prices started off 2007 at their weakest and finished the year at their strongest. After starting the year around the $630 level prices declined toward the $600 level between 1 January and 11 January. After this initial decline, however, prices began their first ascent. Prices climbed rapidly to test $690 on 26 February before a bout of profit-taking drove prices back to $640. From this point prices would climb once again, nearing $700 in the middle of April. After testing this level gold traded in a sideways fashion between $641.10 and $693.30 from 26 April to 31 August.

In September gold prices broke past $700 for the first time in history. Gold rose 9.9% from the end of August to $742.80 on 28 September. Prices rose steadily throughout the month, moving higher on a settlement basis on all but four trading days during the month. On 18 September the U.S. Federal Reserve cut its benchmark federal funds rate, for the first time since June 2003, by 50 basis points to 4.75%. Gold prices settled at $717 that day. The monthly average price of gold was a record $716.74 in September.

Gold prices continued to trend higher during October, averaging $760.95, 6.2% above the previous record from September. On the first day of October prices moved up from the September

Real and Nominal Gold Prices

Quarterly, Through Fourth Quarter 2007.

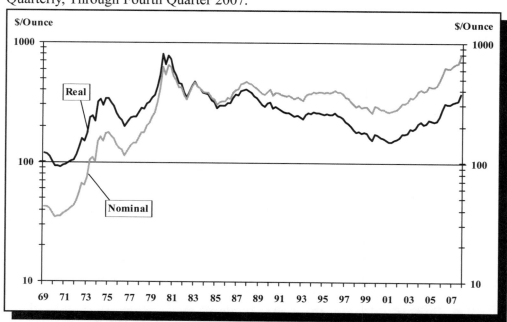

close. Prices then fell slightly to test the $730 level during the first week of the month. Prices crossed $800 on an intra-day basis on the final day of the month, for the first time since January of 1980, before settling at $795.30. That day the Federal Reserve cut the federal funds rate for the second time. This rate was cut by 25 basis points, to 4.50%.

On 2 November gold prices settled above $800 for the first time since January 1980. Gold prices closed at $808.50 on 2 November. The 2007 intra-day high of $848 occurred on 7 November, in the midst of a falling U.S. dollar, rising oil prices, and rising polit-ical tensions in the Middle East. Prices declined from this level to settle below

$800 at $795.30 on 30 November, down 1.6% from the October close of $782.20. Prices averaged a record $807.09 in November, 6.1% above the previous record from October. November was the most volatile month for prices in 2007; price volatility registered 27.3%. It also was the most volatile month since July 2006, when price volatility averaged 27.8%.

Gold traded around $800 during the beginning of December before staging one final rally before the end of the year. On 11 December the Federal Reserve lowered the federal funds rate for the third and final time in 2007. This was the second consecutive 25 basis point cut, bringing the federal funds rate to

Monthly Gold Price Volatility

Through December 2007.

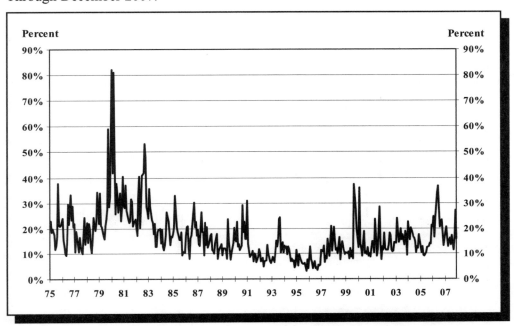

4.25%. Gold prices closed at $817.10 that day. Prices dipped below $800 on an intraday basis on 13 December and settled below this level on 14 and 17 December, for the last time in 2007. Gold prices moved higher to close out the year and set the stage for further increases in early 2008.

From 24 December through 31 December gold traded firmly above $800 in a $35.80 range between $811.60 and $847.40. On 28 December prices for the nearby active contract settled at a record $842.70. This record was broken on the first trading day of 2008 when prices broke past $850 to reach $864.90 intraday and close at $860. From 3

January through 7 January gold traded around $860 before breaking higher once again on 8 January. That day prices reached $884 and settled at a new record $880.30.

Prices surged even higher during the remainder of January. On 11 January prices crossed $900 for the first time on an intraday basis and settled just below this level at $897.70. Gold prices forcefully broke past this level 14 January, the next trading day, to reach $915.50 intraday and settle at $903.40. Prices moved above $900 on an intraday and settlement basis on 15 January and on an intraday basis on 16 January before falling to a settlement of $882 that day.

High, Low, and Average Gold Prices
Annual, Through December 2007.

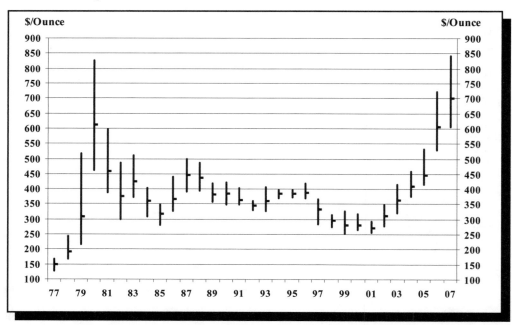

From 17 January to 23 January gold traded in a wide $47 range between $849.50 and $896.50. On 24 January prices once again broke past $900, where they remained through 1 February. During this period gold prices reached a record intraday high of $941.80 on 1 February and settlement high of $927.10 on 28 January.

As gold prices were marching toward $800 early in the fourth quarter of 2007 many people with a bullish bias toward gold talked about how prices had to go back to their 1980 peak. These same people are now saying that gold prices have to go there in real terms. In 2006 dollars the price of gold averaged

$1,639 in 1980. There is no natural, economic, or mathematic law that says that the price of an asset must revert to a previous peak, in real or nominal terms, and stay there. It is especially strange that gold bulls would think this given that the price of gold was at $873 only momentarily on 21 January 1980, spent only two days settling above $800 at that time, and averaged $611.98 for that year.

High, Low, and Settlement Prices in 2007

Daily, Through 22 January 2008. Basis nearby active Comex contract.

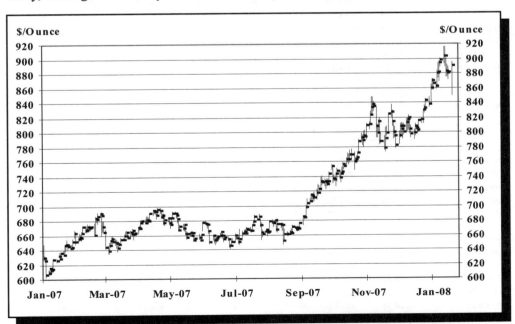

London Gold Prices

Dollars per Ounce

	1968	1969	1970	1971	1972	1973	1974	1975
January	$35.20	$42.30	$34.94	$37.87	$45.75	$65.14	$129.19	$176.27
February	35.20	42.60	34.99	38.74	48.26	74.20	150.23	179.59
March	35.20	43.20	35.09	38.87	48.33	84.37	168.42	178.16
April	37.90	43.30	35.62	39.01	49.03	90.50	172.24	169.84
May	40.70	43.46	35.95	40.52	54.62	101.96	163.27	167.39
June	41.10	41.44	35.44	40.10	62.09	120.12	154.10	164.24
July	39.50	41.76	35.32	40.95	65.67	120.17	142.98	165.17
August	39.20	41.09	35.38	42.73	67.03	106.76	154.64	163.00
September	40.20	40.87	36.19	42.02	65.47	102.97	151.77	144.59
October	39.20	40.44	37.52	42.50	64.86	100.08	158.78	142.76
November	39.80	37.40	37.44	42.86	62.91	94.92	181.66	142.42
December	41.10	35.17	37.44	43.48	63.91	106.72	183.85	139.30
Annual	$38.69	$41.09	$35.94	$40.80	$58.16	$97.33	$159.26	$161.06
Percent Change	--	6.2%	-12.5%	13.5%	42.5%	67.3%	63.6%	1.1%

	1976	1977	1978	1979	1980	1981	1982	1983
January	$131.49	$132.26	$173.18	$227.27	$675.31	$557.39	$384.13	$481.29
February	131.07	136.30	178.16	245.67	665.32	499.76	374.13	491.11
March	132.58	148.23	183.66	242.05	553.58	498.76	330.25	419.70
April	127.94	149.17	175.28	239.16	517.41	495.80	350.34	432.88
May	126.94	146.61	176.31	257.62	513.82	479.70	333.82	438.01
June	125.71	140.78	183.75	279.07	600.72	464.76	314.98	412.84
July	117.76	143.39	188.73	294.74	644.28	409.28	338.97	422.72
August	109.93	144.95	206.30	300.82	627.15	410.16	364.23	416.24
September	114.15	149.52	212.08	355.12	673.63	443.75	437.31	411.80
October	116.14	158.86	227.39	391.66	661.15	437.76	422.15	393.58
November	130.46	162.10	206.07	391.99	623.46	413.37	414.91	381.66
December	133.88	160.45	207.83	455.08	594.92	410.09	444.29	388.34
Annual	$124.84	$147.72	$193.23	$306.69	$612.56	$460.05	$375.79	$424.18
Percent Change	-22.5%	18.3%	30.8%	58.7%	99.7%	-24.9%	-18.3%	12.9%

	1984	1985	1986	1987	1988	1989	1990	1991
January	$370.89	$302.79	$345.38	$408.26	$476.58	$404.01	$410.11	$383.64
February	385.92	299.10	338.89	401.12	442.07	387.51	416.81	363.83
March	394.26	303.94	345.70	408.91	443.61	390.15	393.06	363.34
April	381.36	325.27	340.44	438.35	451.55	384.40	374.24	358.38
May	377.40	316.37	342.38	460.23	451.07	371.05	369.05	356.95
June	377.67	316.49	342.72	449.59	451.33	367.60	352.33	366.72
July	347.47	317.22	348.34	450.55	437.63	375.04	362.53	367.69
August	347.68	329.79	376.60	461.15	431.28	365.14	394.73	356.31
September	341.09	323.35	417.73	460.35	413.46	361.75	389.32	348.74
October	340.17	325.84	423.51	465.36	406.79	366.88	380.74	358.69
November	341.18	325.30	397.55	467.57	420.17	394.26	381.73	360.41
December	320.16	321.72	390.92	486.24	419.05	409.39	376.95	361.73
Annual	$360.44	$317.26	$367.51	$446.47	$437.05	$381.43	$383.47	$362.20
Percent Change	-15.0%	-12.0%	15.8%	21.5%	-2.1%	-12.7%	0.5%	-5.5%

London Gold Prices
Dollars per Ounce

	1992	1993	1994	1995	1996	1997	1998	1999
January	$354.45	$329.01	$386.88	$378.55	$399.30	$355.20	$289.10	$287.31
February	353.91	329.31	381.91	376.64	404.83	346.76	297.49	287.07
March	344.34	330.08	384.13	382.12	396.21	351.81	296.18	285.96
April	338.62	342.15	377.27	391.03	392.85	344.47	308.29	282.62
May	337.24	367.18	381.41	385.22	392.09	343.84	299.10	276.44
June	340.81	371.89	385.64	387.56	385.27	340.76	292.32	261.31
July	352.70	392.19	385.49	386.40	383.66	324.11	292.87	255.81
August	348.74	378.84	380.35	383.81	387.35	324.01	284.11	256.69
September	345.43	355.28	391.58	383.05	383.13	322.82	288.98	265.23
October	344.38	364.18	389.77	383.14	381.06	324.87	295.93	311.10
November	335.02	373.83	384.38	385.71	377.70	306.27	294.12	293.39
December	334.80	383.30	379.29	387.44	368.98	288.74	291.48	282.67
Annual	$344.20	$359.77	$384.01	$384.22	$387.70	$331.14	$294.16	$278.80
Percent Change	-5.0%	4.5%	6.7%	0.1%	0.9%	-14.6%	-11.2%	-5.2%

	2000	2001	2002	2003	2004	2005	2006	2007
January	284.26	265.58	281.46	356.86	413.79	424.03	549.86	631.17
February	299.60	261.99	295.40	359.47	404.88	423.10	555.02	664.75
March	286.43	263.03	294.06	340.55	406.67	434.32	557.09	654.90
April	279.69	260.48	302.68	328.18	403.26	429.24	610.71	679.37
May	275.19	272.35	314.24	355.68	383.78	421.87	675.39	666.86
June	285.73	270.23	321.56	356.35	392.21	430.60	596.15	655.49
July	281.66	267.53	313.40	351.02	398.08	424.32	634.30	665.30
August	274.47	272.37	310.25	359.77	400.51	437.91	632.59	665.41
September	273.55	283.47	319.49	379.07	405.49	455.59	598.19	712.65
October	270.16	283.06	316.46	378.92	420.46	469.90	585.78	755.47
November	266.02	276.33	319.21	389.13	438.81	476.15	627.83	806.25
December	271.45	275.85	332.61	407.63	442.08	510.36	629.79	803.20
Annual	$279.02	$271.02	$310.07	$363.55	$409.17	$444.78	$604.39	$696.73
Percent Change	0.1%	-2.9%	14.4%	17.2%	12.5%	8.7%	35.9%	16.0%

Note: Average afternoon price fix by London bullion dealers. There may be some
discrepancies due to rounding.
Source: Metals Week, CPM Group.
January 7, 2008